LIBRARY HUMOR:
A Bibliothecal Miscellany to 1970

Edited and Indexed
by
NORMAN D. STEVENS
Director, Molesworth Institute

The Scarecrow Press, Inc.
Metuchen, N.J.   1971

Z
682
.5
.S7

To R. S. and G. W.

The Librarian by Giuseppe Arcimboldo

Table of Contents

v

vii

ix

Items Not Found in This Anthology or,
Permissions Not Forthcoming

The following items represent contributions to the field of library humor that ought to have been included in this anthology. They are not reprinted simply because the necessary permissions from the authors and/or publishers could not be obtained. It is regrettable that these items could not be included and apologies are extended to the reader who will have to turn to the original source to locate and enjoy them. The reader, however, may be assured that these have been carefully selected and that he will find it well worthwhile to look these up.

Imaginary Librarians

Frank J. Anderson. "The Library Key Club." Library Journal 89:1918-21, 1964.

Herbert Bruncken. "Posthumous Papers of Sophronia Tibbs." Wilson Bulletin for Librarians 11:682-3; 1937.

John Wakeman. "An Interview with Arbuthnot." Wilson Library Bulletin 36:835, 1962.

Censorship

Barbara Toohey. "Song Found Written on the Back of an Old Order Card." Library Journal 88:3555, 1963.

Library Education

Paul S. Dunkin. "Look to the Closet, Friend." Library Journal 92:2539, 1967.

Jabberwock. "Modern Librarian in the Making." South African Libraries 9:129, 1942.

Library Administration

"Important Innovation for Librarians Only." Bulletin of Bibliography 9:134, April 1917.

The Librarian and the User

Frank J. Anderson. "Trends in Book Selection and
Readability Determination." Library Journal
76:268-9, 1951.

Paul S. Dunkin. "Books Please." Library Journal
92:2373, 1967.

Alice Payne. "Ein Kleines Bibliothek-Lexicon."
Library Journal 83:163, 1958.

John C. Pine. "Carnegie Public Library." Library
Journal 91:4578, 1966.

Cataloging and Classification

"The Catalog Is 'Only Secondarily a Reference Tool'."
Library Journal 81:23-4, 1956.

Lenore S. Gribbin. "Infernal Cataloging: a Retrospect."
Library Journal 87:1731, 1962.

Alison Hall. "Hobgoblins, or a Students' Guide to
Classification." The Assistant Librarian 57:60, 1964.

Automation and the World of the Future

Harold Wooster. "Machine Versatilis--a Modern Fable."
Library Journal 94:725-7, 1969.

Introduction

Librarians, like people, often turn to the writing of humor in an effort to escape their day-to-day problems and sometimes to develop schemes that will solve those problems once and for all. The results are by no means outstanding contributions to the general field of humorous writing and, in most cases, probably seem as dull to the non-librarian as most serious library literature is to the librarian. Much of what passes for humorous library literature is not even funny to the librarian. The literature is replete, for example, with short anecdotes recounting encounters with patrons, [1] items left in returned books, [2] and miscited titles, [3] virtually all of which are dismal examples of humor. There is much, however, that is entertaining and this anthology is an attempt to gather together some of the best examples produced by the end of 1969 for the amusement and delight of my fellow-librarians. This anthology is not designed to serve any useful purpose and should not be used in an attempt to analyze the librarian's self-image or other such nonsense. While we too often search our body of recorded knowledge for solutions to problems, we too seldom search it for entertainment and amusement. I hope that this anthology will encourage others to delve further into this field.

That is, in large part, a selfish hope. Although I undertook, over a period of years, a thorough and detailed search of the literature in my quest for humorous items, I am sure that I have overlooked many items. The approaches to this subject are not easy despite the existence of numerous indexing sources. The literature, to begin with, has not been adequately indexed from this standpoint. Even with a thorough search, including a scanning of the entire volume for some years of Library Literature, I doubt that everything of potential interest in the indexes was located. Then much of this material, even when it is in the standard journals, is simply not indexed. I had neither the time nor the patience to undertake any extensive scanning of journals but some spot checking of this kind did turn up a number of interesting items. Finally it is clear that the editors of library journals have not always been too receptive to humorous writing for there exists, to a far greater degree than is true for serious writing, a considerable body of miscellaneous pamphlet-type material that dwells far beyond the ken of the indexing and abstracting services. Staff newsletters, and other similar ephemeral publications, are a most fruitful source of humor and they, too, are largely unindexed, and indeed are often unrecorded and unavailable. In short I can think of no other area of librarianship that is so difficult of access. The omission of your favorite material, therefore, may be a matter of rejection on my part but it may just as easily be a matter of ignorance. Citations to, or copies of, material not included here that strikes others as humorous will be gratefully received.

Those difficulties mean, of course, that this anthology owes a great deal to the assistance which I have received from others in identifying and locating material. Special thanks along these lines go to Bernice Bollenbacher, William L. Coakley, Peter Gann, Gerald McDonald, Leslie J. Mitchell, Mary Pearce, Arnold P. Sable, Tony Shearman, and Robert Usherwood. Thanks are also due to the authors, editors, and publishers who have given permission to reprint copyrighted material in this anthology.

Works by bibliographers, documentalists, indexers, and information specialists, as well as by librarians, have been included in this anthology. For the most part works by non-librarians about libraries or librarians have been excluded. This distinction has been made not because of any feeling that the humorous material by non-librarians tends to become too sarcastic but because of a feeling that there is an abundance of humorous writing about libraries and librarians by librarians to be enjoyed. Oddly enough except for Edmund Lester Pearson, who is perhaps too briefly represented here, most librarians who have contributed to this area have done so infrequently. The items included here are most often the only piece of humorous writing by a particular librarian. That is too bad for many of them seem to have had a real talent for entertainment. It is also disappointing to note the absence of contributions from any of the major figures of librarianship. Such items simply do not exist. One would have hoped that even they could have sometimes taken their work somewhat less seriously.

The organization of this anthology is simple, yet it is essentially meaningless. The material could just have easily been arranged in a straight chronological or alphabetical sequence but one does, after all, expect a librarian to organize his material. Perhaps I should have taken a lead from present day computer technology and arranged the material in no particular order so as to provide for random access. The reader who is so inclined may ignore the organization and may approach the material in any order that he wishes.

Finally I should warn the reader that the index, for any work by a librarian must have an index, is only partly serious. It is patterned after the delightful index by G. V. Carey, Past-President of the Society of Indexers, in his pamphlet Making an Index. 4 The technique and a number of actual entries have been lifted from that index with the kind permission of Mr. Carey and of the Cambridge University Press.

Notes

1. Do not see, for example, Edith Wyatt's "My Day" Southeastern Librarian 12:94-6, 1962.

2. Strips of bacon, both cooked and uncooked, (73) have edged out girdles (13) easily in the literature to date.

3. The earliest printed version I have been able to find of the most famous of these (The Scarlet Ship, or The Ruby Yacht) appeared in The Librarian 9:153-4, 1919.

4. G. V. Carey, Making an Index (3d ed. ; Cambridge, 1963).

IMAGINARY LIBRARIANS

Mr. Abelthwaite Looks to the Future

O. C. Ibidem

Reprinted from Indiana University Library News Letter v. 2, n. s., No. 2, p. 7-8, November 1966. Reprinted with permission of the Indiana University Libraries.

Mr. Abelthwaite, as the leading candidate for the new post on our library staff, your paper qualifications appear to be unexcelled. This interview, I assure you, is a mere formality, and will be as brief as possible. I'm sorry to rush things, but before my meeting with the Vice Dean for External Affairs, I'm going to have to make a brief study of work-flow charts in American Universities. Texas excepted.

Most interesting! It's the kind of thing I'm very fond of doing.

I'm glad to hear that you are. I'm not. We feel we're a bit behind times here--practically all we know about is books and periodicals, cataloging, charging and discharging, that sort of thing. I'm what you might call a "practicing librarian" myself. That's why we're looking for people like you--with your background, pipe, and all that. What exactly was your title at Billingsgate State?

Expert in Terminology.

I like that. You might as well keep the title if and when you come here. Would you mind telling me something about your work?

You mean you want me to fill you in?

Exactly. How well you put things. In other words-- there are other words, I presume?

That goes without saying. We must explore the situation. Problems must be approached from all angles.

21

We must discuss the matter which is under consideration.
Things must be taken out into the open. You brief me on
your needs, and I'll give you a rundown. Certain foundations
must be established--the prime concern is communication.
In short, we must exchange each and every idea--preferably
new ideas--with free and open minds.

Without prejudice?

Exactly!

I suspect you're the man we're looking for, Mr.
Abelthwaite. Do you mind if I begin by asking a few elementary questions?

Of course not. Everything must be brought out into
the open.

I hardly know where to begin.

Begin with something basic to the issue. Start by
asking me what the principal responsibility of a librarian is.

Very good. What is the principal responsibility of a
librarian?

The principal responsibility of a librarian is to bring
the right book to the right person at the right time.

Thank you. And is that what you do in your present
position, Mr. Abelthwaite?

It would hardly be practicable. Not in this age, considering what this is an age of.

And what is this an age of, Mr. Abelthwaite?

This, sir, is an age of specialization.

I feel that way too. And this specialization affects
libraries?

From the ground up. There are public libraries,
school libraries, college libraries, university libraries,
national libraries, and special libraries.

Splendid! And what would you say these different
libraries are on?

They are on various levels.

What do some of these libraries go into?

They go into their subject areas in depth.

Right. Now, may I ask you what librarians are not?

They are not properly recognized. They are not adequately paid.

Precisely. And what do we make in order to ameliorate these conditions?

We make studies.

And attend--?

Meetings.

What do we do in our studies and at our meetings?

We lead towards.

Towards what?

Solutions to our problems.

Thank you. I think you understand about librarians. Would you mind giving me the definition of a university library?

A university library is the heart of the university.

I think that definition a very good one, Mr. Abelthwaite. Now speaking in general terms, what are libraries not?

They are not adequately financed. They lack.

What do they lack?

Sufficient space. Adequate staffing. A realistic budget with which to meet their needs.

Specifically, Mr. Abelthwaite, what kind of needs?

Ever-expanding. For instance, the demands of.

Yes, indeed.   The demands of what?

Of study, research, and recreational reading.

What, at the present time, can we not do with these demands?

Cope.

I think we are reaching the point.   What methods are most libraries using in what age?

They are using horse and buggy methods in a jet age.

Very good, Mr. Abelthwaite, I'm glad to hear you say that.   Is there (1) any hope, and (2) if so, in what does it lie?

(1) Yes.   (2) Automation.

You mean machines?

What else?

Like escalators, for instance, and electric book lifts?

That's not what I had in mind.   I was thinking of computers, retrieval systems, et cetera.

I see.   And have these systems been tried and proved?

I hesitate to answer that query, because we are still in a stage.

What stage would you say we are in?

The stage of experimentation.   We have programs.

Can you mention a specific program, Mr. Abelthwaite?

Certainly.   There is Marc.

Mark?

Yes, Marc.

I'm sorry, Mr. Abelthwaite, but as I explained, I'm only an oldtime, practicing librarian, not up on my abbreviatology. What exactly does "Mark" stand for?

It stands for Machine Readable Catalog.

"Machine Readable Katalog. " I see. Isn't there a misspelling there some place?

There may be. So what? Computorization doesn't fool with such minutiae as spelling and punctuation. We aren't the English Department, you know.

Of course not; you're quite right. But to get back to automation. What would you say it is in?

It is in the future. It is the handwriting on the wall. Moreover, it is a challenge to our profession.

And what shall you do?

We shall meet that challenge.

I certainly think you're going to do, Mr. Abelthwaite. How are we meeting the challenge at present?

By making studies and attending meetings.

Then libraries are definitely planning for automation?

Not even death and taxes are surer.

Sir, this has been a great pleasure. We shall make you an offer at twice the salary you are now getting, whatever that may be. Before we adjourn, would you care to make a final covering statement on automation in the library--one that I might use in my annual report?

Gladly. You may quote me. Planning for automation in the library is here to stay.

Twinkle, Twinkle, Little Scientific & Technical Aerospace

Diana R. Gorman

This is a revision of an article which appeared in The Assistant Librarian 59:234-6, 1966, under the name of Diana Williams.
It is reprinted here by permission of the author.

"What is the use of a book without pictures or con-
versations?" thought Alice as she read her Esdaile. She
began to drowse, when suddenly a White Rabbit ran close
by her and disappeared down a large rabbit hole. In another
moment Alice was after it, and soon she found herself falling down what seemed to be a very deep well. As she fell,
she noticed that the sides of the well were covered with
bookshelves. She snatched a book as she passed: 'Definitions of Terms in Cataloguing & Classification.' She opened
it and began to read:

1. Characteristics:

   'fish' divided by the 'colour' characteristic = red
      herrings
   'fruit' divided by the 'temperament' characteristic =
      'Wild Strawberries'

2. Phase-relations:

   playing for time / tea for two

3. Foci:

   the 'alcohol' facet of 'drink' brings about varying foci

4. Intra-facet relationship:

   a 'white lady' followed by a 'chaser' resulting in a
      'pink lady'

Just then Alice landed with a thud. All around her
it was dark, but she could just distinguish miniature shelves

filled with books. She took one and made out the words READ ME. On opening it at the title page she saw printed 'British Museum Catalogue,' and immediately shrank to three inches in height. Alice realised that she was now just the right size for wandering around the library. She glanced at the books, but the titles seemed unfamiliar: 'Usage and Abusage: A Guide to Good English,' by Kenneth Tynan; 'Put Out More Flags,' by Percy Thrower; 'Antic Hay,' by Victor Silvester.

Alice turned a corner and almost walked into a pile of books heaped on the floor. She stretched herself on tiptoe and peeped over the edge; her eyes immediately met those of a large, blue Colophon, which was sitting quietly smoking a hookah. They looked at each other for some time, till at last the Colophon took the hookah from its mouth and said, "Who are you?"

"I think I'm a librarian" replied Alice, "but everything is very confusing."

"It isn't," said the Colophon.

"Well, perhaps you haven't found it so yet, but when you've been changed into an imprint, I should think you'll feel a little queer."

"Not at all. But why have you changed?"

"I can't remember things," replied Alice, "I've tried to say 'How Doth the Little Allibone', but it all came different."

"Repeat 'You are square, Father Esdaile'" said the Colophon. Alice folded her hands and began:

"'You are square, Father Esdaile,' the young student said,
'And the scholars today are all hep.
To pass them the version the censor has read
Is to show that you're quite out of step.'

'You are young,' Father Esdaile replied, 'and confused;
You refer to transmission of text--
Which means the original words have been used,
And not that the book's been de-sexed.'"

27

"Wrong from beginning to end," said the Colophon decidedly, and slithering off its pile of books, it disappeared out of sight. Alice stood thoughtfully for a moment, but her attention was caught by two fat little men arguing in a corner. On the collar of one was marked De Bure, and on the other De Bury.

"Every reader his book," said the first.

"Contrariwise," remarked the other, "every book its reader."

"You like poetry?" said De Bure to Alice.

"Ye-es, pretty well--some poetry," Alice said doubtfully. "Would you tell me how I get out of here?"

"What shall I repeat to her?" said De Bure, looking round at De Bury with great, solemn eyes, and not noticing Alice's question.

" 'Thesaurus and the Catalogue' is the longest," De Bury replied. De Bure began instantly.

"Thesaurus and the Catalogue--"

Here Alice ventured to interrupt. "If it's very long," she said, as politely as she could, "would you tell me first how I get out--" De Bure smiled gently and began again:

"Thesaurus and the Catalogue
Both worked at BNB,
And talked of the A. A. C. R.
And Seymour Lubetsky;
And sometimes when in jocund mood,
Of 17th D. C.

'O subjects come and talk with us,'
Thesaurus said with glee:
'Then we'll recall the relevance
Of Cranfield [C. R. P.];
But if you think that that's not FAIR,
Then leave it all to me.'

But four young subjects hurried up
All eager for the treat:
Their Coates were brushed, their facets washed,
Their foci clean and neat:

28

In fact the tidiest array
You'd ever hope to meet.

Four other subjects followed them
And yet another four;
And thick and fast they came at last,
And more, and more, and more--
Till all the subjects sat around, in
Loose assemblage on the floor.

'The time has come, ' Thesaurus said,
'To talk of UDC:
Of isolates and analets,
of MARC and F. I. D.
And why the levels integrate,
And P. M. E. S. T. '

'But wait a bit, ' the subjects cried,
All sitting in a batch, our
Indications are not relevant
In focus and in match.
Why, we are all coterminous--
This seems to be a catch. '

'A Farradane, ' Thesaurus said
'Is what we chiefly need:
Concurrence and appurtenance
Are very good indeed.
Now if you're ready subjects dear,
We will begin to read. '

'O don't read us, ' the subjects cried,
'O this is all too KWIC:
It seems that we're caught in a MESH
And you've been very SLIC.
We're sure the dear old Kaiser
Wouldn't play us such a trick. '

'I weep for you, ' Thesaurus said,
'I deeply sympathise. '
With false drops rolling down his cheeks
He began to synthesise.
And with no 'noise' he held his spotted
Hanky to his eyes.

'O subjects, ' said the Catalogue
'Have you enjoyed the fun?
Now, shall we talk of uniterms?'

29

But answer came there none--
And this was scarcely odd because
They'd indexed every one."

During this poem, Alice had crept quietly away, and
had not gone very far when she came in sight of a book-
selection meeting. Sitting at a large area table were the
Mad Hatrics and the March Hertis. On his head, the Mad
Hatrics balanced a book with a ticket marked 10/6 on it:
seeing Alice staring at it he said: "It really cost more you
know, but I got discount through the Library Licence Agreement."

"Sit down," said the March Hertis.

"Why is a festschrift like a union catalogue?" asked
the Mad Hatrics.

"I don't know," Alice replied, "what's the answer?"

"I haven't the slightest idea," said the Hatrics.
"Have a book."

"Thank you," said Alice, and opening the book that
he pushed towards her, she began to read:

'Twas Leipzig, and the Slithy Toase
Had titles from the Channel Isles.
All Grolieresque the binder sews
His fascicules and files.

Beware the Thomason, my son!
His Commonwealth, his Civil War:
Exclude the Quaker tracts, and then
The folios abhor.

And as in bookish thought he stood,
The Thomason, with eyes of flame,
Came Padelouping through the wood,
And deckled as it came.

He took his 'stabbing' sword in hand--
The Arber foe turned deathly pale--
Then using Caxton's 'sloping stroke'
He slit it head to tail.

Like copper burr, he raised its fur--
His stabbing blade went Fraktur-Frak.

He left it dead, and with its head
He came a-Blooteling back.

'Twas Leipzig, and the Slithy Toase
Had titles from the Channel Isles.
All Grolieresque the binder sews
His fascicules and files.

As Alice finished reading, she noticed that the Mad
Hatrics and March Hertis were pulling a Dormouse out of
B. B. I. P. , and shaking it into shape again, said: "Tell us
a story."

"Once upon a time," began the Dormouse, after thinking for a minute or two, "there were three little classification schemes, and their names were B. C. , C. C. , and
D. C. , and they lived at the back of a catalogue--"

"What did they live on?" asked Alice.

"They lived on catalogue cards," said the Dormouse.

"They couldn't have done that, you know," Alice
gently remarked, "or the catalogue would have been useless."

"So it was," said the Dormouse, "completely useless."

"Why did they live at the back of a catalogue?" Alice
went on.

"Take another book," the March Hertis said to Alice
very earnestly.

"No thank you," replied Alice, "I think I shall go
now," and getting up from the meeting, she hurried away as
fas as she could.

Soon she came upon the Gryphius and the Mock Tottel,
the latter sitting sadly on a rock, crying.

"What is his sorrow?" asked Alice.

"Oh, he has nobody to talk to--he's too clever. He
went to Library School, you know."

"What did you learn?" said Alice addressing the

31

Mock Tottel.

"Oh, the usual things: our main classes were classification and boobliography. There were different kinds of boobliography I remember: antomical or clinical, remunerative or systaltic, and hysterical. We had a few lessons in conjuring too."

"What for?"

"You really are very dull," said the Mock Tottel angrily, "to learn our Hatrics of course."

"I wasn't at all clever," muttered the Gryphius beginning to cry, and he began to sing quietly:

"'Tis the voice of the tutor: I heard him complain 'Your last essay was bad, you must do it again'."

"Have you any idea what a delight a Reference Quadrille is?" asked the Mock Tottel. "First you form two lines; then, when you've cleared the H. M. S. O. pamphlets out of the way--"

"That generally takes some time," interrupted the Gryphius.

"--you advance twice, each with a Hansard. Shall we try that much? Who shall sing?"

"You sing," said the Gryphius, "I've forgotten the words."

So they began solemnly dancing round and round Alice, now and then treading on her toes, while the Mock Tottel sang very slowly:

"'Will you print a little faster?" said a Willings to a Times,
'There's an Ulrich just behind me, and it's smudging all my lines.
See how eagerly the Walford and the Winchell both advance,
They are waiting on the matrix--Bucop come and join the dance.'
Bucop, Lulop, Bucop, Lulop, Bucop join the dance,
Bucop, Lulop, Bucop, Lulop, Lulop join the dance.

32

'You can really have no notion how delightful you
    will look,
When you're placed upon a Warfedale and made up
    into a book.'
But the Times replied, "Bodoni, no!' and gave a
    look askance,
Said he thanked the Willings kindly, but he wouldn't
    join the dance.
    Bucop, Lulop, Bucop, Lulop, Bucop join the dance,
    Bucop, Lulop, Bucop, Lulop, Lulop join the dance.

"Thank you, that was very interesting," said Alice.
Just then a cry of "The trial's beginning' could be heard in
the distance. "Come on," cried the Gryphius, and taking
Alice by the hand, hurried off. But as they ran, Alice
caught sight of Sir Ladsirlac, the White Knight, lying in a
ditch, where he had fallen from his horse. She broke away
from the Gryphius and ran to help him. Dragging him out
by the feet, she laid him on the bank. "Are you all right?"
she asked.

"Oh, yes thank you--I was thinking," replied the
Knight. "You look sad though; let me sing you a song to
comfort you."

"Is it very long?" Alice asked, for she had heard a
good deal of poetry that day. "I have a trial to go to you
know."

"It is long," said the Knight, "But it's very, very
beautiful. It either brings tears to people's eyes, or else--"

"Or else what?" said Alice, for the Knight had made
a sudden pause.

"Or else it doesn't. The name of the song is 'Beneath the Tree of Porphyry'." Alice stood and listened very
attentively, but no tears came to her eyes.

    "I'll tell you everything I can;
    It was like this you see:
    I saw an old man squat beneath
    The tree of Porphyry.
    'Who are you aged man?' I said,
    'And what is it you do?'
    He said 'I'm flogging aspect cards,
    Especially Peek-a-Boo.'

33

He said, 'I search for microprints
In differential facets,
Then make them into filmorex
By hitting them with mallets.
I sell them all to men who deal
In seminal mnemonics,
Who process them by carbon heat
And set them all in onyx. '

He said, 'I look for classes
That are mutually exclusive,
But in the Stoic triad
They are really most elusive.
One of the schemes I came across
Was analytico-synthetic,
But when compared with UDC
I found it most pathetic. '

He said, 'I drink intaglio
When I begin my revels,
But then my zone analysis
Goes into rounds and levels.
I hunt notations quite a lot,
Especially radix fraction,
But the one I really want to find
Has got some retroaction. '

'I co-ordinate my indexes
Most usually by Battening,
Which somehow I disseminate
By Bradford's law of scattering.
I build up compound subjects
Where possible by synthesis,
And reference my catalogue
By always using syndesis. '

But now I've amplified my phrase,
I'm taking to the road.
I've indexed my citation,
And I've packed my Zatocode.
I'm going to follow that old man
Who meant so much to me:
That dear old man who sat beneath
The tree of Porphyry. "

As he sang the last words of the ballad, the White
Knight gathered up the reins, and turned the horse's head a-
long the road by which Alice had come. "You'll soon be at

the trial," he said, "but you'' wait and wave your handkerchief when I get to that turn in the road?"

"Of course I'll wait," said Alice, "and thank you for
the song." They shook hands, and the Knight slowly rode
away. Then Alice turned and ran as fast as she could to
the trial.

The King and Queen of Hertis were seated on their
throne, and all around them a crowd was assembled--all
sorts of councils, committees and co-operative schemes, and
a library-full of books.

"Herald! Read the accusation," said the King. The
White Rabbit stood up and announced: "The Knave of Hertis
stole the 'Acess to Information' pamphlet, thereby depriving
us of the formulation and development of a national plan, and
the proposals for action for the planning function carried out
by a national bibliographic advisory council and the executive
function carried out by a national bibliographic centre."

"Consider your verdict," said the King.

"Not yet! Not yet!" the Rabbit interrupted hastily,
and he called the first witness; this was the Mad Hatrics.

"I am a poor man--" he began.

"Off with his head!" screamed the Queen, "the Mad
Hatrics and the Knave of Hearts are in league, and have
been providing each other with information by means of co-
operation through public, technical and commercial libraries."

"Call the next witness," said the King.

The White Rabbit stood up and called out, "Alice."

"This is ridiculous," thought Alice, and then aloud
she said. "I can't give evidence--I never studied the information explosion properly--I didn't think I'd ever need to
know anything about it in the future."

"That's your own fault," shouted the Queen. "Do you
plead guilty or not guilty?"

"Rubbish," cried Alice, "it's nothing to do with me
anyway. It's the responsibility of the government to establish efficient organization of information and documentation

on a national footing."

"She's read the pamphlet," shrieked the Queen, "she's stolen it--she's guilty--off with her head!"

"Nonsense," retorted Alice, "anyway, you're nothing but a lot of books," whereupon all the books rose up and came flying down at her.

Alice found herself lying on the grass, and some dead leaves from the trees were fluttering down on to her face. "What a curious dream," she thought as she got up and walked into the house. Just before she closed the door, she thought for a moment that she saw the White Knight sitting precariously on the garden gate.

Valete Mrs. Finkleblintz

John A. North

Reprinted from Doorway 6:13-4, January 1968. Reprinted
with permission of the author and of the Co-operative Book
Centre of Canada Ltd.

"It is with mixed feelings of immense gratitude and
overwhelming sadness that we, the staff of this library, are
gathered here today to commemorate the retirement of our
Head Cataloguer, Mrs. Gertrude Finkleblintz. In the 61 years
Mrs. Finkleblintz has been with this library, she has served
faithfully and lovingly in her unlauded role beyond the view of
the public.

Although many of you will remember Mrs. Finkleblintz's first day with us, some of the newer staff members
may not be so cognizant with her many contributions to the
vitally important art of cataloguing. It is due mainly to Mrs.
Finkleblintz's magnificent efforts that this library has today
a catalogue unparalleled anywhere in the world. She has never been afraid to pioneer new movements in the art, and we
remember with pride the ten years of selfless research,
which culminated in her valuable monologue on the "standard-
ization of catalogue-card hole sizes." This profound and
stimulating work, published at a time when the profession
was concerned with more ephemeral and sensational topics
such as standards of service, establishment of reference collections, and co-operative storage of periodicals, was never
accorded the recognition it deserved. Always unassuming,
Mrs. Finkleblintz never used her deep understanding and vast
resources of energy to become well-known in library circles.
Her entire professional life was devoted to making the catalogues of this library unique. Her indelible mark will remain with this library for generations and drawer upon drawer
of 3 x 5 cards are her memorial to readers and staff alike.

Painstaking care in descriptive cataloguing has been
the keynote of Mrs. Finkleblintz's work and each book in this
library has been so accurately catalogued that we have more

37

punctuation marks per card square inch than any other library. Mrs. Finkleblintz's high regard for the fine art of annotation enabled her to successfully resist the blandishments of advocates of short cataloguing. Some of Mrs. Finkleblintz's annotations extend to 8 or 9 cards, and although this tends to enlarge our catalogue space requirements, the clarity and insight for which the notes are famous is a boon to the reader. One reader mentioned that the notes were of such tremendous value that he rarely needed to leave the catalogue to consult the shelves.

Neither should we forget the administrative capabilities for which Mrs. Finkleblintz was justly famous. Realizing that cataloguing was of such vital importance, she built up over the years a departmental staff which equalled, and then surpassed, that of the combined strength of the Lending and Reference Departments. We are proud to recall that through the years when this library was unjustly criticised for the alleged paucity and quality of its holdings Mrs. Finkleblintz managed to spend, and spend wisely, almost one half of our library budget in a manner which enabled us to display to such worthwhile advantage such books as we had.

In a brief ceremony such as this, it is impossible to mention all the instances in which the guiding hand of Mrs. Finkleblintz steered our library away from possible disaster. However, a few must be mentioned--her resistance to the principle of "open access" which kept library users from desecrating our shelves until early in the nineteen-sixties--her careful deletion of words and passages in all biology books and certain other works which has protected the youth of this community from the influence of certain prurient publishers and political thinkers--her continuing crusade to impress upon younger staff members the fact that librarians are entrusted with the guardianship of books, and that the more books which can be kept in the library, the better the standard of service which we provide.

It is to such people as Mrs. Finkleblintz that we are indebted for any esteem in which our library is held by the community. By continuing to work together along the tried and trusted lines of our own experience, we shall continue to provide the standard of service which our readers have come to expect. It is true that certain sensationalist techniques have been employed by book stores and neighbouring libraries, and that some of the more fickle and gullible residents of the community have transferred their patronage to these other

38

sources. However, we exist to give the public what they should have, which, as we all know, is not what they think they want.

We must close ranks to fill the large blank left by Mrs. Finkleblintz, and join together to fulfill the motto of our Staff Association "Ever serve you right."

Mrs. Finkleblintz, as a gesture of our appreciation, I ask you to accept this gold-plated catalogue-drawer rod as a symbol of the deep regard in which we hold you. Also we would like you to accept this fourteen volume bound set of your wonderfully explicit instructions on annotation from the Procedures Manual. May I say in conclusion that your retirement is mourned by us all, and that this library will never be the same again. Thank you."

Inside Librarianship: No. 5--
The Apotheosis of Galloway Fyrne

Stanley Snaith

From Librarian and Book World 46:205-9, 1957. Reprinted
by permission of the author and James Clark & Co., Ltd.

Few of our calling have "sat" for a full-length biography. Librarians are content to live unlaurelled and unsung.
They are born, they grow up, they embrace their profession,
they give themselves ungrudgingly to the public weal (all too
often for a peppercorn reward); in due course they shuffle
off this mortal coil, and then--the poppy of oblivion performs
its traditional office. There is, then, a sub-flavour of irony
in the announcement that a memoir of Galloway Fyrne is in
the press. (Galloway Fyrne: a tribute to a life of service,
Clarke and Co., 21S.) For Galloway Fyrne's peculiar distinction was that he rose to a position of peculiar distinction
by a peculiar lack of distinction. His career was, so to
speak, the aggrandizement of the lowest common denomina-
tor. Do not misconstrue me. It is far from my desire to
be provocative. I have seen the proofsheets of the forthcoming biography. The work is of a piece. The documentation
is thorough. The tone, if hagiographical, is not blatantly so.
I am decently reluctant to trespass upon the author's preserve. But it happens that Miss Mullivant, though well
versed in Fyrne the myth, seems to have had no acquaint-
ance with Fyrne the man. I had. Hence this modest gloss.

*   *   *   *

My starting point is the time when we were both in
the throes of Qualifying. In contrast with my own methods--
in which Guess and God figured immoderately--Fyrne went
nap on honest toil. To compass a single Section (this was
the era of the old syllabus) he would scorn delights and live
laborious days for six months on end. Correspondence
courses? He toiled and spun at them. Textbooks? He
lived, moved and had his being in textbooks. Note-taking?

He note-took with quenchless and uncomprehending ardour, with the student's pathetic trust that somehow the mere art of committing a thing to one's tablets made it an inalienable personal property. Like the mills of God, his brain ground slowly but exceeding small. He even, in the manner of Byron, went in for nocturnal labour, fortified by exotic drugs-- in Galloway's case, aspirins and coffee. . . .

In after years I was often to recall the episode of the Literary History examination. Galloway, armed to the teeth, with names and dates, movements and schools, arrived at his Phillipi with (sheer nervousness, I suppose) an hour to spare. "I dropped into a teashop," he told me, "and to pass the time I had a last look at the breviary. Take it from me, old horse, I had a shock. There was one whole chapter-- reams and reams of it--packed to bursting with dashed poets and what have you--that I had clean overlooked."

"Clean overlooked," he repeated ruefully, somewhat as one of the biblical virgins might have confessed to an oversight in re the trimming of the lamp.

"Rather late in the day to find that out," I remarked.

"It jarred me, I admit. There was no time to memorise the stuff, so I shoved it down on my fingernails--my writing is small, you know--all that apple-sauce about who had written what, and when. And, believe it or not, old horse, the very first question--a Compulsory--was on this same period."

"Well--!"

"I simply romped through it."

"You did!"

"Yes."

"And they disqualified you?"

He coughed. "Well, no--."

"You mean to say--?"

"It knocked 'em sideways. I got a Merit."

I am a chronicler, not a moralist. I confess I looked

41

my admiration. This was Big. This was Napoleonic resource. I perceived for the first time that there were
Depths in Galloway Fyrne.

*   *   *   *

So much for Galloway the student. Now for Galloway
the job-hunter. Whenever anything was "going," Galloway,
with the curious unshakable insensate stubbornness of which
only the unheroic are capable, was staking his claim. Nor--
for he was spacious in his ambitions--did he confine himself
to the municipal field. It only needed Moccasin's the Chem-
ists to advertise for a book-department manager, for Galloway to launch his broadsides into the citadel. Did the Alpine
Club yearn after a cataloguer for their monumental library,
Fyrne was theirs for the taking. All this got him, in a
mensurable sense, nowhere. But it made him Talked About.
And in our profession, to be Talked About is to be half way
to--so to speak--fame and fortune. Well, anyway, fame.

It would hardly be too much to say that, for a time,
no Short List was complete without the name of Fyrne.
Which is the more odd in that he was at a signal disadvan-
tage. For just then an abundance of brilliant aspirants had
descended upon the library scene like the shower of curates
in Bronte's Shirley. To them Fyrne was a moonlight unto
sunlight. Yet whenever one of those--you know 'em--rare
and covetable situations was in the market, Galloway was up
with the head of the field. "Who's selected for Pudlington?"
we would enquire of the booksellers' travellers, ever our in-
fallible grapevine. "Fotheringay of Southampton, Camis of
Winchelsea--and of course Galloway Fyrne," they would say.
It was always "of course." That very "of course" was an
implicit acknowledgment of the formidable ubiquity of Fyrne.
On these occasions he was, as the booksellers' travellers
testified, constant as the Northern Star of whose true-fixed
and resting quality there is no fellow in the firmament.

Those out of the know often pondered the mystery of
Galloway and the Short Lists. Miss Mullivant, preoccupied
with the Apotheosis, takes it for granted. But we who were
his contemporaries did not take it for granted. We put our
ears to the ground. We tapped sources. And presently it
emerged that the explanation lay in his Testimonials. Those
who have seen them say these breathed fair as myrrh and
frankincense. The connoisseur of irony might reflect that all
the chiefs under whom Galloway trained had the most luke-
warm opinion of his capacities. Nevertheless, while librar-

42

ians are not disposed to squander praise that is not earned, in the case of Galloway the most incorruptible relaxed the tensity of their virtue. "He's a muddler, of course," they would confess. "Concrete from the adam's apple northwards. But, hang it, he's a trier. And anyhow he's such a nice chap."

That was the kernel. He was a nice chap. Of the arts and the humanities in general he knew nothing--indeed, hardly suspected anything; and his social accomplishments had no patine. But that cherubic countenance, that bland and innocent regard, that slow and self-effacing manner, disarmed one at the outset.

*   *   *   *

What impulse led Fyrne to put himself up for election to the Council of the Association of Assistant Librarians, must remain conjectural. My own guess is that he was inveigled into it by misguided friends. The appearance of his name on the voting paper caused widespread discussion. "Fyrne? Isn't that the tomato who gets on all the Short Lists?" "That's him. Take my tip, he's an up-and-coming man." (Whereas the generality of us were plain down-and-going.) His election, among such refulgent planets as Sandry and Seymour Smith, had a considerable element of surprise. I would hazard that the most surprised person of all was Fyrne himself. At all events, as a councillor he was liked. Some members--particularly the espousers of suspect causes --were inclined to say too much. Not so Galloway. Galloway never said too much. In truth he never said anything. His forte was flashes of brilliant silence. In two years of office, his most sustained oration consisted of one word: "seconded."

*   *   *   *

At the same period our hero contributed some articles to a professional sheet. In the teeth of his biographer's staunch advocacy, candour obliges me to say that they were not outstandingly good articles. They were not even good articles. They were just mediocre enough to be admirable specimens of their genre. The ideas were exhausted--and exhausting. The style was deficient in the precious quality that Mr. Polly compendiously described as "epithet." But it happened (Galloway was fortunate in his timing) that at this time--I am speaking of a couple of decades ago--some clever and original but intolerant newcomers had been kicking up

43

their heels in another periodical; a quite choice hoo-ha had eventuated; book, bell and candle had been invoked; and the natural reaction had set in. Everyone was suddenly looking askance at clever and original but intolerant newcomers. Fyrne came as a reassuring change. As a young fogey, he seemed to have inherited the mantle of Thomas Gray, who according to Dr. Johnson "was dull in a new way, and that made many people think him great. "

* * * *

To some of us who knew him it seemed that poor Galloway (one somehow got into the habit of this condescendingly affable epithet) would spend the rest of his days attending selection committees--so near his goal, yet so far, like the Peri at the gates of Paradise. So that it came as a mild shock when he finally succeeded to the woolsack. True that the Librarianship of Much Clipping was not a pearl of the first lustre. Mr. Gordon would have raised his eyebrows at it. Mr. Lamb would have treated it as the idle wind which he regarded not. Much Clipping was a backwater. Much Clipping even took a civic pride in being a backwater. The Library Committee was apathetic. The burghers, never having enjoyed a progressive library policy, did not think to ask for one. The library had been going full steam astern for years--and our Galloway gave it a helping push. (He was in no danger of courting odium: even under the worst management a library, as Bacon said of the world, "goeth of its own motion, beyond the rules of wisdom. ") One might have said that Fyrne was buried alive--lost beyond reclaim.

In fact some of us did say it.

But he knew better.

He proved us wrong.

He had established a bridgehead. Now he commenced to fan out.

The next few years saw this diffident and ingenuous individual whizzing to and fro about the sphere of librarianship like one of those mythical couriers of Homer. An East coast resort, a Yorkshire mining town, an overgrown Surrey village, each in turn made what it could of the ambiguous privilege of his employment. And each summer they rifled the ratepayer's money-box in order to despatch him to the Library Association Conference, where he attended the ses-

sions with a solemn and unremitting assiduity. He learned
nothing (nor did I, when my turn came). He gave nothing
(like most of us, if it came to that). But, I am told, for
him it was always Early Doors, and a seat plumb spang in
the centre of the orchestra stalls. (The really sagacious
strategists--I have in mind the Thirsts and the Morning-Af-
ters--opt for the gangway end of the back row.) While other
delegates were living in sin at the Pictures or in the beach-
chair, Galloway would be harassedly choosing between simul-
taneous afternoon meetings, rather as a Hindu flagellant might
balance the attractions of alternative forms of torture.

Then came the turn of the university city. At this I
was as startled as the young man of St. Bees who was stung
on the nose by a wasp. I--being, like Galloway, self-unedu-
cated--would never have aspired to a university city. I will
swear that Galloway too had never aspired to a university
city! His candidacy was pure habit. Yet there he was! In
situ! Monarch of all he surveyed! Chancing to encounter
him soon after his appointment, I sought enlightenment.

"Fact is, Stanley," he said with that Innigkeit--that
unselfconscious simplicity--which distinguished him, "my
predecessor was a bit of a screwball. Highbrow and all that.
He read Greek philosophy--for pleasure! He was difficult to
get on with. Perhaps you'll remember him--Obadiah Root. *
Yes, I though you would. I found out afterwards that the
Committee had set their hearts on getting an Ordinary Sort
of Chap. So they picked me."

That was reasonable enough. All the same, imagination recoils from the spectacle of Galloway Fyrne as librarian to a university city. And who, knowing him as I did,
could have thought of him as the recipient of a literary honours degree? The thing was without precedent. It was stag-
gering. It was undiluted fantasy. But it was true. The new
Doctor of Literature gave an address--prepared for him by
his Reference Assistant, who was by way of being a scholar
--on "The Place of Literature in Life." I was impecunious-
ly debarred from this feast of reason and flow of soul. But
a colleague gave me details. "The text was sound," he said,
"but it cried aloud for colour in the presentation."

"And Galloway's lacked colour, I take it?"

---

*Known to his immediate circle as 'Square Root. '--S. S.

"Colour?" He gave a roopy laugh. "It was whiter than--you remember the old madrigal?--the whitewash on the wall."

"Pity."

"What our Galloway knows about the place of Literature in Life wouldn't fill the hole in a doughnut. As for the slippered pleasantries, they were not so much delivered as strangled at birth."

"So the address was a flop?"

"H'm. I wouldn't say that. In academic company you're on an easy wicket. If you're stodgy it passes for erudition. If you ball-up your notes, they laugh indulgently, suspecting a recondite jest. So Galloway got by."

*   *   *   *

The Doctorate, though implausible, can be swallowed --just. But that further apogee, the Knighthood? Here Miss Mullivant might have vouchsafed some light. But she does not. This is to be regretted. For Knighthoods are not commonly lavished upon librarians. Heave a brick in the Annual General Meeting, and it's odds on you'll hit a librarian who has not been knighted, and never will be. Admittedly, the award was an encouraging sign that our vocation is not entirely unknown in high places. But all the same--! Galloway of all people--!

Earth has not anything to show more fair than a newly-created knight; and Galloway burgeoned. He assumed a courtly distance. He put on girth. He sacrificed his convenience to collars of a breath-taking height and rigidity. He grew a beard, and even the most prudish agreed that it became him. To those of us who had, so to speak, run about the braes with him and pou'd the gowans fine, there was something baroque in the spectacle of Galloway as an Elder Statesman of the profession. But who were we to jeer at a President of the Library Association?

For, of course, he was offered the Presidency. Sir Galloway, with crushing magnanimity, accepted it. To be true, the Presidency meant sitting on committees; but Galloway, as a whilom councillor, was a hard-bitten campaigner. The Presidency meant Speeches. Galloway could not speak. But then few speakers _can_ speak. He was seldom en rapport

with his audience, but how many speakers are? Dash it all,
Sir Galloway, apart from being so extravagantly belaurelled,
was known to be Solid.   Custom could not stale his infinite
sobriety.   Besides, as a fosterling of the Groves of Academe
he divined by instinct the sovereign importance, in formal
orations, of--how to put it?--<u>parvo in multum</u>.

*   *   *   *

I can add nothing more that is not common knowledge.
For Galloway's apotheosis took him beyond the ken of us
groundlings. We plotted his vertiginous career, but at several removes: his appointment to the Librarianship of the
House of Lords (a desirable post apart from the occupational
risk of a nervous breakdown through underwork), followed by
the inevitable Barony; his consequential association with
Unesco; his tours of America and Australia; his lectures to
the English Association ("The Place of Literature in Life")
and the International Pen Club at Vienna ("The Place of Life
in Literature"); and so forth.   His roseate platitudes were en-
shrined for the delectation of posterity in the columns of <u>The
Times</u>; and at least once--this has escaped Miss Mullivant's
net--he was cartooned in <u>Punch</u>.   No librarian before him
had been cartooned in <u>Punch</u>.   It was a dazzling consumma-
tion.   Galloway had entered his kingdom.

The public memory being what it is, I doubt whether
Fyrne is more than a name to the younger generation.   It is
to be hoped they will make themselves acquainted with the
forthcoming biography.   Its subject is still worthy of study:
though whether as an Example or an Awful Warning, each
reader must decide for himself.   But I hope I have said
enough to indicate that our author has documented a quite
unique chapter in library history.

The Placid Puddle Rest Home: A Proposal

Schroeder Gahuvnik*
as told to Lester J. Pourciau

From South Carolina Librarian 13:14-5, October 1968. Reprinted with permission of Mr. Pourciau and of the South
Carolina Librarian.

(*Mr. Gahuvnik was for many years Director of Libraries on Bouvet Island. He retired in 1966 and
came to the United States to promote the "PLacid
Puddle Home." He was last known to be in or a-
round Noonan, North Dakota, attempting to purchase
property for the "Home." Mr. Pourciau is a doc-
toral student, Graduate Library School, Indiana University.)

The long history of the vicious attack and downright
insult heaped upon the noble art of cataloging is very well
known and regretted by many librarians. Much of this injurious dialogue has been subtle; some has been open and
hostile. Concern over this situation prompted a number of
prominent people to convene, in 1965, on Bouvet Island to
discuss possible means of compensation to catalogers for the
ills they have long suffered. After many hours of debate
and consideration, it was decided to propose the "Placid
Puddle Rest Home" as a reward for those who had managed
to live through the trials and tribulations of a life and career
as a cataloger. What a joyous abode this would be! The
tentative site of the "Home" is about ten miles due north of
Noonan, North Dakota, and about four miles west of Hades.
Already a committee is busy at work preparing rules of con-
duct and activity for the fine group of people who will eventually inhabit the "Home."

From the onset of the meeting on Bouvet Island, there
was some opposition to the "Home" and in addition to questioning its necessity, there were some who actually chal-
lenged the fact that catalogers have a tradition of being ma-

48

ligned. Such, of course, is completely untrue. Consider, for example, the statement of Enoch Sneed that it is "better not to compile a catalogue, both as an unavailing bother and moreover as the absence of it makes you more secure in your office ... "[1] This horrid statement was first printed to infect the minds of librarians in 1773!!! Others have attempted to identify catalogers with the popular and frivolous. One of these attempts is a wretched discourse entitled "There's figures in them Dewey Decimals; or, Hi Ho Silver Screen."[2] Still another anti-cataloger proposal is that of the Molesworth Institute. They want to publish a journal titled Ibid., and have publically stated that entry of this journal will be a constant source of confusion! The Molesworth people are true enemies. They want to manufacture catalog cards that will disintegrate in twenty years.[3] Such cards would enforce catalogers to evaluate their work and engage in re-cataloging five times in each century. Even if this hellish battle is lost and these cards come into widespread use, the typical cataloger's career will span several sets of them.

Back to the "Home!" Preliminary plans will require that each cataloger bring his own Cutter-Sanborn Table, nothing more. Darling Dewey will be supplied to all, as will be a bone, and a huge metal bin in which experimentation in sedimentary filing systems may be made. The first exercise required of all will be a self cataloging task so that all membership records will be accurate and neat. Main entry in this self cataloging will, of course, be the name of the cataloger who is admitted to the "Home." Place of birth, name of parents, and date of birth will be substituted for the usual imprint information. Added entries will take the form of the title held while employed, such as "Chief, LC Card Adaptation Division." Once a new cataloger has joined the group in the "Home" and has completed the self cataloging project, the resulting cards will be filed in his or her own, personal "Kittytwig" (diminutive of "Catalog"). An adequate supply of volumes withdrawn from other libraries will be supplied to each person so that idleness will not interfere with one's efforts. Plans are now being made to contact the National Library of Jan Mayen to inquire about the possibility of obtaining their discards.

While the above is presently only in nebulous planning stage, sincere efforts are being made to make the "Home" a reality. Hopefully, these efforts will shortly culminate in its existence. When this joyous time arrives, revenge will be had; detractors will be spited, and each and every cataloger who desires will be able to rest assured that when he or she has finally arrived at that blissful, golden gate of retirement, the end of the road will not be waiting, but rather, a new life can be greeted at the "Placid Puddle Rest Home."

Notes

1. Edmund L. Pearson, The Old Librarian's Almanack ... (Woodstock, Vermont: Elm Tree Press, 1909), p 23.

2. Mrs. M. Y. G. Rothman, Wilson Library Bulletin, XXI (December, 1946), 296+.

3. Norman D. Stevens, "The Molesworth Institute," ALA Bulletin, LVII (January, 1963), 75-76.

Early Days

Charles Grapevine

From Librarian and Book World 42:159-60, 1953.   Reprinted
with permission of James Clarke & Co. , Ltd.

I well remember my first day at Boozlington.   It was
in December 1900, and so cold that, at four o'clock, "Bullseye" Martin, who had succeeded the great C. G. H. Bates as
chief, ordered me to light his fire.   "But, sir," I said, "I
have never done it before.   Where shall I find paper?"   "Tush,
boy, use your ingenuity.   Tear a couple of pages out of The
Times.   No one will notice."   And that is what I did, whenever he wanted a fire.   Years later, I was to regret this,
but, at the time, I did not realise that the Morning Post
would burn better.

Most people think that "Bullseye" was so named from
his habit of offering sweets to members of the staff who had
pleased him, but actually it was due to the accuracy with
which he spat into an old paste pot placed beside his desk.
I only knew him miss once, and then I don't think he liked
the colour of the Chairman's shoes.

"Bullseye" was a stickler for punctuality.   Anyone arriving after six-thirty was for "the carpet," and he once
made me do two hours extra inkwell-cleaning for returning
three minutes late from breakfast.   He was less keen when
the time came for us to go home.   Everything had to be tidy,
and woe betide us if a book was out of place when he made
his nightly inspection at ten o'clock.   He could sense a mis-
placed book.   "Never have time to look inside, but I know
'em from the outside," he'd say.   "Smell a wrong 'un a mile
off.   Know 'em from the outside I do. "

He wasn't a great bookman, but he made his mark in
other ways.   One of his ideas was for a gadget which em-
bossed an anti-gambling quotation at the same time as it

51

blacked out sporting news. And he made an indicator which
not only showed if a book was in or out, but if it was worth
reading anyway. People came from miles to look at this indicator. He had room to spare at one corner, so he put in
a clock showing what time it was in Sydney. And he had a
flag on top, to show visitors if he was in or out. When it
was up, he was in, when it was down, he was out. The day
Queen Victoria died, he had it at half-mast.

Yes, the library world lost a character when "Bullseye" Martin retired. There aren't many librarians left who
ride to work on horseback.

Another character at Boozington was Cyril Blisterley.
He became chief when "Bullseye" retired, early in '09, but
when I started he was Deputy. He'd wanted an office to himself, but "Bullseye" wouldn't let him have one. So he had a
desk in a corner, and when we wanted to speak to him we had
to tap on the side of the desk before he would answer. I had
to go out every morning to get him a halfpenny bun, and if
the chief was out of the way I toasted it on my penknife in
front of the office fire. Once, while doing this, I became so
engrossed repeating cataloguing rules to myself that the bun
got badly burnt. At this moment, "Bullseye" came back unexpectedly, and I only just had time to thrust the bun into
my trouser pocket. "Well?" he asked, and then saw the
smoke. "Drat the boy, he's on fire!" he shouted, and emp-
tied a fire-bucket over me.

After that, Blisterley had his bun sent in already
toasted, but, as he said, it wasn't the same. The last time
I went to see him, years after he had retired, he insisted on
my toasting him a bun, on my penknife, in front of the fire.
The poor old chap had an awful job eating it, as he'd lost his
teeth, but he enjoyed it. We had a good laugh about the time
I burnt his bun, and he gave back the halfpenny he'd made
me forfeit.

Unlike "Bullseye," he was a bookman. He was genu-
inely fond of books, and, after his first few months as chief,
did little else than "keep up to date with current literature,"
as he put it. He was so fond of books that he couldn't bear
to part with them, and his office was always crowded with
volumes he wanted to "have one more look at." Eventually
it got so full that, to make more room for books, he had to
move out of the office to his old desk in the corner. As he
was chief now, though, he didn't like us tapping on the desk,
and he had a little bell-push there instead. When he retired

we got so many books out of the office that we didn't buy any for eighteen months. And right in the far corner we found some bones. At first we thought they were from the Museum, but we later found they'd belonged to the caretaker who disappeared in '14. We'd thought he'd joined up, but he must have lost his way in there one night.

The chief was very annoyed when he realised that we'd had the drains up three times in '15 for nothing.

Gulliver's Library Travels

William Moore

From The Librarian and Book World 22:195-6, 1933. Reprinted with permission of James Clarke & Co., Ltd.

The King of Laputa, learning of my interest in literature, had often promised me a visit to the famous Laputan
Academy of Librarianship. "The Laputans are a nation of
book borrowers," said the King, "and our keepers of books
have devised wondrous complex systems for the regulation of
book circulation which have to be taught to students. We go
to-morrow."

I was received very kindly by the Director and went
many days to the Academy. Every room had something curious in library science and I believe I visited no fewer than
five hundred rooms. The first professor I saw was of wild
aspect with a foxy face, his whole appearance being modelled
on some character in a book called Sherlock Holmes. He
wore a cap with two peaks. He had been ten years upon a
project for the correct taking of library statistics by finger-
prints. "Every book borrowed from a lending library," he
said, "has only one issue recorded whereas that book might
be read by a dozen persons. All wrong! My system is perfect. Let every reader have his finger-prints recorded.
When the book is returned let it be sprinkled with this powder
and all the finger-prints will show up at once and be counted.
There is no end to the value of finger-prints which are at
the root of all librarianship. All new readers have to do is
to place their fingers on an entrance form and the library
has a record of him for life." He rattled a small box below
my nose and the Director made me understand I was to give
him a small donation. I left him muttering something about
"Scotland Yard."

I went into another room, but was ready to hasten
back being almost deafened by a horrible noise. My guide
hurried me forward conjuring me in a whisper to give no

54

offence which would be highly resented by the professor in charge and therefore I durst not hold my ears. The room was filled with gramophone records shelved everywhere and carefully numbered. About a hundred and fifty gramophones were blaring and bellowing at once and a teacher stood on a platform, a vacant smile on his face. He was trying to give a lesson on library extension, I was told. The students did not pay the slightest attention but occupied themselves with practical joking. Every minute some left the room and there was a constant coming and going of students.

It seemed the professor had had records made of lectures in librarianship. All the students needed to do to pass the examination at the end of term was to consult their notes and refer the examiner to the number of the record concerned. For instance, if a question was asked, "What system of recording fines and other penalties would you recommend, and why?" the student simply wrote "D 1143," and passed. If honours were aimed at, the student was asked to produce his gramophone and play the record. This record system was invaluable to them in their career as librarians. If they had a difficult problem to solve at their library they simply ordered a record from the Academy which was sent by return of post at special prices to members of the Laputan Library Association. A catalogue was published annually with prices, and I understand was availed of liberally especially by the honours men. The gramophones, of course, were bought from the Academy and their purchase was compulsory.

There was a most ingenious lecturer on library planning. He had visited a city in Laputa called Hollywood. There he had made films of every department in a library. Scenic artists had designed complete library systems of cardboard according to the latest rules of planning, tables, chairs, bookstacks, complete, and all students in Laputa had to do was sit and watch the library grow on the screen. I do not remember much of the film I saw, but I recall that all exits in "open access" libraries were within view of the staff and the number of superficial feet allotted to every borrower was most cleverly arrived at. All the libraries were top-lighted. Each student had to provide his own cinema outfit provided at special terms by the Academy.

In another room I was highly pleased with an X-ray projector designed to be stationed at all exits of lending libraries. The unsuspecting borrowers had to pass through the rays and the librarian could see at a glance whether he--

or she--had books concealed about their persons or not. My
guide informed me that some Laputan libraries--Irish I think
he called them--had refused to install the X-ray projector on
ethical grounds and their staffs--male and female--in consequence were bitterly disappointed. I had to give the inventor
a small donation to his research fund.

Another room I visited was full of dog-kennels. Here
were trained a special type of bloodhound which traced missing books by smell. Every book in the library was sprinkled
with a rare, pungent perfume which harmonized with the
book's usual odour and the dogs could trace it even when a
book had been in circulation for years.

Then there was a special invention of the Director's
which consisted of a sensitive motor-van which paraded the
streets and accurately located in which house stolen books
from the library were hidden. I had seen one of these vans
in operation in connection with unpaid wireless licences and
thought the new development was excellent.

The robot librarians were wonderful. I can only say
here if machinery develops much further there will be little
need in the future for librarians or assistants. "Go up to
that figure," whispered the Director, "and whisper, 'Co-
operation and co-ordination.' " I did so. The robot smiled
vaguely, opened his mouth and intoned as if repeating a
psalm: "The successful administration of a county library
system depends entirely upon the co-operation and co-ordination of the respective areas." I made further experiments
with other robots and I remember one who when asked,
"where can I find a book on plumbing?" replied, "Our classification system depends upon the mutual exclusion of terms
and their essential characteristics and the extension and in-
tension of words, not to speak of their denotation and conno-
tation. Correlation of properties has not been forgotten and
---" There was a lot more, but I failed to understand what
he was driving at and came away without learning where I
could find a book on "Plumbing."

I was privileged on the third day of my visit to see
an extraordinary sight, the final test for the highest possible
honour in the Laputan Academy of Librarianship. It was a
most searching and strenuous test and the candidates looked
pale and careworn as the Director gravely rose to address
them. "Gentlemen," he said, "this is a solemn moment for
you all. The severe test you must now undergo is one, if
you pass it, which will be of incalculable value to you at

every moment of your lives as librarians. It is indeed more valuable than all the rest of your technical studies put together. Do your utmost, I beg of you all, and your reward will be great. It is as you know the Diploma with Honours and permission to use the letters F. L. A. , a Fellow of the Laputan Academy. In addition, the best candidate has his portrait painted which will be hung in the Great Hall. Each candidate must await my word before beginning and stop when the bell rings. You have all been provided with tough-skinned bladders with ivory mouthpieces. You know what you must do. GET READY! SET! BLOW!" At the word "BLOW!" all the candidates blew into the bladders, their heads visibly swelling in the process and the winning ones blew balloons of immense size and capacity. After the test was over it was lamentable to see how exhausted the candidates became for everyone collapsed into their seats and the wind in the bladders sighed itself out in Straussian discords.

But I soon grew weary of the Academy and, leaving the Director, I was instructed to creep on my hands and knees to his desk and strike the ground with my head forty-two times saying the following words, "Poonkbosh, Dreiffellbloof, Veendbagg," which means in English, "May your Highness outlive the sun twelve moons and a quarter."

Transmogrification in the Library

Tony Shearman

From The Assistant Librarian 57:43-6, 1964. Reprinted with
permission of the author and of the editor of The Assistant
Librarian.

'Stock and staff will be readily interchangeable'--
McColvin Report, p. 119

Joseph Pale was like most library assistants: he was
extraordinary; and he belonged to a generation which was
honest enough to try to hide this quality behind a façade of
humility. He hated the 'new' description assistant librarian,
considering it lacking in the natural modesty necessary for
the practice of his profession. His appearance, however,
did not help him in this. He had large dark coloured eyes
whose strangeness was accentuated by thick, black-rimmed
glasses; also he had bushy eyebrows which stuck out at either
side like a colonel's moustache ends. This effect was increased by an odd-shaped nose which incorporated both snub
and Roman, as well as by an unexpectedly sensitive mouth.

For the last two days he had not been feeling well and
he found this showing in his work. He had handed a woman
a book called Red-hot Spurs after she had plainly asked for
something 'nice;' and yesterday afternoon he had given wrong
tickets to fifteen people. After tea he had stamped 'withdrawn' a large batch of books set aside to be sent for rebinding. There was no doubt at all that he was unwell. At first
he had credited it to overworking. In his spare time he was
studying on his own for the examinations, and he knew that
to ensure success even at pass level meant necessary and de-
liberate overwork. For this reason, although he had realised
he was not well, he had decided not to relax his five-hour
stint although at the risk of aggravating the mysterious illness. A stubborn force advised complete disregard of whatever was wrong inside his body.

This evening he felt more peculiar still and had considerable difficulty in holding on to the reality of objects around him. He puzzled about his condition as he sat in his armchair studying. It was not like any other illness he had ever had: there were no spots, or a rash, no cough or congestion, above all nothing that the doctor could diagnose, requiring this or that medicine. Perhaps it was a mental disease. Somewhere Joseph had read that 7 per cent of the library profession ended in the loony bin. Certainly this was not overwork as he had experienced it before. Then there had been headaches, eyeache and a complete disinclination towards anything that required thought. It really had been a miracle he had passed the other three parts of the examination. This time he had a lightheadedness accompanied by clear-sightedness and as well an overwhelming sense of not being himself. The question came to him--who was he if he was not himself.

The words on the page he was reading blurred and went away from him to a great distance. It as as if his mind were being detached from his body. He could feel that he was still sitting in a chair but also that he had no control over it. Now his body too was changing. His legs were contracting... stiffening; his clothes felt as if they had been starched in a most extravagant way. There was a tightness along his backbone--it was stitched and glued in a manner that made him urgently want to scratch himself. But he had no hands--they were bound to his sides and covered over so that he could not move them. There followed a flattening out, a comforming to pattern, and more tightening up. His whole person was completely rigid. What seemed odd was that whereas his mind had been confined to his head before, now it seemed free to move where it liked. It was, as it were, his inmost essence.

The chair was gone. He stood, wedged tightly, shoulder to shoulder, with many other objects like him, on a wooden ledge. In front was darkness; behind, a reassuring wooden wall against which he could lean if he wanted. His left-hand neighbour was solid and dependable, whilst the one on his right was flimsy and unquestionably feminine. She was well worn and seemed tired. She sighed involuntarily and Joseph wanted to jump out of his skin but realised he was bound hand and foot to his place on the ledge. The sigh was the first sound he had heard since his translation to this place. He longed to ask his unfortunate companion about her troubles.

59

'Being of a resourceful nature,' he said, considerably surprised at himself; 'it is possible that I can be of assistance to you, madam.' There was no answer and no movement. He must have imagined the sigh. He sighed himself. When would this unreality end? His mind cavorted around inside him, convoluting and spiraling most alarmingly as it sought an answer. Suddenly he sniffed suspiciously and at the same moment realised two things; that he was in the library and that he was a book. Admittedly he was not quite like other books--they could not talk for instance--but as near as it was possible for human beings to approach book form. In the distance he thought he heard hearty laughter. He remembered the sigh. So! books had emotions. They could not talk, but according to their nature they could express their feelings. The love story next door sighed again.

The following morning at the library where Joseph worked the rest of the staff were arriving at the back entrance. The first to go through to the lending library was Lawrence Stumble. He was not a coward or easily intimidated, but when he found Robinson Crusoe waiting for him at the counter he gave a great shout of fear and turned back and ran towards the staffroom.

Miss Mumble was just coming down the stairs when Lawrence appeared wild-eyed and distraught.

'T--There's a man in the lending,' he stammered.

'So what,' said Miss Mumble. 'Come to repair the telephone I expect.'
'N--No. He has a huge beard and strange clothes and ... you have a look.'

Miss Mumble marched into the lending with Lawrence treading almost on her heels. She turned white on seeing Robinson, muttered 'Art thou from Heaven or from Hell' and walked rapidly back, treading fearfully on Lawrence's heels.
'Who is he?' she asked as soon as they were at a safe distance.

'I haven't the faintest,' Lawrence answered.

Mr. Rumble, the chief assistant, had arrived by now and he was breathlessly informed of the being in the lending.

'What being are you talking about? Tumble the caretaker?'

'No! No! He has an enormous beard and the most
peculiar clothes ...'

Mr. Rumble strode through to the lending. The other
two waited to tell their colleagues as they arrived. After
five minutes Mr. Crumble came in and walked straight past
the assembled staff without waiting to hear why they were all
gathered outside the entrance to the lending.

They heard Mr. Rumble say: 'Ah, here is the deputy
librarian, Mr. Crumble. This gentleman is--er--Robinson
Crusoe. I've just had the situation explained to me, Mr.
Crumble. Apparently Mr. Crusoe is a temporary substitute
for Mr. Pale I understand it is a case of transmogrification' ('What the devil does that mean?') 'and will last for
several days. I suggest Mr. Crusoe is given a change of
clothes and a haircut and is shown the routines of library
work.'

The rest of the staff had come out and were gathered
round listening attentively.

'This is a case for the Chief Librarian,' Mr. Crumble pronounced solemnly, 'when he arrives.' Meanwhile, I
think your suggestion is a sound one. May I leave Mr.
Crusoe in your hands Mr. Rumble? I think he had better
appear in more civilised garb before he sees the Chief Librarian. And the committee do not approve of beards.'

Mr. Humble, the chief librarian, arrived punctually
at half past nine and was made aware of the situation as
soon as he had taken off his hat and coat.

'Transmogrification eh? Poor old Pale. What does
it mean?'

'As a matter of fact I'm not too sure. However, the
reference librarian should be able to find out. I'll get her
on it right away.'

There was a knock at the door.

'Mr. Crusoe to see you Mr. Humble.'

'Thank you, Rumble. Now what is all this about,

Mr. Crusoe?' the chief librarian asked in his kindest tones.

'Transmogrification,' replied Crusoe, firmly and to the point.

'Ah yes, to be sure, transmogrification. Well, let me see. Your predecessor, Mr. Pale, is down on the time-table this morning to work on the counter. I'm afraid you will have to take your turn at this work, just as the others do.'

'I understand you perfectly, sir,' said Robinson, gallantly submitting to this ruling.

'Miss Mumble will help you out should you encounter any difficulties. I am sure she will be only too pleased to show you the ropes.'

Robinson executed an exquisite eighteenth-century bow despite his twentieth-century pinstripe suit, and left his new superiors shaking their heads at each other. 'Did he expect me to get up to reply?' Mr. Humble asked, 'Me with my middle-aged spread.'

The eighteenth-century manners which Robinson exhibited to the astounded readers began to attract attention and Miss Mumble decided, charming as they were, they must be stopped. As one of the middle-aged housewives was about to leave, having had her book date-marked, Robinson kissed her hand with an extravagant flourish of the left hand, declaiming: 'Good morrow, mistress.'

'Come on, 'urry up, or I shall miss my 'bus,' said the next woman in the queue.

'Certainly, good mistress. I hope you do not miss your--what was it you said?'

'Bus. B. U. S. Ooh, you mustn't kiss my hand like that.'

'Robinson,' said Miss Mumble distantly, 'this is the way to stamp the ladies' books.'

She stared stonily ahead and energetically stamped the date stamp on the book labels then back on to the inking

pad. As each reader went out, she casually remarked
'Thank you' in case anyone was interested.

'That is all that is required,' she said pointedly,
looking at Robinson and thinking of the wife and children Defoe had given him at the end of the famous book.

'Thank you, Mistress Mumble, for your advice.' He
bent to kiss her hand, but she withdrew it and stalked to
the 'in' counter where a queue had formed. The readers
in it were gazing interestedly at the scene before them.

Shortly after this, an effusive woman asked Robinson
if he would recommend a novel to her. 'I have such difficulty in getting to sleep at night and find that if I read the
right sort of book it will work wonders. The doctors give
me drugs but they have absolutely no effect at all, you
know.'

'Indeed, mistress,' Robinson murmured, wandering
along in front of the shelves and wondering which book to
give her. Suddenly he noticed his own name on one of the
books.

'I don't mind what it is as long as it doesn't keep
me awake half the night. I had one called War and Peace
--that was a good one. Forever Amber--that was no good
at all ... what is this? Robinson Crusoe by Defoe. I
have never heard of the author. Is he good?'

'Oh yes. Pray mistress, do take this book. The
author writes with a distinction I would not accord any other.
You might almost believe the hero a real person as you
read about him. And after you read of the heroic deeds I
--he carried out, and then think of the comfort of your bed,
I am sure you will sleep more soundly than you thought possible.'

'You are very persuasive, young man, for a library
assistant. Still, I think I will try your recommendation.'
Robinson was delighted and thumped the book several times
to make sure the date could be read.

'I shall bring it back if it is not good,' the woman
warned him.

*   *   *   *

Joseph found himself packed in a shopping bag between potatoes and a cabbage. The bag was being swung about in a most alarming manner and the dust from the potatoes was making his back itch incorrigibly. Eventually he was brought to rest, taken out and thrown on the table. There on his side he remained until lunchtime feeling giddy and sick. At the meal-table his first page was read--without much interest--the reader's concentration being mainly on the beef and two vegetables, but half-way through the second page she became interested and when she picked up her knife and fork again she sent a shower of gravy over the paper.

'Tut tut,' she reprimanded herself, and smeared the gravy in trying to wipe it off with her table napkin.

Joseph was left again until late evening, when he was taken upstairs to bed. By now he was tired of being an inanimate object and wondered how he could escape. He tried violent wriggling and so surprised the woman who was reading him that she tore out part of page ten in her fright. The woman's husband on the other side of the bed asked what she thought she was doing.

'It moved, I tell you, it moved.'

'Don't be daft, books can't move by themselves.'

'This one did, I felt it.'

Joseph kept still, though his mind whirled around inside him searching feverishly for a way out. There was a dull pain on his chest where the datemarker had been thumped and now he could feel a line of pain where page ten had been torn. Involuntarily he moved again to relieve the pain. The woman screamed and threw him across the room, where he hit the wall with a thud. To his astonishment he went through the wall and fell an immeasurable distance, down, down ... into his own chair where he studied every evening.

It was an ordinary dream made very real because his mind was tired through overworking. He had picked up a copy of Robinson Crusoe to see how much of it he remembered from the time when he had read it as a child. What was odd though was that the dull pain on his chest still lingered and also there was a sharp pain in his side. When he undressed to go to bed he found a long and quite deep scratch mark and also he noticed gravy marks on his suit. The following morning he checked the library copy of Robinson Crusoe and was not surprised to find that page ten was torn. It was difficult to account, however, for the faded marks of blood left on the part that remained. Joseph quickly took the book and stamped it clearly in several places WITHDRAWN.

The Molesworth Institute

Norman D. Stevens

From ALA Bulletin 57:75-6, 1963. Reprinted with permission of the author and of the American Library Association.

As the result of numerous inquiries concerning the
activities of the Molesworth Institute in recent months, the
board of directors of the institute with considerable reluctance has authorized publication of this brief article describing its basic goals and some of its library-oriented projects.

The Molesworth Institute was found in 1956 as a privately supported nonprofit organization. Its basic objectives
are to foster the growth and development of Molesworth
studies in the United States, to combat the subversive and
antihuman activities of the Treens, to encourage the spread
of general knowledge and raise the general standard of intelligence throughout the world, and to destroy the basic
fabric of bibliography. Our research workers, who are
dedicated to these objectives, serve entirely on a volunteer
basis, working on particular projects which they feel will
best meet these objectives. For that reason, and because
the Institute is interested only in pure research and will not
accept financial aid from outside sources, work on most projects proceeds slowly and we do not envisage their completion in the near future.

One project currently occupying much of our time and
efforts is the development of a paper stock for use in a
program designed to force librarians to reevaluate each item
in their collection after a given period of time (we have
been thinking in terms of a twenty-year period but have not
yet finalized our decision) which will, at the same time, reduce the costs of recataloging, withdrawal, etc.

Under the expert guidance of Dr. Timothy Peason,
formerly of St. Custard's, we are developing a paper stock

66

which will change its color automatically after, say, nineteen years. It will then totally disintegrate one year later. This paper is designed primarily for use as catalog cards. When the card changes its color from white to bright purple, it is a signal that the book which that card represents is to be reevaluated. If the book is to be discarded, it simply may be set aside for a year and then thrown away. The library records may be ignored because they will disappear automatically. If, on the other hand, the book is to be retained, it will have to be recataloged according to the latest code (what a boon!). The new cards can then be filed while the old ones are forgotten.

Until the cataloging-in-source project fell through, we had been working on a scheme to use a similar paper for books. We are now holding this phase of development in abeyance until an acceptable scheme for distribution of catalog cards with books as issued by the publisher is perfected. Ideally, with both cards and books on our special paper, the library would have to put those items which it felt necessary to keep after the given period into some type of microform. These items could then be recataloged, while other items could be ignored. These would remove themselves without further work on the part of the library staff. Of course, a larger custodial staff equipped with vacuum cleaners might be needed to remove the accumulated dust.

Research of this nature, however, is only a small part of our activities. Our major efforts to date have been devoted to publishing projects. First, we plan to solve a major space problem for libraries by microfilming all Braille books, perhaps the bulkiest of all library items. Second, we are preparing an octolingual interlinear edition of the famous 1721 Chinese encyclopedia, the Ku Kin T'u Shu Thi' Ch'eng, which was originally published in 5020 volumes. For some time, a team of outstanding world scholars have been translating this major work into English, French, Spanish, Russian, Arabic, Swahili, and Treen. The Chinese text will be reproduced from the original wood blocks. Our third project is the publication of all books from the long-lost Librairie Saint Victor which were recently rediscovered in the basement of the Vladivostok Free Public Library. This will include, among other titles, La Gualimaffree des Bigotz and L'Histoire des Farfaditz.

Perhaps our major project, completed but lacking publication funds, is a periodical designed to amaze and confound the bibliographic world. This periodical, to be issued at the whim of the editor, will be entitled, purely and simply, Ibid. Its format will be so plain that it will be impossible to distinguish reference to it from other, more legitimate references using the term Ibid. In other words, by properly citing the periodical Ibid., with or without page references, any statement appearing in it can be attributed to any author. All of our articles, untitled and unsigned, naturally, will be brief, general, and of the highest literary quality. In an effort to further confusion and spread the influence of Ibid., each subscriber may make whatever corrections or additions he desires to the contents of any issue. We hope to include in an early issue the famous Molesworth-Peason Universal Statistical Table which completely supersedes and makes totally unnecessary such works as Statistical Abstracts and similar pieces of nonsense which have hitherto hindered would-be scholars and research workers.

The Institute's nonlibrary-oriented projects are equally important, but cannot be mentioned here. Suggestions for other projects of value to libraries that would further the aims of the Institute are always welcome, as are research workers who are willing to devote their time and energy to any of our ongoing projects.

Molesworth Institute Revisited

Norman D. Stevens

From ALA Bulletin 63:1275-7, 1969. Reprinted with permission of the author and of the American Library Association.

Since 1956 there has existed in various locations in the United States a little-known, privately-supported, non-profit research organization known as The Molesworth Institute. Some of its earlier activities were reported on in the ALA Bulletin.[1] Since that time work on many of the important projects described there has continued unabated by our small staff of dedicated volunteer research workers. Some significant, albeit minor, contributions have been made by the Institute in recent years.[2] Progress in general, however, has been somewhat slow and, in some areas, distressingly unspectacular, but we now expect at almost any time the kind of breakthrough in our project to microfilm all Braille books that will bring the Institute the recognition it so richly deserves.

As sponsored research elsewhere has turned increasingly to automation and information retrieval, as well as to other more significant areas, the Board of Directors of The Molesworth Institute has felt that the non-sponsorable research of its workers has fallen somewhat too close to reality and that a fundamental reassessment of the Institute's goals was long overdue. Consequently they recently decided to move the headquarters of the Institute to a more bucolic atmosphere; and, in conjunction with that move, they sponsored the Spring Hill Conference on the state of the art. As a result, the basic goals of The Molesworth Institute were reaffirmed. These goals are: "To foster the growth and development of Molesworth Studies in the United States, to combat the subversive and anti-human activities of the Treens, to encourage the spread of general knowledge and raise the general standard of intelligence throughout the world, and to destroy the basic fabric of bibliography."[3]

69

The goals were also broadened to include "the investigation and application of techniques being developed in other scientific disciplines to the world of books and libraries."[5]

In the few short weeks since this conference was held a number of significant new projects are already under consideration, and the work at The Molesworth Institute has developed a new atmosphere of intensive application, dedication, and rededication. As always one of the major problems is finding enough capable, dedicated research workers with a fundamental commitment to the basic goals of The Molesworth Institute. The Board of Directors has, therefore, contrary to its usual policy, agreed to announce the basic details of some of the new areas currently being investigated in the hopes that this will stimulate a number of people to become Fellows of The Molesworth Institute. We earnestly solicit applications from interested parties who feel that they possess the necessary qualifications.

One of our most significant new studies will be carried out in academic institutions as soon as enough volunteers can be found. It has often been said that "The library is the heart of the institution." To test this statement we now have a team of research workers investigating the possibility of heart transplants. We propose, for example, to move intact the library from a large ARL institution to a small college to see if the latter is suddenly rejuvenated and if the former can survive the shock. The prospects for transplants are numerous and only a few such exchanges should furnish much valuable information on the size of a "heart" which is needed to maintain institutions of varying ages, sizes, and natural conditions.

Another study involves the development of a non-citation index in which it is proposed to list regularly all scientific papers which have not been cited by another author.[6] This work may then be used either in identifying work that may be completely ignored since it has never been cited, or, by the more imaginative, in identifying important work that ought to be pursued further. Along somewhat the same lines we are considering the establishment of a number of NIGEL centers in parallel to the ERIC centers. The NIGEL centers (Negative Information on Godawful Educational Literature) will be concerned with the collection and destruction of educational reports and literature in a number of different areas. These centers will publish weekly bibliographic listings. Some consideration is being given to the possibility of the preservation for historical purposes only of the reports selected for destruction probably by publication in microfiche form at a reduction ratio far beyond the capacity of any reader now available.

Still another line of investigation concerns itself with the collection of picture postcards of libraries to assist in two projects. The first involves the use of a Hinman collator to identify the common features of library buildings in an effort to design the perfect library building. The second involves a consideration of the use of laser beams, and other advanced techniques in the field of microminiaturization, to develop programs for the solid state transmission of books and readers from one library to another.

Finally one of our most important new studies is CRAM III (Clear and Readable Automation Manuals). Because of the urgent and difficult nature of the problem, the initial stages of Project CRAM and CRAM II were by-passed since our preliminary studies revealed that CRAM III is the first level at which any significant improvements are capable of being shown. Many of the details of CRAM III are, at the moment, either confidential or not fully worked out, but we can indicate that one line of research involves the mechanical translation of a number of automation manuals into Treen.

Let me conclude simply by stating that The Molesworth Institute is now earnestly seeking research workers who wish to devote their energies to these, or similar research projects of their own making, vital tasks.

Notes

1. Norman D. Stevens, "The Molesworth Institute," ALA Bulletin 57:75-76, 1963.

2. See, for example, Library Journal 90:2916, 1965; and 92:945, 1967.

3. Op cit. p. 75. N. B. , Op cit. supersedes Ibid. see Op. cit. p. 76.
    In response to numerous requests from readers who have not seen Ibid. and whose libraries may not have complete files, I thought I might report here on one of the most significant accomplishments of The Molesworth Institute which has previously only appeared in

Ibid. That is, of course, the famous Molesworth-Peason Universal Statistical Table.

Figure 1

The Molesworth-Peason Universal Statistical Table[4]

1	2	3	4	5	6	7	8	9	10
11	12	13	14	15	16	17	18	19	20
21	22	23	24	25	26	27	28	29	30
31	32	33	34	35	36	37	38	39	40
41	42	43	44	45	46	47	48	49	50
51	52	53	54	55	56	57	58	59	60
61	62	63	64	65	66	67	68	69	70
71	72	73	74	75	76	77	78	79	80
81	82	83	84	85	86	87	88	89	90
91	92	93	94	95	96	97	98	99	100
*	#	&	—	—	—	—	—	—	—

* Figures not available
\# Latest figures --- (e.g., 1938)
& Estimate based on sample of --- % (e.g., 3.7)
___ Users may provide their own symbols and notes for notes for the remaining spaces

Special note: Through the use of these tables the research-er can immediately provide himself with any statistics he desires, and by properly quoting Ibid. can attribute them to any authority he desires. (e.g., The researcher first quotes a legitimate statement from Archer's book Matableland Today; he then states that the consumption of peanut butter in Matableland in 1965 amounted to 250 lbs. per person which statement he footnotes to Ibid.)

4. Abbreviated version; for complete table and further explanation see Ibid.

5. Spring Hill Conference on the Future of The Molesworth Institute, December 9-13, 1968. Proceedings, p. 13.

6. Our initial proposal was to list in the NCI works that had not been cited in another paper; our preliminary sample indicated that 97.3 percent of all authors cite their own works in later papers.

The Private Papers of Edwin Pooter
(Borough Librarian of Slow-on-the-Uptake)

W. R. McC.

From The Library World 52:79-80, 130-2, 165-6, 187-8,
214-5, 236-7, 1959/1950; 53:8-9, 67-8, 1950/1951. Reprinted with permission of W. H. Smith & Son, Ltd.

I.

I always read the professional journals very carefully. It's just like my new-broom Deputy to dismiss the articles as 90 per cent drivel and froth turned out by young
hopefuls anxious to catch some Chief's eye, but as I told
him, he would not have got on my staff at Slow-on-the-Uptake if he hadn't done that bibliography on milling. (And I
think that remark he then made about catching an old bird
with chaff verged on the impertinent.)

Anyway, I was very impressed with what Mr. Sydney
had to say recently in the Library Association Record about
non-fiction and fiction issues, so I sent for Miss Vague to
find me my last annual report. At first when I worked it
out it didn't seem that Toronto was doing too well, and I was
thinking of writing to the L. A. R. to point out that our figures were even more favourable. I believe in keeping my
subordinates closely informed about my intentions, so I rang
for Simpson to check through my calculations. He started
his usual carping straight away. I must admit that I hadn't
noticed that Toronto didn't include the estimated open shelf
Reference issues as I had done, but it was rather gratuitous
of him to show me how to work out percentages in simple
stages. Anybody can get a fraction upside down. He does
think he's a mathematical wizard and no mistake.

It's very bad to let one of your assistants, even your
Deputy, catch you in an error, so I had to take him down a
peg or two before he went out of the office. I told him that
he had made it quite clear to me that our non-fiction percentage was much too low. I said that he had been appointed in the hope (since proved vain) that he would find time

73

and energy to improve the position. I said that a young
man who wanted to make a name in the profession ought to
be able to create a better class demand and that a lot more
could be done by such things as making reading lists of history text-books and biographies, so that the borrowers
would be led gently from The Borgia Testament to Gibbon's
Decline and Fall, and when Simpson said that he couldn't
see that reading one was more worthy than reading the other,
I told him that he was trying to tear down everything I had
fought for. The nincompoop finished by saying that we
could soon get a 100 per cent non-fiction issue by refraining
from buying fiction. He doesn't know much about my committee if he thinks they would go on voting the money if the
issues dropped by 80 per cent! Where would our jobs be
then?

No, Simpson has still got a lot to learn. And he
needn't think that I shall let the matter drop. Dr. Savage
was right: this is going to be an everlasting campaign.

II.

There is nothing to equal foresight in librarianship,
and I pride myself that events never catch us napping at
Slow -on-the-Uptake Public Library. Library work is just
like a series of military campaigns. Simpson says that
speaking as an old soldier, he thinks that it is just about as
efficient. I'm not quite sure what he means, but I rather
suspect that he is having another of his sly digs at authority. Anyway, to get to the point, I have been making plans
for our cataloguers and classifiers after the British National Bibliography gets under way in January. We shall want
to keep them up to scratch, and as they would have a lot of
time on their hands I propose to get the Reserve Store
books fully catalogued. (They are so old they have only
been listed on sheets chronologically when withdrawn from
ordinary circulation.) I am also toying with the idea of
changing over from classified to dictionary cataloguing.
That alone will keep them going for years. We can also do
a little more with weekly, monthly and quarterly lists of
additions.

I rang for Simpson to inform him of my intentions
and pointed out that he would have to raise his stationery
estimates for the next financial year, as we should be using
very many more catalogue cards. Simpson asked if he
ought to put down a few hundred for cabinets as well, because we should have to file all the extra cards somewhere.

A sensible idea for once you see, and I said of course he
must, but, as usual, he went right off the rails and said
that he had been labouring under the delusion that the British National Bibliography, from the librarian's point of view,
had been introduced as much to save "cataloguing" as to provide more "catalogue." He said that he would count the
scheme a failure unless our saving on cataloguers' salaries
was greater than the cost of subscription and any other inci-
dental expenses.

You can't let your Deputy get away with that sort of
talk. I was quite firm. I said that he wasn't going to tear
down the organisation I had built up with such care, in order to introduce his own new-fangled ideas. I had been doing the thinking for Slow-on-the-Uptake for the past twenty
years just as my father had done before me, and we should
get on better in future if he confined his outrageous suggestions to matters within his province.

Simpson said in that case he needn't exactly change
the subject, as he was being pestered by the chief cataloguer for more shelf-room for the British Museum printed
catalogue. I told him that he mustn't turn right round and
start bothering me with little things like that. Simpson said
that the B.M. Catalogue wasn't a little thing now, and that
it would be quite a big thing when it was finished. I told
him that not being unacquainted with it I knew the uniform
volumes looked very imposing on the shelf, and that it was
my intention to have it moved into my office when it was
completed. Simpson asked if he understood that I wished to
have the finished Catalogue A-Z in my projected office in
the New Central Library when it was built. I said that he
had grasped the matter wonderfully quickly, as that was exactly what I meant. Simpson replied that the completion of
both the B.M. Catalogue and the new Slow-on-the-Uptake
Central Library might well coincide, but he doubted whether
I should have the incumbency. I must have turned pale with
anger at such a preposterous statement, but I let my expression change to patient pity when he continued with the
nonsense that he calculated that as it had taken 18 years and
42 volumes to get as far as COR, at the present rate of
progress the whole thing would require 100 volumes occupying 100 cubic feet of shelf space, and that the early volumes
would be 200 years out of date when "Z" was reached, and
it was all safely installed in my office in the year of our
Lord 2131.

How can an otherwise sensible man get hold of such

ridiculous ideas?

III.

I wonder if you have ever tried to match up the holes on two bus tickets supposedly punched for the same journey. My Deputy Simpson and I were riding out to the Sloppy Park Branch and I noticed that as usual the conductor had failed to register a bull on either or both of the tickets I held. (The committee at Slow-on-the-Uptake are really quite generous about little expenses.) I don't think that it does any harm to improve the shining hour, so I drew Simpson's attention to the conductor's carelessness, and remarked that I should never tolerate such a state of affairs in any organization working under my jurisdiction. As usual, Simpson had to go one better, and said that as the conductors invariably failed to punch the correct destination, he thought that the operation could be omitted altogether, although it was doubtless as soothing to the conductors to ting their little punches and as comfortingly orthodox to their directors, as many of the routine processes meticulously repeated for decades in public librarianship. That's typical of Simpson. He's a very good man, with lots of energy, but he's much took quick to turn well-meant advice into quite a different condemnation of real solid library work.

I said to him (in a very kindly way, of course) that the techniques of Brown, Jast and the other great librarians of the past had stood the test of time and that he could run a library without any records at all, which seemed to be his ambition, when he had gained enough experience to be appointed Chief Librarian somewhere. And not until. Simpson said he didn't expect to convince me that we ought to amalgamate the shelf register and the classified catalogue as he had only been advocating it for six months, but he thought that it would be a step in the right direction if I agreed with him that nine entries for each new non-fiction book smacked of the Circumlocution Office. I said that I was pretty sure that we didn't have anything like nine entries,[1] and that exaggeration didn't bolster a weak case. Simpson tried to say something, but I help up my hand for silence and told him that each of our records was designed to give certain essential information and despite all that he said, to omit any record or to combine any of them would lead to a lowering of our efficiency. Simpson tried to interrupt again, so I told him that the subject was closed, and that if he wished to converse I should be obliged if he would change the subject. Simpson said that he had been trying to

76

change the subject for the last mile, and that as the meeting had become formal he would ask my permission to return to my original remarks about bus tickets. He said that his point that the punching of bus tickets was virtually useless had been proved by the fact that we had successfully passed our stop some time ago.

Why hadn't the ninny told me before?

IV.

I was looking for my Deputy this morning, to tell him my plans for celebrating the Centenary and to see if he could conceivably add anything worthwhile to them. Of course two pages of pious aspirations which end with the customary demand for a Treasury grant go down well enough within the profession, but are quite useless elsewhere. We must have something to grip the public imagination, something that will bring home to the ratepayers the bestial nature of life before the founding of Public Libraries as compared with the spaciousness of 1950. And we must have little models of some kind on show too.

Anyway, it seemed about time that Simpson started to work out the details of my conceptions. I rang for him repeatedly but failed to locate him for nearly an hour. Thought I had my usual morning's self-imposed task on my desk to occupy me while I waited, as I had nearly finished it I began to get a little bit impatient, so naturally I asked Simpson where he had been when he condescended to put in an appearance in time for his elevenses. Of course he wasn't to be caught in the wrong, oh, no! He had the nerve to cite a chance remark I made to him last week, to the effect that he ought to get out into the public departments and see what good work the system was doing instead of spending all the day in his office vainly trying to prove there was something wrong with the methods which I have so carefully built up.

I told him that he had singularly misunderstood my meaning if he had construed my reprimand as carte blanche to waste his time at the Lending Library counter doing routine work that would be better performed by any Junior at a quarter of the salary I paid him. Simpson mounted his high horse at once and replied that he had been satisfying himself that Slow Ref at any rate was not overflowing with sock darning, guzzling tramps, but that it was the Mecca of students and research workers like the annual reports said.

77

I told him that to claim that we were harbouring and sustaining such obnoxious characters would be a strange response to appeals for favourable publicity during Centenary year, while denials would only give wider currency to the stories already circulating--qui s'excuse, s'accuse! I added in my most freezing manner that one glance should have been sufficient to reassure him, but the Artful Dodger countered that he had spent the time assisting a genuine student who had the most varied interests. He had wished to verify the quotation from Butler's Hudibras

> Learning, that cobweb of the brain,
> Profane, erroneous, and vain.

and then he wanted to know the name of the latest element--made by man. Simpson said that after some thrilling research he had been able to supply his students with "Berkelium." Simpson went on to say that his morning hadn't been wasted and that he had happily proved the comprehensive nature of the Reference stock because he had been able to tell his student (who was apparently studying geography also), that the state capital of Arizona did begin with "P" as he had thought, though Simpson couldn't understand what he meant when he said "Of course, 'Immolates itself on a funeral pyre'."

I picked up my pencil and finished my self-appointed task by writing three words on the paper in front of me. Then I told Simpson he shouldn't become too self-congratulatory about the vital assistance he had rendered to the student, at any rate until he had looked at the bottom right-hand corner of the back page of the Daily Telegraph.

I gave him the Centenary plans to work out: the job ought to wipe some of the cobwebs from his brain. Because of the idiot's intervention I had to look for some new occupation to fill up the time to lunch.

I rang for the file copy of The Times and did the one in that.

V.

After due reflection I have come to the conclusion that Simpson made up that story which I reported in the April issue, about the crossword enthusiast in the Reference Library. The spiteful nuisance must have come into my office when I had gone out for a few minutes, seen the words

that I was stuck on, divined the answers by some miracu-
lous means, and then come back when I had returned and
embarked on that ridiculous cock and bull story with the
specific intention of spoiling my morning's enjoyment. I
went through to the Ref. to see if there were any traces of
Simpson's mythical reader but before I could make any
guarded enquiries I noticed that there was a lady waiting at
the service counter. I thought it would be setting a good
example to the staff if I took her query myself. Besides
which, it's so easy to lose touch with the actual service by
becoming immersed in theoretical considerations, but, as I
impress on my subordinates, I make a regular habit of doing a little work in each department in turn. I don't mean
that I am put down on the time-table or anything like that,
but I render a little assistance and advice as I am passing
through.

The lady said that she wanted some information on
"stone frigates," so I got Jane and Brassey but I couldn't
find anything. Then I went to Murray and waded through
the columns under "stone" and "frigate." Though I was almost carried away by the wealth of information that I gleaned on possible uses of two simple words, I must admit that
none of it was apposite. If only one of the Ref. staff had
come back I could have saved my face by passing over the
query and saying that I was wanted urgently on the telephone.
Isn't it exasperating the way assistants can disappear just
when they are most wanted! I was almost at my wit's end
when Bastoe came back. It was on the tip of my tongue to
blow him up about being away for so long while I was trying
to solve such an abstruse enquiry, but I thought better of it
because you must never let your staff think that they know
any more about the job than you do yourself. It's bad for
their morale. It was very fortunate that I didn't give Bastoe a clue about my unsuccessful search because when I told
him in an airy way what was wanted (as though I had only
just been asked myself) he answered immediately that he
thought we should find the meaning in Partridge's Dictionary
of Forces Slang. Sure enough it was there. I handed it
over in triumph to my perfectly genuine student who said
that she was most awfully grateful for my invaluable assistance and would I please find out for her where San Blas was
because she was "doing the most interesting quiz." Complete collapse of Elderly Gentleman, as Punch used to say.

Oscar Wilde was right when he said that nature imi-
tates art.

I admit that I was a trifle piqued that a young whipper-snapper should chance on a scrap of information which
I had failed to find, so I decided to chasten him by enquir-
ing where his colleagues on the Ref. staff were. I first
asked him where Miss Jones was, and he replied with what
looked suspiciously like a smirk that she left us soon after
Christmas to get married. I told him not to be facetious
for I was perfectly well aware that Miss Jones had been
left some time, and that he should have known that I meant
Miss Smith. Bastoe said that she was expected back shortly. I looked at the clock and said that she should have been
back from her elevenses long ago, and if things weren't
tightened up I should stop it altogether. Bastoe said that it
wasn't elevenses that she was coming back from. He added
in the expressionless voice of a stage butler that she was
expected back from Library School sometime this summer,
as the Committee had given her a year's leave of absence
last September.

I didn't stay to ask Bastoe where he had been while
I was attending at the Ref. counter. He might have said
he'd been away doing his National Service.

VI.

I re-introduce the topic of provision of fiction without
apology. As you know, I strongly disfavour any vulgariza-
tion of Our Cause. I've had some pretty heated arguments
on the subject with my ardent Deputy, Simpson, and though
I say it myself, I have never lost my point. And as I've
told him time and again, there are bigger guns on my side
than on his. There is scarcely a prominent member of the
profession, or at least of the L. A. Council, who has not
come down heavily in print on the side of the angels. And
now I come to think of it, there have also been many non-
public librarians of distinction who have implored us to ab-
jure the poison. (That malcontent Simpson says that they
ought to mind their own business.)

Anyway, I was most gratified last week to read in
The Bookseller that the Commercial Libraries Association
was advocating that Public Libraries should not be permitted to circulate any new fiction and that their non-fiction
should be restricted to that which booksellers deem to be of
educational and cultural value.

I could hardly wait to show Simpson the passage and
kept my finger on the bell push till he ran into my office.

He murmured something about where was the fire, or had someone asked to use the microfilm reader at last. Naturally, I ignored such impudence and thrust The Bookseller under his nose. When he had read the relevant paragraphs I asked him why he should persist in his miserable desires to cheapen our great work by the provision of ephemeral fiction while older and wiser heads than his, including many disinterested men of acknowledged brilliance, urged a sounder course. Simpson gave me a queer look and replied that if the Commercial Libraries Association was disinterested, then he was Jimmy Durante, Patron of the Arts. He then asked if he might change the subject, a sure sign that he had no sensible answer to my contention.

He said that he had seen in the May issue of The Library World that it appeared there might be a country-wide surplus of junior candidates over vacancies. I told him that it wasn't news to me and that there was a long waiting list of candidates eager to enter my service in Slow Library. Simpson asked me if I had thought why this had come about, and I replied that it was perfectly obvious that the reputation of librarianship rested on the dignity of the profession and upon the high regard which all sections of the community had for the chief officers, not least at Slow-on-the-Uptake. Simpson said that might have something to do with it, but for his part he thought that it was more likely due to the spread of psychiatry. I asked him what on earth he meant, and he continued by saying that about two-thirds of the Slow waiting list (and therefore, he supposed, a like proportion throughout the country) was composed of those unfortunates who based their applications on the advice of the psychiatrist who was attending them after their nervous breakdown whilst training for the teaching profession, or after they had taken to biting their grandmothers in the leg. Simpson then said that he thought that the said psychiatrists presume that their patients will feel at home in a profession where the chief officials, not least at Slow-on-the-Uptake, though not translating verbiage into action, do yet extol the virtue of rushing lemming-like to self-destruction.

I get so annoyed with Simpson, I often feel as mad as blazes.

VII.

Who said the age of miracles was past? Simpson and I are in agreement--in a way. We've come to the conclusion that it's no use trying to please everybody. Simp-

81

son said that in his limited experience it seemed to be useless to try to please anybody. It's so strange to be in
agreement with my professional sorehead deputy, Simpson,
that I feel compelled to report how it came about. I showed
him, not without a little pardonable feeling of triumph, that
an anonymous correspondent to The Library World had taken
objection to captious criticisms by young members of the
profession who think that they can take a short cut down the
road to fame and fortune (fortune, save the mark!) by criti-
cising all the salient features of good honest librarianship
which have been established and nurtured by the many illustrious librarians of an older generation.

Simpson said that he had seen the note I was refer-
ring to, but that he wasn't exactly abashed because he was
of the opinion that the younger man worth his salt had always been an iconoclast. He asked me if I had seen an article in The Library Assistant which complained on the other
hand that the daring revolutionaries of the last generation
had settled down into hibernating chiefdom and achieved none
of the promise their facile pens had threatened. I took
Simpson's word for it, but naturally I hadn't seen anything
appearing in a periodical with such a title. Assistant indeed! Simpson asked me if I didn't commit some written
indiscretions in my flaming youth: didn't I cross swords
with Brown when he raised the iron curtain at Clerkengrad.
I told him that he was trying to make me a little too ancient, but I supposed that some of my remarks during the
great Tuppenny Library controversy must have been taken
as criticism of something and therefore I suppose also of
somebody.

As it was rather a slack Saturday morning, I suggested that we ought to try and write an article together
which couldn't be taken as criticism either direct or im-
plied, by any old fossil with a guilty conscience. We started
off by saying that we might write in praise of gramophone
record libraries. We didn't pursue the matter further because it occurred to us simultaneously that it might be resented by all the benighted authorities which, like Slow-on-
the-Uptake, might have been embroiled with the wine and
the women but had managed to eschew the song. It's quite
obvious on close inspection that you can't criticise anything
without causing offence, and you can't praise anything which
is not universal without implying criticism where the subject of your praise is not featured. Impasse.

I know it's rather unusual, but as I was feeling

rather pleased with Simpson and as we were both lunching in town, I asked him to accompany me. We went across to "The Crown" and had a couple each in the bar first to get up an appetite. I said surely we can think of something for that article. Simpson said let's kick off with a demand for a Treasury Grant, that's always greet with enthusiasm. I said that we could continue with support for salary increases for assistants and Simpson said that a few words for underpaid chiefs wouldn't be amiss, and wasn't it my turn to get the next round. I said we could conclude with a grand hurrah for the Centenary and isn't progress wonderful. I asked Simpson what about it and he said all right, the same again. I said we ought to be able to put our paper to music, and Simpson said we could then add it to the gramophone record library. So we had one more for the road and agreed to cut our joint article down to something much shorter.

"God's in his heaven, all's right with the world."

VIII.

I'm not like the celebrated parliamentarian whose impromptu speeches were not worth the paper they were written on, but I do believe in reflecting deeply on some topic before the annual conference. It's quite safe to ignore the titles of the papers, which are usually uninformative, and gamble that some speaker will introduce the subject I have chosen or at least go so near it that I can comment on the facts with which I have made myself familiar without being accused of irrelevancy. Of course it's not a gamble but a dead cert that masses of speakers will discuss one hundred years' progress within the profession and compare it with the progress in the general life of the country.

I have decided that the key to all progress lies in the spread of democracy: public libraries have spread democracy and the spread of democracy has led to the development of public libraries. A perfectly balanced sentence, I must certainly get it in somewhere.

I was sitting at my desk clarifying my ideas still further and making a few notes (not to take with me to London, only because I find I can remember things better when I have written them down). My hands were so cold that I could hardly hold my pencil and when it started to rain I rang for Simpson and asked him why on earth he didn't use his brains and get the boilers started when it turned cold in the autumn. I added that he had thought fit to keep the furnace blazing during some of the hottest days of the year which occurred at the beginning of May. But you know Simpson as well as I do. He wasn't to be put in the wrong, now or ever. He replied that there was a Borough Council order that the central heating wasn't to be started up until September 25th. I said I couldn't remember any order that open fires in offices were not to be lighted and that he was to get Bonehed the janitor to light mine immediately. Simpson had the audacity to say that it might not be appreciated by the rest of the staff who were coping with the arctic conditions without any artificial heating, and that went for him, too. I replied quite icily (a good one, that) to the effect that the rest of the assistants could keep themselves warm working on the counter and shelving returned books, and that if my Deputy felt himself in danger of frostbite he might lend a hand in the lending himself. And in the meantime he could jolly well get that fire started for me.

Bonehed came in with the paper and sticks and a bucket of dusty coal and soon had the fire laid. He then produced a bottle and said that on Mr. Simpson's instruction's he was going to pour paraffin on to ensure that I should have a good blaze. My heart warmed a little to Simpson and I told Bonehed to pour plenty on, but to be careful he didn't set the whole place afire. He stood well back, almost by the door, and threw a lighted match on. It didn't catch right away so he came a little closer and tried to light it again. Not a flicker. An awful doubt assailed me. I snatched up the bottle and smelt it. The silly fool had got hold of the wrong bottle and drowned the whole mass of kindling (all there was in the library) with Clearo disinfectant.

Later
I didn't get to the Conference so I wasn't able to say my little piece about the wonders of democracy. I got to bed with a bad chill instead. There's one consolation, though. I'm not starting back to work till September 25th.

Notes

1. Pooter is wrong, but Simpson was not right. Slow-on-the-Uptake Public Library has these entries for each new non-fiction book: order card, order book, accession register, shelf register, author catalogue

84

card, classified catalogue card, weekly list of additions, printed monthly list of additions. The order book and the accession register are in duplicate, however, and there is an additional author or subject reference card on the average for each book added. Twelve entries in total. --Editor.

The Meditations of Joe Soap
"A. L. A. , North West"

From The Assistant Librarian 53:44-5, 1965. Reprinted
with permission of the editor of The Assistant Librarian.

There was an advert. for a Deputy Branch Librarian
here, and it's not a bad town, so I applied for it and got it.
We'd been living with my Mother-in-law, but we've two kids
now and we wanted a house of our own.

It's a decent authority and the staff are a grand lot--
the only snag is the Boss, Samuel Barker, A. L. A. , the
Branch Librarian. Goodness knows where he learned his
librarianship, but he just isn't on the same wavelength as
the rest of the profession. After 10 months of it I'm wondering if it's me that's out of step, but I look at my admin.
notes and read the articles in the Record and the Assistant
--and even the instructions from HQ (No. 64/211/B/Fl To
be read and initialled by all members of staff, etc.)--they
all tie up. And when I go to meetings the other library
types seem to speak the same language. Not Old Sam,
though. "You can get by without all this fancy stuff, dis-
plays and what not . . . And there's no need to run after
the borrowers either. If they are keen they'll ask for
things. It's not up to us to tell them when we get new
books in: we don't want dozens of reservations . . . I've
no time for folk that are too proud to get down to the routine work. We want none of that professional and non-pro-
fessional nonsense here. You decided those books were to
be discarded--well get on and discard them . . ."

So I do, right up to stripping them for salvage, while
the last but one junior (18, 6 "O" levels, F. P. E. , and
flighty with it) is parked by the catalogue looking up readers'
requests in the B. N. B. Half of them will come back from
HQ marked "In your own stock," "More details please,"
"Not yet published," etc. , but it's not my worry--or is it?

Here's the Big Boss. "Good morning, Mr. Soap.

Settling in alright are you?" "Finding my feet now, sir."
"Good. No worries, then?" "Well, sir, Mr. Barker and
I don't always see eye to eye. That worries me a bit."
"Must have a bit of give and take, Mr. Soap, musn't we?
Can't expect us to change the system overnight just to suit
you. Talk it over with Mr. Barker. There's always room
for compromises between reasonable people." "Yes, sir.
That's what my Uncle Polonius up in Oldham said." "Wise
man, your Uncle. Well I'd better get in to see Mr. Barker.
Thing I admire about him, you know, is his complete loyalty to his staff. He'd never dream of breathing a word to
me against any one of them. Carry on, then, Mr. Soap,
and remember--any problems, anything at all, don't be a-
fraid to come to me with them." So in to the office and
Old Sam gets the whiskey out.

"Come to me with your problems!" I can imagine it!

"Yes Mr. Soap?" "Well, it's Mr. Barker, sir. He
hasn't got the right attitude, somehow." "In what way, Mr.
Soap?" "Well, for instance, he wouldn't let me send a card
to old Mrs. Peabody to tell her that 'East Lynne' was there
for her, because he said he wanted to save postage, yet he
himself rang up the manager of the local garage to tell him
we'd got the latest 'Angelique.' And there was a teacher
who wanted 3 books on toadstools for his class when he only
had one ticket and Mr. Barker wouldn't give them to him.
But the Doctor brought 7 books back and he only had 3 tickets and 4 bits of card with his name scribbled on them.
And I don't think we ought to put the fines money in the tea
fund when there's any over; and we could offer to get books
for people instead of just saying 'Sorry, we've not got it';
and we could look for books on the shelf for them instead of
saying 'Room at the top' by Braine, 3rd shelf up on the 2nd
bookcase--if it's in.' And . . ." "Really, Mr. Soap, this
wasn't quite what I had in mind when I asked up to bring me
your problems. Mr. Barker is a very experienced librarian, and he must have good reason for these things. It's
not for you to question his methods. Loyalty, Mr. Soap.
Trust and Loyalty are the essence of our English Way of
Life. We mustn't have all the staff developing into sea lawyers, must we? . . . And if there's nothing else?"

What else could he say? It must sound pretty feeble.
You can't describe the atmosphere of secrecy and furtive-
ness about everything, particularly correspondence and policy decisions; the undermining of your position with the junior
staff--all your instructions altered at once if he knows you've

given them, staff you've started on a job taken off it immediately and given something else to do. The frustration of working against the readers and not for them; the sickness you feel when a child peeps round the door and is afraid to come in because the Boss is on duty. All the pinpricks that make it hell to work here. But what to do? I can't afford to move under about four years or I'll lose heavily on the house. (Besides, after buying stair carpet, curtains etc., at the moment I couldn't afford the fare to an interview if it was more than a 4d. bus ride away.) Looking for another job in under a year wouldn't go down too well either, even if there were many to be had in these parts. Can I stick it until the old man retires? What's 5 more years going to do to me? What's it doing to the junior staff now? The old man oozes charm when he likes, and already they see with his eyes in so many things. Perhaps the Schools will straighten them out, if any of them manage to get in. Meanwhile, Carry on, Joe! As long as the pay cheque keeps coming through, you're laughing. Shut your eyes and take nothing to heart. Give yourself a real interest in life to keep your mind off work. Start off on photography, or local history or something. And if at the end of 5 years you don't care any more--well, nobody but you cares now, so what does it matter? Forget your A. L. A. mate, and get those repairs done. If you don't do them nobody else will. . .

How I Do Library Work Real Good

Petunia F. Worblefister*

From Southeastern Librarian 15:212, 1965. Reprinted with permission of the author (Lenore S. Gribbin) and of the Southeastern Librarian.

Once upon a long, long time ago (to be exact, when I was nineteen years old and living in Run Amok, Alaska), I decided to go to the public library for the first time. It was an interesting experience since the library was housed in an abandoned igloo, contained 59 paperback books, and had signs stating "No Reading in Library." I selected a small tome entitled Calvin Coolidge: Man or Myth, and that is what started me on a lifetime of public library use. A whole thrilling new world of books and reading opened up. From Calvin Coolidge I proceeded to Sun Yat-sen, Alf Landon, and Carlos M. Gusto.

When I reached the age of discretion, I migrated to the big city (Big City, Georgia, it was) and there visited the biggest public library I had ever seen. It had 12,000 volumes and four employees, two of whom were sober. With great trembling and trepidation I approached the desk lady and asked her if she had any good books to read. She asked me what I thought all them things on the shelves were, and I was delighted with her gay repartee. (Actually her name was Miss Gay Repartee.) Miss Repartee showed me how to use the Duo Decimal system to find books on certain subjects, and, as a very special favor, she allowed me to check out a copy of How to Service Your Essex which was kept in a locked cage with the other sex books. Thus I continued my reading career. From Essex I proceeded to Pierce-Arrow, Cord, and Edsel. By that time I had almost used up the small inheritance that I was living on, so I decided I must train for some profession. I then scampered

*Readers' Advisor, Al Fresco Public Library, Florida.

to the public library and read books on home economics, parapsychology, algae farming, brick-laying, and sand sculpture. Then one day, it struck me: with all my varied reading, catholic interests, and vast fund of knowledge, I had already embarked upon the profession of library service. And so I enrolled (if you're over 30, you enroll; under 30, you matriculate) in the John C. Calhoun Junior College in Due Course, South Carolina. I majored in English with a minor in nepotism, receiving a B. A. A. From there I went to Sickening Thud, Tennessee, and started my graduate work at the Scopes-Darrow University. I took an M. S. L. with specialization in modern cataloging techniques. I then started a D. Ts. (Doctor of Trivialities) and wrote my dissertation on "The Significance of the Author Statement on the Verso of the Title-Page." In doing my research I was in correspondence with Melvin Melvil, Sanford Cutter, H. Wilson Wilson, et 'Al, 'Al being my source of information from Iran. My thesis received the Lèse-Majesté Award for Excellence of Punctuation.

My first job was in an Army Library, under the command of General Debility, and my primary task was to count the number of enlisted men who left the library before 8 P. M. I found this very interesting, but when the opportunity arose, I returned to my first love and took a job in the public library in Al Fresco, Florida. This was so satisfying that I am still there and may stay until my retirement, especially since that is only eight months away. I cannot express the thrill, the excitement, which flows through me when a new, and often nervous, patron enters the library and asks me for some good books to read. Then I join my illustrious forerunners, my present cohorts in libraries everywhere, even the future disciples of learning, as I proudly say, "What do you think all them things on the shelves are?"

CENSORSHIP

The End of a Perfect Illusion
(A Drama of Predestination)

Duncan Aikman

From Texas Library Association. News Notes v 2, No. 3: 5-6, 1926. Reprinted with permission of Mrs. Duncan Aikman and the editor of the Texas Library Journal.

Scene: A Public court room in the year 1946. Democracy has by this time progressed to a point where a Public Library's proposed book purchases must be submitted severally to a public hearing, with the provision that no book objected to by an organization composed of two or more persons may be bought. The stage is appropriately set for such an orgy, with the judge of the court of criminal appeals by law presiding, the librarian arraigned at the bar as defendant, and a host of forward-looking world improvers, both long haired and short haired, appearing with their legal advisers, as plaintiffs.

Crier: Oyez, oyez, oyez, the case of the state of Moronia against Literature.

Judge of the court of Criminal Appeals (harshly):
Madame Librarian, are you ready with your proposals?

Librarian (trembling so that she lisps noticeably):
May it please your honor, out of consideration for the feelings of our constituents, it has been decided this year not to buy any books of current publication. People differ in tastes, conventions and opinions, and until its reputation is established as a classic, practically any book may be regarded as controversial and injurious to the community's neurosis. (Murmurs of approval in the court.) Therefore, it is only proposed to use our funds for the re-placement of a few works of long established respectability. First on the list, if

93

there are no objections, we should like to acquire
a new set of the novels of Charles Dickens--

First Volunteer Censor (angrily): Your honor, there certainly are objections and I take pleasure in assert-
ing them on behalf of the Anti-Saloon League.
Every work of this discredited British wine-bibber
contains passages which present tavern life attrac-
tively to our youth. Ther are, furthermore,
whole paragraphs in the Pickwick papers from
which a clever revolutionist against the constitution of the United States might devise recipes for
making punch, and--

Judge: Objections sustained.

Librarian: Our set of Bulfinch's Mythology is in ruins.
Are there any objections to re-placing that?

Second Volunteer Censor: It has long been the policy of
this community to provide no reading matter for
the public which reflects discredit on the account
of the origins of human life given in the book of
Genesis. Ancient mythology may be less consciously vicious in this respect than evolutionary
atheism which was so fortunately banished from
our library 15 years ago. Nevertheless, it runs
counter to the teachings of the Holy Writ and I am
against playing any favorites. On behalf of the
World Fundamentalist Expurgation League, I protest.

Judge: Objection sustained.

Librarian: The dilapidated condition of our 1913 copy of
Gibbons' Decline and Fall of the Roman Empire
suggest that--

Fourth Volunteer Censor: I had the pleasure seven years
ago of assisting at the removal from the library
of the works of Voltaire. I may say now that if
even this dilapidated copy of Gibbons' dastardly attack on the Christian faith of upstanding, redblood-
ed Americans is not thrown into the ash-can at
once, I shall inspire, through the power of the
Evangelican Ministerial Alliance, the hostility of
every newspaper in this community against the library.

94

Judge: Objection sustained. The offender must be removed within one hour, or the court will find the
librarian in contempt.

Librarian: (growing slightly acid): Is there a possibility
that we may be allowed to re-purchase the Diaries
of George Washington?

Fifth Volunteer Censor: The Reverence-our-Heroes
League of America does not propose that our young
people, the voters and law enforcers of tomorrow,
shall be corrupted with the suggestion that the
father of his country indulged in such regrettable
vices of his time as dancing, drinking, card-play-
ing and distilling. This work in the interests of
patriotism should never have been published, your
honor and fellow citizens, to render the effects of
its unfortunate publication null and void.

Judge: Objection sustained. The court furthermore ad-
vises that the Diaries of George Washington be removed and burned at the city crematory.

Librarian: I have but one more request, your honor, to
which I feel sure there can be no objections. Our
library badly needs a dozen more copies of the
Holy Bible.

Sixth Volunteer Censor (a brown little man with slant eyes
and broken English): The Shinto-Buddhist-Moham-
medan Alliance of this progressive city submits
that its members are as good and as typical
Americans as our fellow citizens here. We object
to the purchase of more copies of this work on the
grounds that its circulation encourages disrespect
for our religions, hurts us in our business, tends
towards the denial of our constitutional rights under the first amendment, and in addition that several of its passage come under the ban of the Pure
Speech Act.

Judge (glaring benevolently over the court-room's up-
roar): The objections are not sustained. I find
the aliens guilty of contempt of court, and hereby
sentence them to a year in jail to be followed by
deportation.

Librarian (wearily): All of my suggestions but one have
been rejected.   What are we to do with the balance of our book purchasing fund, amounting to
$111.11?

Judge: The court orders that the balance be divided
equally between the Uncontaminated Illiteracy Fel-
lowship and the Society for the Assistance of Volunteer Prohibition Snoopers.   This hearing stands
adjourned.

Exit librarian wilting on the arm of a stiffly officious
bailiff, and the forward-looking world improvers chanting in
unison, "Oh, yes, we have no bananas."

How to Burn a Book

Richard Armour

Nothing causes so much trouble around a college as
books. Professors have to write them to get promoted. Students have to read them to stay in college. Trustees have
to raise money to build libraries to house them. No wonder
there is so much interest today in reducing the number of
books by burning them--on a selective basis, of course.

Book burning is a charming old custom, hallowed by
antiquity. It has been practiced for centuries by Fascists,
Communists, atheists, school children, rival authors, and
tired librarians. Like everything of importance since the invention of the cloak and the shroud, its origins are cloaked
in mystery and shrouded in secrecy. Some scholars believe
that the first instance of book burning occurred in the Middle
Ages, when a monk was trying to illuminate a manuscript.
All agree that book burning was almost non-existent during
the period when books were made of stone. With the coming
of papyrus, book burning made a long stride forward.

One of the most famous literary references to book
burning occurs in Shakespeare. In The Tempest (Act III,
scene ii), Caliban gives the following helpful advice to his
fellow conspirators when they are plotting to overcome Pros-
pero:

Why, as I told thee, 'tis a custom with him
I' th' afternoon to sleep. There thou mayst brain him,
Having first seized his books; or with a log
Batter his skull, or paunch him with a stake,
Or cut his wezand with thy knife. Remember

97

First to possess his books; for without them
He's but a sot, as I am, nor hath not
One spirit to command: they all do hate him
As rootedly as I. Burn but his books.

Since this custom is so ancient and has been practiced so continuously, it might seem strange that there is
need at this time for instruction regarding how to burn a
book. The need, however, is not only real but urgent.
Many of those currently engaged in book burning are not
themselves readers or possessors of books, and thus are
unable to cope effectively with the destruction of these unfamiliar objects. For those who are able to read, it is
hoped that these instructions will be found helpful.

Unless the fire has already been brought to an extremely high temperature, it is not advisable to burn a book
whole. The first step is to remove the binding, which is
the outer part and has very little printing on it. If this
should happen to be buckram or leather, it may be necessary to pour gasoline upon it to increase its flammability.
(These instructions may be ignored if the book--as there is
an increasingly good chance will be the case--has a paper
binding. Moreover, the book burner may wish to spare such
bindings out of deference for the women who are depicted upon them.)

Once the binding is removed, the book's pages should
be taken out a few at a time. If the pages have been cun-
ningly stitched together, instead of glued, this may be a laborious process, but one well worth the effort. Fifty or a
hundred pages fastened together will be found to burn with
exasperating slowness, and the expenditure of a considerable
amount of gasoline may be required. On the other hand,
five or ten pages will burn quite rapidly. Although it may
take a little more time at first, removal of the pages one by
one will pay off in the end. Each individual page will burn
quickly, give off a lovely flame, and leave almost no ash.
The page-by-page method of book burning is strongly recommended.

Where to burn books is a matter of individual prefer-
ence. Some experienced book burners report that they use
an ordinary fireplace or backyard incinerator with good effect. Although less efficient than wood, coal, or peat, books
make a bright flame and will warm a small room if the fire
is fed continuously. Except for books bound in morocco and
calf, they do not leave clinkers. For cooking, and especial-

ly for use in the barbecue pit, books are of convenient size but have certain serious drawbacks. They give off an unsteady heat and lack the lingering glow of charcoal. In an emergency, however, they will serve the purpose.

An increasingly popular place for book burning is the middle of a street or, even better, a town square. This makes possible the burning of a larger number of books at one time, and the fire may become intense enough for the burning of whole books, thus eliminating the necessity of the painstaking separation of pages referred to above. Another advantage is that this type of burning can be watched by a large number of townspeople and can become something of a social event. Community sings often develop spontaneously on such occasions, and many persons stay late to reminisce about other book burnings and to tell stories by the waning fire. It is well to watch the direction of the wind, and to have fire apparatus nearby in case the blaze should get out of hand. It is also foresighted to engage additional street cleaners to sweep up the ashes and partially burnt bindings the next day. Some towns have returned a handsome profit by selling the concession for refreshments, souvenirs, and other items likely to be desired by the crowd of onlookers.

Since the invention of printing, book burning has lagged seriously behind book production. Suggestions have recently been offered from all sides, especially the left side and the right side, about how to close this dangerous gap. Burning the individual book is slow and toilsome, and many scores and even hundreds of copies of a book may be produced while half a dozen copies are being burned. One proposal, under serious consideration in some quarters, is to burn libraries instead of books. Another plan envisages burning publishing houses.

In this brief treatment of the subject, there is no space to discuss in detail the merits of these various proposals. The burning of individual books has an element of sport in it, and permits a considerable amount of what is known as audience participation. The burning of libraries is a large-scale, practical solution to the problem, and the resulting conflagrations woud, it is admitted, be spectacular. The burning of publishing houses is an admirable idea, although since most publishing houses are in New York City, persons in other parts of the country would have to be content with watching the blazes over television.

The simplest and most efficient method, and one that would afford a great deal of pleasure to a large number of persons, seems to us to have been overlooked by the specialists in this field. It would get even closer to the source, would be nation-wide, and would be without hazards or ill effects. It is so obvious that we wonder it has not gained general acceptance long before this Why not burn authors? We are confident that, now that this has been proposed, the delightful simplicity of the method will be apparent to everyone. Author-burning is likely to become widespread, and it is hoped that the authors themselves will enter in wholeheartedly. It may be the greatest thing since Gutenberg.

Mother Goose Rhymes

Kendall Banning

Selections from his Mother Goose Rhymes. New York, Mother Goose, 1929. Reprinted with permission of Mrs. Kendall Banning.

Dedicated to

The Censors

who have taught us how
to read naughty meanings
into harmless words.

Old Mother Goose

Old Mother Goose, when
    She wanted to ***1
Would **** a fat goose
Or a very fine gander.

(An odd conceit for an old lady.)

A Dillar, A Dollar

A Dillar, a dollar,
    A two o'clock scholar,
What makes you **** so soon?
    You used to **** at two o'clock,
But now you **** at noon.

(The precipitate scholar.)

1. In reading aloud it is most convenient to pronounce
**** as u-m-m-m-h.

Peter, Peter, Pumpkin Eater

Peter, Peter, pumpkin eater,
Had a wife and could't **** her;
He put her in a pumpkin shell
And there he **** her very well.

Peter, Peter, pumpkin eater,
Had another and didn't **** her;
Peter learned to read and spell
And then he **** her very well.

(Knowledge is power!)

There Was An Old Woman
Who Lived In a Shoe

There was an old woman who
    lived in a shoe
Who had so many children she didn't
    know what to do;
So she *****************
And ********************
And ********************

(There's less rhyme than reason in
                    this one!)

Charley

Charley loves good cake and ale;
    Charley loves good candy;
Charley loves to **** the girls
    When they are clean and handy

(Cleanliness is next to godliness!)

Deep Soundings

John Felltimber

From The Assistant Librarian 46:153-4, 1953.   Reprinted
with permission of the editor of The Assistant Librarian.

Now that it is generally accepted that the profession
is firmly stuck in primeval mud until the Clearwaters wash
the way forward, we must pronounce upon the hitherto confused question of book rejection and censorship. Having
studied the history of book rejection (earlier the burning of
rolls, the breaking up of bricks) from the fairly early times
when Noah banned polygamous and polyandrous books as antedeluvian, we now have proposals which we put forward with
the authority of our collective age (roughly 150).

Contemporary pronouncements are not helpful. Blutner
of Garton has decreed that Kinsey vol. 2 should be lent only
to citizens over 24-1/2 who can produce certificates of health,
marriage and birth, together with evidence of need, while
Wrist of Hortal declares that this work should be studied by
all who can prove a total absence of relevant experience.
The staff of Hortal are presumably working out methods (suitable for the public service point) of establishing this absence.
We have no doubt that Mr. Water of Carrington has shown in
the pages of the Bookseller that thrillers provoke crime while
on the other hand "J. F. W. B." has proved with reference to
statistics from all countries except Greenland that prisoners
should be given not only crime books but also textbooks on
poisoning and safe-breaking. Is the profession (he asks) qualified to select such specialist literature?[1]

It seems to us that there is an incurable difference of
view here. Who can tell what would have happened if the
Mancunians had been allowed to read that poisonous book before instead of after? Our proposals make such speculations
idle. We suggest the immediate setting up of the N. L. D. L. --
the National Library of Dreadful Literature. Sufficient copies
of all disturbing, dangerous and doubtful books must be made

available for loan to all those citizens who have been turned away from local libraries and can prove it. Certain people such as Bishops, Cabinet Ministers and John O'Leary would be admitted unconditionally. One copy of each dreadful book will be preserved for posterity, provided that posterity is somehow made to understand that there are or were other libraries. (In Eire, of course, the N. L. D. L. would rapidly outgrow the other relatively tiny collections).

At this stage, detailed administrative proposals are premature. The inevitable and more or less Appropriate Body will be set up. There will be a committee to which busybodies with special knowledge of the dreadful will be co-opted. For instance, the secretary of the League of Genteel Maidens, Messrs. Cohn and Schine, Sir Waldron Smithers, Arthur Deakin and Sir Alfred Munnings would probably be willing to serve provided that they could be allowed to denounce almost everybody once a month. (This would ensure a rapid growth of collections.) The librarian will, of course, be T. Clearwater[2], while the staff will need special training in distinguishing polymorphic types. [3] This would be necessary for survival. Various departments at once suggest themselves: e. g., photographs (close classification required here);[4] prints and drawings; manuscripts (unpublished documents) and two special departments, one for books on the Index and books on devil-worship and witchcraft, and another closed to the public where will be gathered bowdlerised and mutilated books, e. g., innumerable spurious editions of D. H. Lawrence, Ovid, Robert Burns, Shakespeare, Rochester and Brown's Manual of Library Economy. These harmful works will be available to research workers only.

Stock will be built up initially from the restricted shelves of existing libraries, thus making available several miles of shelf-space in Chief Librarians' offices throughout the country.

The classification scheme will have to be devised so that borrowers are properly segregated. For instance, the minor religious sects will have to be carefully scattered about the room while the works of Leopold von Sacher-Masoch will have to be separated from those of the divine Marquis himself; otherwise the public will become intolerably confused. Fiction and autobiography (treated as one) must be classified and no distinction made between Literature (Henry Miller, Genet, Frank Harris, Norman Douglas) and literature (Micky Spillane, James Hadley Chase and Angela Thirkell).

Enough has been said to indicate the scope of our great project. The mind boggles at its possibilities.[5] The profession can now go forward hand in hand into uncharted seas along unexplored avenues and unscaled heights, to advance at last into long-sought terra incognita of fulfilment-- the union of the dreadful book with the dreadful reader every time.

Notes

1. When cornered in his palatial suite of offices at the Librarian, and asked for his answer to this important question, "J. F. W. B." rudely replied, "What do YOU think?"

2. T. Clearwater, by his brilliant and consistent use of high-sounding flannel, booming rhetoric and grinding repetition, has demonstrated a fitness for this important post not possessed by any other librarian. Ex nihilo nihil . . .

3. Apted's Angela will be taken on the staff without delay, thus saving her from the awful fate of meeting Mr. Hepworth on short lists 16-57 sometime before he or she retires (whichever is the earlier).

4. We are indebted to a little man in the B. N. B. basement for classifying a rare historical photograph depicting the well-known aberration, prevalent in Carmarthen, of fixation on ordinary egg-shaped sewer pipes. 131. 342124090006282240914298[1].

5. Dafft-Flubbing has pointed out in succinct language, however, that boggling is an inverted form of dissociation producing traumatic disorders such as shelving books spines inwards. See his Felicity does it again, Chills and Boom, [n. d.], pp. 456ff.

LIBRARY EDUCATION

Forsythia Not Cherry Blossoms

Edmund Lester Pearson

From his column "The Librarian" in the <u>Boston Transcript</u>
May 5, 1915.

"Young ladies," said Miss Tush, principal of the Philander School for Children's Librarians, addressing the senior class, "remember that the future of the country is, in
the larger sense, in your hands.   A wrong decision on any
point may be very grave.   Consider carefully are you sure
when you put up a picture bulletin that it is in the right
spirit?   It represents daffodils, let us say, against a pale
green background.   Would honeysuckles be better?   Do not
make a false step.   Ponder everything.

"You will meet with opposition, of course.   In every
library, I am glad to say, the children's department maintains a gentle but firm opposition to all others.   They have
not received the light yet, so we must be patient.   Patient
and sweet.   Be very sweet.   They are rude, of course, and
uncouth, and it is by sweetness that we conquer them in the
end.

"Hold firm to the ideal.   The most significant department of the library must receive its due recognition.   And
that is what we represent, --the most significant department.
How picturesque, ladies, is the well-equipped children's
room!   How pleasing to all who follow the ideal!   How educational!   How well adapted to the photographer's art!

"The story-hour, --can anything be sweeter than the
young lady with the eager little ones about her, listening to
her recital of that charming tale, --Section 12, Group 2,
Plan 8, Story A, of the prescribed Course for Armenian
and Italian Children, mixed, from 9 to 10 and a half years,
during the Easter Vacation, afternoons only.

"I will now assign the subjects for four more of the

109

graduation theses.   Miss Dipsy will take as her theme:
The Cultural Value of White Crocuses on the Charging Desk
as Contrasted with Pink Azaleas.   Miss Pippin will write
on: Should the Assistant-Children's Librarian-in-charge-of-
Story-Telling wear Mauve or Pale Blue?   Miss Bunn will
discuss: Dealing with the Scoffer.   And Miss Lippitt will
treat: The Cooing Voice, and How to Cultivate it.   That is
all today.   At the next lecture please all bring a sprig of
forsythia, in order to be in the right mood toward what I
have to say.   It--

A Voice: "Would cherry blossoms do, if I could not
get forsythia?"

Miss Tush: "I am afraid not.   That is, of course,
if you do not wish to destroy the atmosphere I shall try to
create.   Are there any more suggestions which anybody has
to offer?   No?   Very well, then.   It is understood about
the forsythia, I think?   Good afternoon."

Mr. Jooley on the Library School

Charles F. Porter and Charles E. Rush

From <u>Library Journal</u> 33:141-3, 1908.

"Tell ye what, Dunnessy, wisht I'd been there," said Mr. Jooley.

"Where d'ye say?" asked Mr. Dunnessy.

"Ever heer tell of a thrainin' school f'r libryians, Dunnessy?"

"Sure I know what ye mane, if it's annything like thrainin' f'r the ring down at Mike's" said Mr. Dunnessy.

"Ye'er wrong again! Spose I'll have to tell ye. I tell ye iverything else, and' I'll have to lay this out f'r ye."

"In the first place, they's differunt kinds iv thrainin', They's th' thrainin' that college boys takes in trottin' th' tin mile relay. (Hosses, Dunnessy, thrain f'r th' same thing.) They they's th' thrainin' that anny seventeen year old M. D. X. Y. Z. docturette takes in order t' cut ye up f'r appindisoitis. An' they's th' thrainin' that Father Kelly, bless his sowl, give ye'er childer, an' th' thrainin' Mrs. Dunnessy gives ye'ersilf whin ye don't do th' manners to soot 'er; they's various kinds, even to th' thrainin' me frind Jay Whitcom Rilley spakes about whin he says:

Some kredulous kronicklers tell us
Of a very tall youngster named Ellis,
    Whose Pa said, Marier,
    If Bubb grows much higher
He'll have to be thrained up a trellis.

But forchunitly, Dunnessy, this thrainin' at Albany is differunt. Just how, I don't know, but it is. Lasteways that's what Hogan tells me. An' he says all of thim are

univarsity graduates, an' are gradually workin' by degrees
f'r B. L. Ss. Hogan says that sthands f'r Bacherlor Libryians. But Hogan's mistook about that, f'r I seed one me-
silf down to John Crerar's libry, Dunnessy, an' it wasnt a
Bacherlor at all at all but as fine a young laady as ye iver
laid eyes on, me boy. An' I've diskiver'd th' maning of the
B. L. S. Sure an' it's Bloomin' Litherary Sikloopeedia.
Niver will the impreshun which was produced on me under-
sthandin' upon that occasion be oblitheratid from me mimory,
Dunnessy. I felt so edified, instruchted an' edikatid that I
was compelled to give vent to me feelin's in this effoosion:

    Heer's to th' chaarmin' young laady libryian
    With a mind elevatid from coortin' an' maaryin.
    She's acquainted with histhory, art an' biography,
    Philosophy, science an' bibliojography.
    Her larnin's piled up like the high Adirondacks,
    An' her insight's as piercin' as if she sat on tacks.
    She can look at th' back iv a book f'r a minit
    An' tell ye interrin'ly all there is in it.
    She is quick with her mind, an' excadin'ly ackerit,
    An' they's no sort iv larnin' but she'll take a crack
      at it.
    At paintin' an' sculpterin', sir, she's a dabbeler,
    An' extramely familiar with rare incunabular.
    But since, at th' pothry I'm not very handy,
    In a word, an' concludin' I w'd say
    SHE'S A DANDY!

    "Lithrachoor as a trade is a great ocupashion. It's
a catchin' epidemick! Spreadin' iverywhere! Me frind
Andrew Carnaygie is adoin it. He's a shovin' books, cahrt
loads iv books, under the specktacles iv ivery man, woman
an' child in th' country, an' unless ye have volumes of books
on all sides of ye, volumes to right of ye, volumes to left
of ye, volumes in front of ye, in all ye'er pockets, in ye'er
hand sachel, und'r ye'er pillow at night an' in ye'er coffee
in the' mornin', ye'er too ignorant to sit down to a square
meal o' vittles with Tiddy Rosenfelt. Lithrachoor is
sthrenuous, Dunnessy, an' if Tiddy gits elected to a third
term I'm thinkin' he'el be afther makin' a law that ivery
prisident iv a railroad, inchoorance company, street car
line, ivery thrust magnate an' publick official will have to
make affydavit that he has read tin books a month, or else
go to th' pinitentiary, where he will have leisure to rade
an' improve his mind. An' Carnaygie is buildin' white Ind-
jianny Bedford limestone sepulchers all over the Sthates to

hold the volumes; an' in ivery wan of these rayciptacles there must be wan, two or twinty B. L. Ss. to guide th' thought, idales an' radin' timperamint of th' community. An' that's what these Albany people are a thrainin' f'r.

An' now, Dunnessy, if ye w'd be afther knowin' what they teach thim at th' Libry Thrainin' School, I will rade ye an exmination paper (Jooley reads):

Ques.   What is a book?

Ans.   A small body of lithrachoor surrounded by kitalog cards.

Q.   What is a desk attindant?

A.   Wan that can smile an' smile an' persuade ye that ye want to rade a book that ye don't want to rade.

Q.   What is a call slip?

A.   Almost always a forlorn hope.

Q.   What is a sthack?

A.   A set of book shelves entirely surrounded by pine boxes.

Q.   What is a reference librarian?

A.   An individool who can find ye something ye didn't niver expect to know in a place ye'd niver expect to find it.

Q.   How would you kitalog a government document?

A.   Put it under the bureau, invart the bureau an' make a cross reference to the fire department.

Q.   What is the Decimal Classification?

A.   A set of pigeonholes into which ye can drop all kinds of information an' niver see thim again.

Q.   How may a conscienchious libryian stem th' tide of fiction?

(Dunnessy promptly replies): "Sure an' he can just
113

dam it!"

Jooley: Now, Dunnessy, w'd ye like to larn to make
a kitalog caard? F'r instance, here's Pat Shaunnessey's old
bettin' book, s'pose we was goin' to kitalog this here book,
th' first thing iver ye do ye write down the call number in
th' corner in blue ink. (Looks in front of book.) Well,
this book 'aint got no call number. Ye see, Dunnessy, nobody niver called f'r this here book, or if they did Pat
widn't let 'em have it on account iv th' bets bein' in it. Put
down three little dots f'r th' call number, in blue ink, mind
ye.

Dunnessy: What's them dots mean?

Jooley: That's th' way they make these here cards.
If they's swear words or annything like that so's thim young
laady's don't like to write it, they just lave it off an' put
down thim three dots. That indikates an exshpurgashun.
Next ye lave th' width iv a junebug. Thim library laadys
call it a centerpade but it manes th' same thing. Then ye
write down th' rid headin', clare at th' tip-top. That's th'
gineral contints iv th' thing. Make it "bad debts."

Dunnessy: What's it a rid headin f'r?

Jooley: Shure, now, an' tha's th' right way. I
s'pose it's because Pat had a rid head 'imself. Then ye
have the width iv a junebug. Then ye write down th' author's
name.

Dunnessy: 'Taint on here.

Jooley: That's all right; just write down "Anon."

Dunnessy: What's that "anon" sthand f'r, Martin?

Jooley: That manes that there didn't nobody write
this here book; it was wrote by a non-intity. Sometimes
ye write it down "psood." That's when a feller writes a
book an' puts down another feller's name f'r th' author. It
means that he's wrote wan book an' been sood f'r it, so's
he dassn't put his name on another. D'ye follow me, Dunnessy? Then ye lave th' width iv a junebug. Next ye write
down th' title. But if ye get tired ye can exshpurgate part
iv it an' put in thim three little dots like three black crows
f'r t' show th' rest iv it's roostin' somewheres else. Then
ye lave the width iv a junebug. Then ye write down th'

114

notes.

Dunnessy: Notes? What's notes?

Jooley: Why, if they's annything annyways pukulier about a book, ye make a note about it. Thim notes is a important part iv a kitalog caard. Now in th' case iv this here volume (holds it up by one cover,) note wan: somewhat dislokated as to th' spoinal collum. Ye write that down, then ye lave th' width iv a junebug. (Looks in book.) Ah! here's a inshripshun. Dont ye niver furgit t' make a not f'r a inksripshun. "Pat Shaunnessey, his book, probably shtole." Put some little coal car cupplins around "probably sthole" indikatin' that it don't say that in th' book but it ought to 'av. Then ye lave th' width iv a junebug. (Jooley opens to title-page.) Note three, pekulier appearance on title-page; (smells of it,) strongly resemblin' tobacco juice. Net ye lave th' width iv a junebug. (Turns pages.) Ah! Note four; wan fly squashed on page twinty-siven. D'ye follow me, Dunnessy? Then ye lave th' width iv a junebug.

Dunnessy: Yes; but what's all thim junebugs f'r, Martin? They's more iv thim on th' card than ye wud see in th' church iv a warm summer avenin'

Jooley: Well, now, I s'pose them's f'r th' tribulashun iv y'r sowl, same's ordinary junebugs is. Lasteways, that's what a kitalog caard's f'r.

Now, I'm not sayin' that this is mere theory, an' nothin' but talk, f'r ye can see f'r ye'r silf that it sthrikes into th' hart iv lithrachoor. It's becomin' a science an' will soon be classed wid th' other ologies an' to know somethin' about this ology wan must be convarsint with all th' others. These B. L. S. s mane business. They's goin' to convart us to th' radin' habit if it takes their last bit iv thrainin'. Wouldn't wonder if frind Carnaygie will soon be buildin' tinimint houses all up an' down Archie Row wid a libry in ivery other room patrolled by a determined, unrelentin' B. L. S. wid' a bottle iv rid ink in wan hand àn' a caard kitalog in th' other. Soon ye'll not have to bother about thinkin', or if ye do, the book will be of great harm to ye. It'll be like thim little boxes of cooked an' predigestid stuff down in the winder to mister Drislane's grocery sthore. There'll be Mr. Carnaygie's libry, an' there'll be a B. L. S. ready to diagnose ye an' prescribe f'r ye, an' there'll be the books done up in purple an' green cowhide; ye step up t' th' loan desk an' press th' button an'--let 'er go Gallagher! Down goes th' larnin' like a boy with a dose iv caster ile.

Ah! Dunnessy, but it's an easy time ye'er grand-
childer will be havin'! Carnaygie an' the B. L. Ss. have
saved future ginerations millions iv years iv exscrewsheatin'
study an' thought.

"Well," said Mr. Dunnessy, "divvle th' bit do I care!
They 'aint inflooenced me yet--but I s'pose they will!"

"Oh! blow ye'er eyes!" responded Mr. Jooley. "Suppose agin they shouldn't! But, as I said wance before, it
takes a thief to catch a thief, which explains the polisman,
an' just so, it takes a libryian to understhand a libryian, an'
amongst thimselves they may know what they are a thrainin'
f'r."

Hymn for Student Librarians

Robert C. Usherwood and John C. Woods

From The Assistant Librarian 57:195, 1964.   Reprinted by permission of the authors and of the editor of The Assistant Librarian.

Much has been written about the professionalism of librarianship.   Public relations (the youngest profession) tried to improve its professional image by having a prayer written for it.   We therefore thought that librarianship, still struggling to obtain a professional image, could perhaps try something along the same lines.   We suggest a hymn for librarianship, and include a sample of such for your perusal.

(To the tune of 'Onward Christian Soldiers')

>   Onward now librarians
>   Marching as to war
>   With old Ranganathan
>   Going on before.
>   See our royal master
>   Leads against the foe
>   Forward into battle
>   See his Colon go.
>   Onward now librarians
>   Marching as to war
>   With old Ranganathan
>   Going on before.
>
>   Bliss and Brown may perish
>   Dewey rise and wane
>   But old Ranganathan
>   Constant will remain.
>   Cat and clas. can never
>   Gainst his will prevail
>   We have Dudley's promise
>   And that cannot fail.
>   Onward, etc.

117

Onward then ye students
Join our happy throng
Blend with ours your voices
Saying Phillips's wrong.
Glory, laud and honour
To the Colon King
This through countless lectures
Shall ye students sing
Onward now librarians, etc.

(We regret that, as so often happens in Church services, this hymn was too long, so we left out the second
verse.)

Odds and Ends
A Recommended Course for Library School

Caroline E. Werkley

From Library Review 22:3-5, 1967. Reprinted with permission of the author and of W. & R. Holmes.

The course I would most like to teach in a school of library science is one very dear to my heart. I would call it 'Odds and Ends', but since odds are that no library school would touch it with a ten-foot pole, as we used to say back in Missouri, that ends 'Odds and Ends', as far as aspiring library students are concerned.

The course, however, is never far out of my mind, and sometimes, as at present, when I am going through a stage of Being Interested in Calligraphy, I jot down an off-beat bit of knowledge for it, such as the fact that the town council of Bodenwerder-on-the-Weser beat the drum for Johannes vom Hagen, one of its home-town boys, when he was advertising as a writing-master at the end of the fourteenth or beginning of the fifteenth century. It vouched for his respectability in a letter patent to the effect that Johannes was born in wedlock, and that he and his parents had conducted themselves 'honestly, devoutly, and respectably.' A little old-fashioned, perhaps, in terms of today's recommendations, but it doubtless got Johannes some pupils who wanted to learn to write 'in gold and silver and any other metal straight from the pen.'[1]

I think I might use as an epigraph on my course-outline a phrase from an advertisement of a cleric-teacher in Toulouse in the middle of the fifteenth century who, after stating his qualifications, wrote irascibly, 'Therefore come ye all here and very quickly; for I am tired of waiting longer and quite weary of telling you so.'[2]

Since, to my mind, the relationship of librarian to book is indivisible as salt and pepper or syrup and pan-

119

cakes, anything pertaining to the book[3]--its history (and this can embrace subjects ranging from tree worship to scapulimancy), its content, its writers, ad infinitum--that interests me could rightly be included in my 'Odds and Ends' course, and I am truly tired of waiting any longer to tell this to any library school that wants to listen.

Last spring, when going through my Early Medieval Scholars phase, I became infatuated with Isidore of Seville. Just think, his encyclopedia was the odds and ends of knowledge for six hundred years. Somewhere I read--not in a history of libraries--that it was Isidore who was responsible for the fascinating story that a unicorn could be captured by a virgin.[4] Once he put his horned head in her lap--snap, the trap! This story made Isidore really come to life for me. What made him think of that combination, a virgin and a unicorn? It inspired a jingle that I thought would make any library school student remember the importance of Isidore of Seville:

> Oh, Isidore and the unicorn,
> The silliest story since man was born.
> There's a Freudian twist to the tale somewhere,
> But it's his neurosis, I don't care.

I told it to a friend of mine, currently enrolled in a school of library science, who, knowing of my interest in the history of books and libraries, had mentioned earlier that, just possibly, the dean of the school she attended might consider me as a part-time teacher of a course in History of the Library. My friend, who is rapturous about automation and library statistics, but has never seen a unicorn, was horrified, 'You won't recite that to her, will you?' she asked.

I did not, but I see no reason why, in our jingle-oriented society, Isidore could not be properly impressed upon the minds of future librarians.

A few years ago I met Boethius, and for weeks went around telling my teen-age son about this wonderful scholar and his Consolation of Philosophy. He was in his Camus period at this time but something must have penetrated, because one day he came home and told me proudly that when his English teacher had mentioned Boethius, he was the only one who knew whom she was talking about. 'Your odds and ends,' he told me, 'are wonderful. I'll bet I know more crazy information from listening to you than any kid in school.'

120

Trees are of vital importance to librarians, of course, because early libraries, in the broad sense that Ernest Richardson[5] and Raymond Irwin[6] and I consider them, were in groves. Also because paper for books is made from trees. And because chairs, tables, desks, shelves and other things in libraries are made of wood (except when they are made of metal),[7] and because the English word 'book' stems from the Anglo-Saxon 'boc,' or beech tree.[8] I would thus certainly devote one lecture to 'Everything about Trees,' including a lot about tree worship, spells, druids and the like. A librarian is not well-rounded who does not know that devils and witches hold an annual dance called the Beneventine wedding under a walnut tree,[9] and that by chewing the leaves of an enchanted tree at Gwalior in India an 'extraordinary sweetness will be imparted to the voice.'[10] Librarians should know about Wood-wives and Moss-folk, and should be cognizant of the fact that a witchpost of rowan built into the hearth will keep witches from passing through the house and up the chimney. And they ought to know about Charles Waterton, nineteenth-century naturalist and eccentric, whose pleasure was to climb up in a great tree to read[11] and watch birds (when he wasn't wrestling alligators).

Well, I don't want to give away all the information in my lecture 'Everything about Trees' here or no one would need to take my course, so I will not elaborate about Erigone (daughter of Icarius to whom Dionysus gave the gift of the vine), who hanged herself from the tree under which her murdered father was buried[12]--but it ends all right, she was changed into a constellation, and so was her little dog, and so was Icarius!

There is no reason why librarians should not be taught about Snoopy and Charlie Brown, in my 'Comic Strips' lecture. I know a librarian in a renowned university who keeps Snoopy cartoons pasted on the walls of her office. She especially likes the one where Lucy is having a crab-in, and Snoopy kisses her and says, 'That's how you break up a crab-in.' The librarian says this helps her not to be cross. I also know a revered scholar-author who pastes these same cartoons on the door of his office, and says that some librarians he has known--especially those who demand the return of books to which he has become attached--remind him of sharp-tongued Lucy. [13]

The lecture on 'Librarians as Temple Priestesses' is a particular favourite of mine. I mean, this is how I really

see the lady librarian: not just an ordinary woman who
rides a bus to work and has people get provoked at her when
she can't find certain books, or a woman who gets provoked
herself when people refuse to return books and swear they
did. Behold her instead as a priestess of the Great God-
dess, as she used to be, a dark-eyed Cretan maiden conducting her strange rites in the Sacred Cave or Grove, surrounded by subterranean gods and by the sacred emblems of
tree, pillar and snake. [14] (All this is a little involved,
you'll just have to come to class to get it properly straightened out.)

     There are a lot of things I haven't mentioned here,
but would in my course, such as Theophilus' tenth-century
recipe for making gold leaf. [15] You have to have a beaver's
tooth or the tooth of a bear or a wild boar for this, and a
purse of vellum parchment, along with pure gold hammered
thin. I almost forgot about the Countess Mahaut, of Artois
and Burgundy, one of the greatest patrons of art of her time
--thirteenth and fourteenth centuries. She had a large
wooden bed with silken sheets and a fur-lined coverlet, and
a lectern for the manuscripts which she illuminated for herself and gave as gifts. She also had a Parrakeet room, the
walls decorated with birds, and one of song with verses
written on the walls, and little gold and silver stars spark-
ling in the ceilings. [16]

     I still haven't discussed Mechthild of Magdeburg, and
Lala of Cyzicus, and John Evelyn (I think I'll use him in the
'Trees' lecture), Merlin, the Ogam script, and King Vorti-
gern--or the copy of the Iliad and the Odyssey written in
letters of gold on 'the gut of a great dragon, one hundred
and twenty feet long.' [17] But if some Library School does
touch my 'Odds and Ends' course with a ten foot pole, come
ye all here and quickly!

Notes

1. S. H. Steinberg, 'Medieval Writing-Masters,' The Li-
    brary, vol. 22, June 1941, p. 5-6.

2. Ibid. p. 11-12.

3. See letter of Inez W. Noyes, 'Where Has the Book
    Gone?' Library Journal, vol. 93(12), 15 June 1968,
    p. 2394.

4. No proper footnote here. Have not the foggiest memory what book it was, something with a pretty dark blue binding. (Possibly published in London? The English know more about unicorns than we Americans do.)

5. Ernest Richardson, The Beginnings of Libraries (Princeton University Press, 1914.)

6. Raymond Irwin, The Heritage of the English Library (London, Allen & Unwin, 1964)--or The English Library, or anything he writes.

7. Note: Unicorns and witches cannot stand iron.

8. Gerald Simons and the Editors of Time-Life Books, Barbarian Europe (New York, Time-Life Books, 1968), p 169.

9. Alexander Porteous, Forest Folklore (New York, Macmillan, 1928), p 289.

10. Ibid, p. 229.

11. When the delicious season of spring sets in, I often get up into the topmost branches of a wide-spreading oak, and there, taking the Metamorphoses out of my pocket, I read the sorrow of poor Halcyone,' Richard Aldington, The Strange Life of Charles Waterton (New York, Duell, Sloan and Pearce, 1949), p. 140.

12. Larousse Encyclopedia of Mythology (New York, Prometheus Press, 1960), p. 179. Note: Icarius should not be confused with Icarus, son of Daedalus.

13. This evaluation of librarians not to be taken seriously. Scholar-author is well-known to librarians as a Puffle-Necked Office Hoarder. See John Sherman and Robert S. Nugent, 'The Birds of Academe,' Library Review, vol. 21 (2), Summer 1967, p. 66.

14. Caroline E. Werkley, "The Reference Librarian: From Temple Priestess to Temple Priestess:" essay unpublished because the subject seems to unnerve most library journals.

15. Just read Theophilus. You will find the whole recipe there.

16. Alice Kemp-Welch, <u>Of Six Mediaeval Women</u> (London, Macmillan, 1913), p. 106-7.

17. Justus Lipsius, "A Brief Outline of the History of Libraries," <u>Literature of Libraries in the Seventeenth and Eighteenth Centuries</u>, vol. 5, edited by John Cotton Dana and Henry W. Kent (Chicago, A. C. Mc Clurg, 1907), p. 55.

RECRUITMENT AND ADVANCEMENT

On Getting Ahead in the Library Profession

Frank J. Anderson

From The Iconoclast Vol. I, No. 1:1-4, 1966. Reprinted by permission of the author and of the editor of The Iconoclast.

No profession should be entered without much malice aforethought. Before making the decision to become a librarian one should do a good deal of considering the future possibilities, comparing alternative professions, and weighing prognosis of success. Once the decision has been made one should not leave things to chance, but a total career picture should be plotted out. The following rambling remarks may be of assistance to the young man, or young woman, who has decided to make a career of book procuring and pandering.

For your professional preparation settle for nothing less than a solidly accredited "name" library school. The name of your school will either haunt you or help you. So you may as well ride it, rather than have it ride you. Get in to a "name" school even if you have to enter on probation, or go into hock in order to finance it.

Once enrolled ingratiate yourself with the director of the school. Do this personage small favors, and be on the alert for publicity concerning him which may appear in professional journals or the local press. Comment personally to him on these items, or send him a brief congratulatory note. Contrary to popular opinion flattery is a swift road to advancement.

Spout off about professionalism and THE LIBRARY PROFESSION at every opportunity, both in and out of class. You can soon become a minor expert on the topic by skimming through LIBRARY LITERATURE to discover the pertinent articles. Read a few. Get several juicy paragraphs down pat and interpolate these whenever the opportunity pre-

sents itself. Be sure to preface your remarks with a por-
tentous "Well, as Downs says . . . " or Asheim or Pow-
ell, or some other impressive name.

Volunteer for student committees which the faculty
suggest might be formed, and also volunteer for any of the
little odds-and-ends jobs that nobody else wants to do. This
will assure you a scholastic reputation of being energetic
and indefatigable. Might even lead to membership in Beta
Phi Mu. Be sure that your name gets into print in school
bulletins and newsletters as being chairman, or member, of
the this-and-that committee. These notices will be "grist"
for your resume when you are job hunting.

Your first job in the field is of vital importance,
since if you play your cards right you can get glowing letters of recommendation from your immediate supervisor,
and maybe even from the chief librarian. You should try to
get your first job in a prestige library system, so that you
may forever after bask in the glow of reflected glory. The
larger the system is the better it will be for you, since it
follows that the larger the staff the lighter the work load.
This gives you some time to observe how the big operators
work, and you can later emulate, or at least mimic, them.

Work hard, at least while being observed, so that in
his monthly evaluation report your department head can note
" . . . this lad is a ball of fire, with an unlimited capacity
for work." Cultivate a nice balance of deferential humility
and aggressive tenacity. Speak out in staff meetings. Back
your opinions with authority by opening your remarks with
such as, "Well, back at Blank Library School Ralph (or Les,
or Larry) seemed to think the underlying philosophy was
. . . " Your listeners are thus impressed with your erudition and infer that you are on a first name basis with the
"big boys" of the library world.

You should be able to manage at least one piece of
library publicity involving yourself as hero. Re-discover
some long hidden book which is perhaps interesting for its
provenance. Or ferret out some little oddity in a manuscript collection such as the out-sized bar bill of some
sanctimonious, but long deceased local notable. With little
research you might be able to blow it up into a good story.
Since it means publicity for the institution the librarian
should be happy to promote it. Be sure your name (spelled
correctly) is prominent in the press releases. If the story
is worthy of pictures be on hand when the newspaper lens-

men appear, since a photo of you and the chief librarian will make excellent material for your job resume folder.

Time your exit from this first job so that the publicity deal is fairly fresh news in the library world. In no circumstances stay more than one year in your first job! Familiarity breeds contempt and after a year your colleagues and superiors will begin to discover the flaws in your professional competence and the annoying quirks of your personality.

You must now seek your "first position." This, your second job, should be as the chief librarian of a moderately-sized system. Not too big, but yet not too small. Seek a Goldilocks type "just right." If the system is too large you might not be able to handle it, if too small you'll have to work too hard.

Before you arrive in the city where your new library is located herald your advent with a fat publicity release which you yourself concoct. Be sure to mention that you are a graduate of Blank Library School, and also that you resigned from a position at the Blink Public Library.

This first position of yours is a very important section of your total career since this is the job in which you puff yourself up into a "big name" in your state and region. It is important that this position be as a chief librarian since this puts you on an equal footing with the head librarians of the larger public and university libraries in your area. You can meet them and converse with them on this basis at library meetings and conventions. Become known to such people. Seek them out at meetings. Follow up with letters, commenting on a bit of (real or imagined) sage advice which you gleaned from being in contact with them.

In your own bailiwick join everything you can think of. Civic, cultural and commercial clubs. If there aren't very many, promote and form some new ones. Let yourself be elected to committees, and even do a little work if you have to. The important thing is to be sure you get plenty of personal publicity. Write your own releases and impinge yourself on the consciousness of the community. Head your stories up with - - - "Joe Blow, City Librarian, graduate of Blank Library School, and formerly on the staff of Blink Public Library spoke to the Blonk Elementary School's PTA on the importance of blunk . . ." After ten or so public exposures you can insert "well-known local

129

lecturer" in your news releases. Clip all these stories for
your scrap book.

Work toward getting some articles printed in professional library journals, so that you may append a list of
"publications" to your job resume. Skill in writing is not
mandatory for such articles, although skill in re-writing is.
A useful device which will supply you with material for articles is to require your department heads to give you detailed reports on their operations. Get them to state specifically their philosophy of service, and to describe the
scope of their department and the methods used to achieve
their service goals. Work these reports over a bit, title
them, and affix your name as author, then spread them a-
round to the various publishers. Technical processes, circulation, reference and children's departments will give you
at least four articles. Combinations, modifications and per-
mutations of the original reports will net you several more.

Suppose the better known, widely circulated journals
have a plethora of articles on hand and reject your offerings.
State and regional library publications are good outlets, and
of course don't overlook the possibility of breaking into print
via the publications of your Alma Mater. If nobody wants
to print your stuff, start up a library publications department and mimeograph your own. Publish the material as a
series of papers. Give the series a jazzy title such as
Horizons, Views, Contributions, or Vistas of Librarianship.
Be sure your name is prominently displayed in the mast-
head as editor.

Publication of a "scholarly" article can help you a-
chieve minor renown as an expert on a particular topic.
Choose something of interest to you and the profession in
general such as recruitment, salaries, or professionalism.
Search out ten or fifteen articles, make a loose outline or
skeleton then drape large chunks from these articles onto
the skeleton. Cite the quoted materials in footnotes with a
few sage comments of your own. If you succeed in getting
this published you'll be "in" as a topical expert. A word of
caution! Don't quote chunks exceeding 500 words or you
will cross the border line between scholarship and plagiar-
ism; and instead of being hailed as an expert are more likely to be classed as a bum and a robber.

One year in this position should give you the reputation of being a "comer," and bright young man in the profession. It will probably provide about all the internal discord,

disruption and financial mismanagement the library can stand too. Move on! Your successor can patch the library together, and your glittering reputation will prevent anyone from listening to your successor's tales of woe as to how you loused things up.

Your second position should be overseas. This will give you an exotic background, a file of 2 x 2 colored slides, notes for articles for the professional journals, souvenirs with which to decorate your home, and material for a couple of years' talks to Rotary, Kiwanis, and others. Stay in this post at least two years. There is an obvious income tax advantage to such a course, and later on you can pose as a small scale martyr who left a promising career in the USA in order to serve as an apostle of modern librarianship to benighted areas in Paris, Rome, or Madrid.

The third, or penultimate, position in your career blueprint should be at A. L. A. headquarters. This not only provides the prestige of official cachet, but the view from the top is all-encompassing and you will quickly become privy to the ins-and-outs of the American library scene. Don't worry about the pay at headquarters since you will stay there only as long as it takes you to spot a prestigious, high-paying job in a pleasant geographical location.

Once you've spotted the job go after it full speed a-head, since this could well be your "snug harbor." Apply discreetly, casually mentioning some of your big name contacts, and offering to supply your resume on request. When the board members take your bait, send your five-pound resume off via airmail, and at the same time a separate letter indicating you've dispatched the resume. This will impress the board with the fact that you are the executive type who knows that time is something more valuable than money. Prepare yourself for the interview by checking into local prides and prejudices of the city where the library is located. This will enable you to make nonchalant references at the luncheon when the board looks you over. Such pre-knowledge will astound them. Brush up on the biographical data of the board members, with special attention to their political affiliations and memberships in service clubs. Wear the appropriate lapel button and practice the jargon of the prevailing political stances. Be convincingly professional and expert, yet humble, when being interviewed. If all these ploys click you'll be offered the job before you leave town.

Act interested--after all this could be the job in which you ride out your career until retirement. Check into the budget thoroughly and make sure it is adequate to provide plenty of staff, including an associate librarian. Memberships, travel and expense money should be sizeable items. A library-owned vehicle of recent vintage, available for your use, would be nice. If all these live up to expectations, dicker for moving expenses and relocation allowance, then sign the contract.

So with a little planning of your career you too can achieve "snug harbor" in under five years out of library school! Soon after your arrival in your "final" job join all the better social, civic, cultural and sporting clubs, out of library funds of course since these are vital areas of library public relations. Delegate all your responsibilities to your associate librarian, except that of check signing, which will keep you in the driver's seat. And now, in this latter segment of your library career, live graciously, rest on your laurels, and tell the years until retirement.

How to Be Brilliant and Successful

S. C. Holliday

From The Library Assistant 44:131-33, 1951.   Reprinted
with permission of the author and of the editor of The
Library Assistant.

Do not--according to your temperament--vigorously
deny or blushingly deprecate what I have to say.   You wish
to become a very senior Senior, possibly a Deputy, perhaps
even a Chief Librarian.   And you want to become known as
an Authority on some aspect of librarianship or on a not
too distantly related subject.   You are wise to admit that
the extra money lures you; otherwise, I might have waxed
satirical at your expense.   As you say--and you are too
right--a chiefship is not only the key to a pauper's Klondyke
but (wherever did you find the phrase?) it has also an alien-
able coruscation all its own.

Well, despite your bad language (you never hoped to
be a civil servant, did you?), I think I know what you mean.
You want to feel able to walk in at Malet Place and shout:
"Hi, Hutch!", "Ho, Charlie!," "Mac, me broth of a
bhoy!"   You want awestricken juniors to buy you large beers
at the Marlborough while you discourse upon Ernie's latest
windmill and what Berwick confided to you.   You aspire, for
you are already corrupted even by future power, to receive
a passing nod from P. S. J. W. himself.   I understand--though
I am amused by your ambition--you want to be on the inside
looking out.

Now it is obvious that I can't tell you how to get the
post you want.   The only advice I can give you there is to
select some expert in jobbery (they are not hard to find) and
watch his methods.   You may be surprised and shocked at
first, but you will learn a lot about human nature.   By diligent study, you will find that only a short time will elapse
before you, too, can crawl through the eye of a needle.
You had better get some Association qualifications, though

133

unfortunately they are not now handed round on a plate as in the days not quite beyond recall. And you had better be educated, for--as you know--to obtain merely a junior's job in a lesser university library or a "senior's" post (at the bottom of the A. P. T. scale) in some obscure Midland town-let, you will need a good Honours degree, a sound knowl-edge of Aramaic, Basque and Cookkoo-oose and be able to write an essay (in Kharoshthi script) upon the left hind-leg of a Tasmanian Devil.

You are professionally qualified, and you are educat-ed--even in the very matters I describe? That is most sat-isfactory. Now, sans fee, and with only your welfare at heart, I am going to tell you how to prepare yourself for Higher Administration, how to become a recognised Author-ity, and how to acquire the reputation of a Sound Man.

First of all, then, I will deal with Higher Adminis-tration. Here you will have to use some thought. Do not let me mislead you, however, for Higher Administration (let me whisper this) is just too easy. You could, if you were foolish enough, pore over the weighty documents pre-pared by the Institute of Management; you could develop a sad, strabismic condition by entering too deeply into the lewd realms of cost accounting, actuarial mathematics and budget forecasting; you could confound yourself with the prob-lems of personnel welfare, with line and staff functions. You could learn to distinguish a therblig from a gantt; you could become word-perfect in the Acts of '50, '52, '92 and 19. Do not indulge in these evil things! To be Successful you must be Sound: you must therefore be in line with the times, or--far better--fifty years behind them.

The best method of preparing yourself for Higher Ad-ministration is not to prepare yourself at all. Instead, you've got to prove yourself capable of H. A. There are ways of doing this. The most obvious--for a junior strug-gling to lift himself from the mire by his bootlickings--is to go to his Chief and say--frankly--"Out! I need the experi-ence and you need a rest. Clear off for a month or two. I'll cope."

This course of action gives rise to occasional diffi-culties, and I will therefore describe a method that has less chance of failure. Don't attempt administrative revolutions within your own library system. However earnest your ef-forts, you will be discouraged by the ribald comments of your colleagues. Instead, you must resort to literature.

You must, in fact, write. To write for the library press you don't have to write very well. Indeed, it is most inadvisable to do so. If you do, and one of the Brigade of Old Guards sees a sentence containing subject, predicate, verb and what have you in correct and apple-pie order, he will snort: "Huh, a wise guy!" and you've lost a point. You see, then, that you've got to develop the common, the very common touch. And for heaven's sake, don't be facetious. Librarianship is a solemn subject--as the Australians would say, a proper Sacred Cow--and you must be serious, dead serious, the deader the better.

But what to write about?--ah, here's where I can really help! You've got to choose a subject that can be appreciated by, and is well within the understanding of all administrators. You will start with your first little essay-- "Correct and Incorrect Methods of Tearing-off Fine Tickets." No Editor will dare reject it. It is, and always has been, a matter of moment. If your essay is sufficiently ungrammatical, and if you conclude with a peroration to the effect that the counter--nay, the fine-roll--is the heart of bibliography, then your article will be read, digested and discussed the length and breadth of the land. Overnight, you will find that you are (not yet a Sound) a Coming Man. True, someone in the British Museum or Library of Congress may die of apoplexy, but pay no attention--they do that all the time.

The succès fou of this essay will almost certainly get you a new job--and--well, here you are, positively leaping up the ladder. Don't worry about Higher Administration any more: you're there, you've done it.

Right. Now for stage two--Soundness. It's simple. You allow a decent, though quite short, interval to elapse, and you slip in your second article. Another subject? Oh, dear me, no! You write, a bit longer, a lot more portentously, your passport to unshakeable esteem: "The Fine Ticket: colour, proportion, perforation."

That's it, my dear chap. Ten minutes after publication, there'll be a letter in the post for you, inviting you to sit (they may even offer you the chair) on a UNESCO committee. Your mail will become a nuisance. They'll want you for the main paper on petty cash at the next Conference, you'll be asked to represent the L. A. on the Standing Commission of Railway Clerks and Cinema Usherettes, and your swift election as a Research Fellow of Chaucer House will be a mere formality.

The transition from Soundness to Authoritativeness is now only a matter of time and ink. Meanwhile, you should exercise craft, and slightly extend your field by writing a severely technical article: "Standards for the Design of Fine-Roll Boxes." When this is printed, you will be recognised as sounder than Sound--as an All-Round Man.

Your moment has come. You have laboured greatly, you have sent questionnaires all over, you have compared, contrasted, tabulated and documented. And with a thrill of personal satisfaction in a job well done, you write the last word of the work that will seal your career: "The Fine Ticket--What of the Future?"

After that, grand occasions only. And when they put the Presidential chain round your neck, perhaps you'll spare a thought for your mentor, who will be there in the background, smirking.

Limericks from Londonderry; A Miscellany

From Times Literary Supplement Sept. 12, 1968 p 1034,
column 5; also Oct. 31, 1968 p 1236, column 2; and from
The Assistant Librarian 61:288, 1968; and from private information. The following items are reprinted with permission of the authors.

I

Advertisement from the September 12 and October 31, 1968
Times Literary Supplement:

Londonderry County
Library
Children's Librarian

A progressive county, very much in the
scene, has need of a librarian, keen, children to enlighten in an area with no blight
on, and the branches to serve are thirteen.
Apply for this job right away, Librarian's
scale is the pay. There is scope and renown in this varsity town, with a new library well on the way.
    Application forms and further particulars
can be obtained from the County Librarian,
County Library Headquarters, Abbey Street,
Coleraine.
    L. J. MITCHELL, County Librarian,
County Library Headquarters, Abbey Street,
Coleraine, Co. Londonderry

II

Upon which Peter Gann wrote to the editor of The Assistant
Librarian:

137

Dear Tony,

Please set up this verse right away
It is topical just for today
If my name you will hide
To keep Mitch mystified
You can tell him on some future day.

Best wishes,
Peter

III

Gann's reply, signed N. W. P. 1951-2, appeared in The Assistant Librarian 61:288, 1968:

A County Librarian of Derry
Was once so inordinately merry,
He wrote adverts in verse
(Though in English, not Erse
Which I think is most fortunate--very!)

What prompted this Limerick use?
Did the Treasurer ask his excuse?
Is staff shortage so frightening
That adverts need brightening
Which sent him in search of his muse?

If you think I am making this up
Then check in Times Literary Supp.
You've no further to delve
Than September Twelve
You will see I've not sold you a pup.

One detail he does not explain
Should applicants wishing to gain
A place on his staff
Persuade him to laugh
By completing their forms in quatrain?

138

IV

While Sir John Heygate of Bellarena, County Londonderry,
a member of the Library Committee, wrote to Mitchell:

> Your T. L. S. advertisement today
> Makes me write, Mr. Mitchell, to say:-
> Do you think I'm too old
> This position to hold?
> If not, please send forms--
> what's the pay?

V

To which Mitchell replied:

> Dear J. H. I don't think you're too old
> You've a great way with children I'm told
> Your uniforms here
> A red cloak and a beard
> As Santa, please come, join the fold.
> The pay is both meagre and small
> In fact it is nothing at all
> But the smile and the joy
> Of each small girl and boy
> Will compensate you for it all!

How to Receive Applicants for Positions

Edmund Lester Pearson

From his column "The Librarian" in the Boston Transcript
February 27, 1918.

Our forthcoming "Manual for Chief Librarians" will be
off the press, it is hoped, in time for the Christmas trade,
either this year or one soon to follow. Number 2 of the
same series, "Manual for Cataloguers" will follow shortly
after, if not before. From Chapter IV of the "Manual for
Chief Librarians" we quote Section 2, on "How to Receive
Applicants for Positions:"

"Retire to your inner office, or, if that is not sufficiently impressive, to the trustees room. Pick out some
apartment large and gloomy; something with marble columns
and onyx panels, something calculated to strike terror to the
stranger.

"Keep the applicant waiting on the edge of his chair,
from three-fourths of an hour to one and one-half hours.
Have your outer sentinels tell him: 'Oh, Dr. Glumpus
couldn't possibly see you yet. He's very busy!'" Have this
very busy motif rubbed into him at frequent intervals. Keep
a line of couriers, pages, messengers, stenographers and
other slaves running in and out. Get the applicant into an
abject frame of mind. Make him feel as if he were a ped-
dler of silver polish trying to butt in at a meeting of the Al-
lied War Council.

"When you admit him at last, retire into a dark corner. Growl a little. Put him where he faces a strong glare
of light. Give him a chair which brings his knees up under
his chin. Say, in gruff tones, 'So you want a position in
this library, do you? Let's see. This is your letter, I
think (selecting it from a bunch of 200). 'Well, well, educational qualifications, what's this? Graduated, head of class,
Yale. Ph. D. at Johns Hopkins, Special studies at Columbia,

Harvard. Three years at Oxford, and Edinburgh. Diploma from Library School at Philander University!"

"At this point, you shake your head, click with your tongue, and mutter 'educational qualifications very meagre! Very meagre!" Convey the impression that perhaps he might get in some places with such recommendations, but never into the dear old Ezra Beesley Free Public Library. Never in the world! Thank God, we have higher standards than that!

" 'Any experience?' you ask. He admits to five years of it. You raise your eyebrows and say: 'That's all?'
"The next question is: 'What salary do you expect?' He timidly suggests thirty-five dollars a month. You utter a hoot. 'Why, my dear Sir, old Mr. Akers, my principal assistant, who has been with us since 1855, gets twenty-two!"

"By this time you should have him in the proper condition. Bring out the application blanks. 'Now, here,' you say, is Form 123A, Form 666B, and Form $x^2+2xy+y^2$. Fill these out carefully and mail them to us. Write with ink. Do not write on both sides of the paper. Use red ink on the left-hand side of the other form, and a violet copying ink on the other. Make them all out in triplicate. Turn them over and brown them on the under side. Then we will mail you Form Alpha Sigma Sigma, and Form K2. If these are made out correctly, and we feel in good humor, you will be placed on the Waiting List for Applicants. That means that when your turn comes you will be permitted to apply again. Good-day, sir."

LIBRARY LITERATURE

How to Write Effectively for a Library Periodical

Philip G. Becker

From Wilson Library Bulletin 31:539, 559, 1957. Reprinted
by permission from the March 1957 issue of the Wilson Library Bulletin. Copyright (c)1957 by the H. W. Wilson Company. Also with permission of the author.

In writing for the library periodical, it is necessary
to keep two main points in mind: determine just what you
are going to say (if anything); determine how to avoid actually coming right out and saying it. These two factors are
the heart and soul of library literature.

The typical article is generally divided into four sections or stages: the introduction, the main body, the summary, and the conclusion. Let us examine them one by one
in order to determine their basic nature.

The Introduction

This section is devoted to a statement or group of
statements, the more the better, dealing with what the author
is either going to explain or discuss in the main body of the
article. Wiggins, in his excellent dissertation, "Administrative Problems of the Winneposh Public Library," succeeded
in expostulating for fifteen pages about what he was going to
say, indeed, he managed to write twenty pages without saying anything at all.

Arbuthnot's article on the study of Freudian symbol-
ism in the cataloging department is an interesting example of
what can happen when a writer makes his introduction a little
too long. Arbuthnot spent his first thirty pages discussing
whether or not it was really possible to say anything positive
on the subject. Arbuthnot has gotten off on the wrong foot
before but never quite as badly as this. On his thirty-first
page Arbuthnot asked rhetorically, fortunately, if the whole

145

business were worth writing about anyway. On the thirty-second page, Arbuthnot, who if he is not brief is at least fair, admitted the subject wasn't much worth thinking about, let alone writing on, and thus he concluded his article in a somewhat more abrupt manner than is customary.

The Main Body

The main body generally occupies itself with a discussion of the theme or themes of the article. Let us use once more Wiggins' excellent article on the Winneposh Public Library because it is a fine example of what an author can do when he really sets his mind to it. Wiggins' main theme was this: the more books you have, the bigger the library collection. In ordinary writing, perhaps, the meaning of this statement would be relatively clear. Wiggins, however, felt that it was a little too clear. Let me quote his opening paragraph in the main body:

> In dealing with the administrative difficulties inherent in problems of this nature, it is essential to bear in mind that the organizational and administrative capacity of the library is governed in a directly proportional manner by the amount of material which the library has collected by means of its acquisitional policy, through gifts and exchanges, as well as through normal acquisitional channels.

After such a magnificent opening statement, it would seem virtually impossible to elaborate still further on this theme, but Wiggins, however, feeling that further discussion was necessary, succeeded in elaborating on this for five pages more.

The Summary

In preparing the summary, the first step is to reread what you have written in an effort to determine just what you have said. Often the author in doing this discovers that he hasn't really said anything whatsoever. For this reason undoubtedly, a great many articles in library literature do not contain summaries.

If you should discover that you have made a point--quite by accident or otherwise--see if you can summarize it, i.e., see if it makes any sense in a general sort of way. Be extremely careful though; do not summarize it too con-

146

cisely as you may have the reader wondering why you took so long to bring out your point instead of having him properly wonder what on earth you are talking about. The best policy, in fact the safest, is to merely reword the point, eliminating a few of the more developmental phrases.

Count the number of pages in your article thus far. If you have at least twenty, you are well on the way toward becoming an expert in the field. If you are a few short-- say five short--the conclusion should bring it up to par with a little effort.

In passing, it is interesting to note that in ordinary parlance the word "conclusion" means "end." However, in library literature this meaning has been broadened somewhat to mean "almost the end but not quite." When the author says "in conclusion" or "let me conclude," you can often assume that he is somewhere beyond the halfway point, but in the case of some of the more experienced writers such an optimistic presumption is not always justified.

In preparing their conclusions, one method used by many writers is to try and clarify the main body of the work. Quite often this is totally impossible. Some writers therefore spend their last pages trying to clarify the summary. This is usually a lot easier to do. Another method of preparing the conclusion is to admit that a great deal more could be said about the subject. You don't have to say how; just mention the fact and discuss it. This is good for five pages at least.

Keep all these points I have mentioned in mind when you write your article. Don't oversimplify the issues, in fact don't simplify them at all. This will only annoy other members of the profession who may well berate you for attempting to set a dangerous precedent. As a matter of fact, you never know when you might have to follow it yourself.

Library Leads

Frank D. Hankins

From Wilson Library Bulletin 37:57, 1962. Reprinted by permission from the September 1962 issue of the Wilson Library Bulletin. Copyright (c)1962 by the H. W. Wilson Company. Also with permission of the author.

Library stories I'll probably never finish reading

Our library had to move 25,000 books in 36 hours!

How to encode by means of digital computers without harming the spines of the festchriften was the purpose of this study.....

In order to obtain the relative percentages between books charged and not returned and those discharged and lost 600 questionnaires were....

We proved that librarians can be glamorous!

Being a librarian is full of surprises....

Booksville Library was bursting at the seams....

One course that is not taught in library school....

Every library school student ought to be required....

Wordsville Library met the challenge....

We faced a challenging....

Challenge....

A survey was made to determine the relative merits of manual vs. machine marking of the codex book....

A survey was made....

As the attached flow charts depicting in detail a breakdown of component steps within the overall book-stamping operation will show....

Anyone can have a book fair!

The importance of interpersonal relationships in the library....

"We must sell the library story," stated....

Librarians are beginning to realize the value of human engineering....

A committee to study recruiting....

Fascinating stories yet unwritten

We sent out 98 questionnaires and then decided it wasn't worth it....

After careful consideration of our time and that of the respondents involved, we junked the proposed survey....

If you want to have a hell of a good time, try the Ford Foundation....

I don't know exactly what my assignment was, but I met a lot of nice people overseas....

After a closed Board meeting today, Librarian X stated that no salary increases were voted by the Board because of a general feeling that the staff members would continue working anyway....

The American Library Association reduced membership dues today....

According to well-informed sources who wish to remain unnamed, the Librarian of the Year doesn't much like people or books. "Actually," he stated, "I read mostly Who's Who in Library Service, plus magazine articles to see who is writing what, so that I will know what to write. People bug me."

149

Library Science - So What?
or
If Dewey Did It, You Can Too

Betsy Ann Olive

From North Carolina Libraries 13:101-3, 1955. Reprinted by permission of the author and of the editor of North Carolina Libraries.

The natural processes of evolution have given us a new creature: the WOPLA. The WOPLA is like other members of the genus Homo in that he has two each of legs, hands, feet, eyes and ears; and one each of head, nose, mouth and heart. The distinguishing characteristic is this: The WOPLA is a librarian, or he has been a librarian, or he Knows Something about libraries. A WOPLA is different from ordinary librarians in that he is Making a Name for himself. A WOPLA is a Writer of Professional Library Articles.

All librarians should aspire to become WOPLAs because a WOPLA Makes a Name for himself, and to Make a Name for himself should be the ambition of all librarians. If more librarians become WOPLAs there will be fewer active librarians. This will be good for the Profession. A simple law of economics will set in: More WOPLAs = Fewer Librarians = Greater Demand for remaining librarians = Higher Salaries. In grave consideration of this elementary law of supply and demand, I am in favor of making more librarians into WOPLAs. Hence, I offer this paper.

The paper is written to give librarians the rules for becoming WOPLAs. Hundreds of journal articles were studied to discover the system and to gather the advice offered herein. It is my considered belief that this is the only place where the rules for becoming a successful WOPLA have been laid down. The rules used most consistently by the best WOPLAs follow:

Rule No. 1: Make proper pyschological adjustment. The successful WOPLA is dedicated. He takes himself seriously. He knows he has something to offer The Profession. He is sure, very sure, he is on his way to Making a Name for himself. Persons who were reared on adages like "The world is full of such, who think too little and talk too much" cannot expect to become expert WOPLAs. It is not true that inert readers are the direct result of inept writing. Ideas like these undermine the WOPLA. Success will not come until they are discarded.

Rule No. 2: Never use a long word when you can find one that is longer. Long words are impressive. The longer, the more impressive. Never say "city," say "municipality." Avoid "use," say "utilization." The proper and constant application of this rule will give your writing a learned and complex air. This is good. Simple, short words make your writing terse and crisp. It is quickly read and understood. This is bad. Do you want to be taken for a simpleton?

Rule No. 3: (This rule is an extension of Rule No. 2.) Never use one word when you can use a clause or a whole sentence. You cannot hope to become a full-fledged WOPLA until you can parlay "Upon verification, the accounts are paid by the order librarian" into the following: "Those invoices received for supplies, books, and other library materials shipped to the debtor institutions by the makers of the invoices will be certified as valid representations of the transactions through precise routines established for this purpose. Thereafter the invoices shall be transferred to the jurisdiction of the head of that department of the institution which is charged with the acquisitions function--who, upon receipt of same, shall draw upon proper funds and make checks payable to the creditor, and thus discharge the obligation--a fact which is noted on the proper records."

Consistent application of Rule No. 3 has two advantages: First, it takes up more space. This is good. Obviously. Among other things, imagine how much it will mean when the journals begin paying by the word. At two cents a word the first sentence is worth only 20c, but the second phrasing would bring in all of $1.88! The other advantage is that involved sentences will puzzle your reader. He must read a paragraph several times to glean its meaning. This is good. Even if he does not read through the whole article--most especially, if he does not read through

151

the whole article, he will have utmost admiration for the writer whose work is so far beyond his grasp. He will know he has discovered another Brilliant Mind. This is good. It is basic that all WOPLAs be thought to have Brilliant Minds.

Rule No. 4: Use the standard library terminology interminably. (This is the one exception to Rules 2 and 3.) Familiarity with the jargon of The Profession and proficiency in its use mark the writer as an old hand at the game. This is good. Here are examples of the application of Rule No. 4:

Good, sound reference books of lasting value are always "monumental works." The successful WOPLA can distinguish between a "monumental work" and a "landmark book." He also knows that every book ever printed falls into one of two classes. It must be either "scholarly" or "popular." A WOPLA never refers to his employment as "work" or a "job," it is always "The Profession." A thorough going, well-trained WOPLA is capable of using several bits of the library parlance in one sentence. An excellent example is: "Reference type situations require detailed specificity catalogwise." In this sentence note particularly the use of "type" and "wise." These two suffixes should be added to both nouns and adjectives wherever possible. They make the emphasis more emphatic. They add polish and elegance to your writing.

If, in addition to the foregoing standard terminology, you can work in other excellent stand-bys like "framework of reference" and "definitive work," so much the better. You are on your way to success. On the other hand, if you refuse to use the terminology in which all the leading WOPLAs write, you will be headed as directly for failure as though you had lost your typewriter. Mark this well.

Rule No. 5: Write upon the same subject and from the same viewpoint as many other WOPLAs have done. This will give you a lengthy bibliography and/or footnotes. This is good. Bibliographies and footnotes lend a certain erudite air which can be achieved in no other manner. A note of warning should be inserted here. After the librarian has become a prolific WOPLA he must exercise caution in the composition of his bibliographies. He should be careful not to list therein the article for which the current one is a near duplicate.

152

Writing upon the same subject which has been treated successfully many times before is also advantageous in that it is very certain, safe and sure. What has been accepted once, usually will be accepted again. New ideas are frowned upon. If a WOPLA insists upon them, he will be called a radical or a visionary. This is bad. A WOPLA wants to Make a Name for himself, but these are not the names.

Rule No. 6: Tell what you have to say before you say it. You call this the introduction. It eliminates all possibility of shocking the reader. Also, the reader who is in a hurry can get the essence of the article from the first paragraph. He will appreciate this and will become one of your devotees. For the benefit of those who have more time to read, the introduction is followed by the body of the article in which will be applied Rule Nos. 2, 3, 4, and 5. You now have told what you have to say before you say it; then you have said what you have to say. You are ready to apply Rule No. 7.

Rule No. 7: Reverse Rule No. 6, and tell what you have said after you have said it. You call this the conclusion. Jointly, Rule Nos. 6 and 7 give the fundamental form used in the writings of all WOPLAs. It is as essential for an aspiring young WOPLA to adhere to this form as it is for a cataloger to stick to the Dewey schedules. Departure from any of the above rules leads to undesirable clarity and tends towards reader interest and appeal. This is bad. Such yielding to popular demands is evidence of a weakness which may be excused in the writing of best-sellers but cannot be tolerated in the works of a good WOPLA.

Though my time in The Profession has been short, my research upon the subject of WOPLAs has been exhaustive. I can guarantee that librarians who follow my WOPLA rules without deviation will become successful Writers of Professional Library Articles. When a librarian has become a good, consistently prolific WOPLA, it is every man for himself to see who can get the most articles into the most journals the most times. If a WOPLA becomes a leader in this publications race, then he will have achieved the goal of all WOPLAs: He will be a V. I. P. This is good.

(Author's note: In the above article all references to persons both living and dead and to the way things are done are purely intentional.)

REPORTS AND QUESTIONNAIRES

The Treasurer's Report

From Wilson Bulletin for Librarians 13:477, 1939. Reprinted by permission from the March 1939 issue of the Wilson Bulletin for Librarians. Copyright (c)1939 by the H. W. Wilson Company.

At one of the state library association conferences in the Mid-West, the following Treasurer's Report was read to the astonished assembly. No doubt it was just as illuminating as most treasurers' reports!

Balance in the treasury of the library association
    as of January 1st, was $10,000.000
    Expenses incurred during the year include:
      Stationary   .10
      Telephone calls (Not all personal)   200.08
      Miscellaneous expenses of officers   750.00
      Postage   1.98
      Damages paid to Rental Libraries in state
        for loss of business   2,000.00
      Bank Nights in various state libraries,
        sponsored by the Junior Members   2,500.00
      C.I.O. to let us alone   .15
      A.L.A. for printing notice of state
        convention   500.68
      Newspapers for keeping Association
        scandals out of headlines   35.75
      Flowers in season for President's desk   345.00
      Odds and ends   1,278.45
      Carfare   305.60
      Fines for speeding of secretary while on
        Association business--plus contempt of
        court   65.00
      Miscellaneous   738.30
      Champagne "rush" luncheons to get more
        members into Association   600.00
      Committee on Resources of state libraries,
        for discovering how many libraries in state
        had copies of Ferdinand   1.25

Receipts:
  For sale of umbrellas left in check room
    after last convention   27. 50
  Refund on annuities, no librarians having
    reached the age of 65   600. 98
  From last convention hotel headquarters
    for contract not to hold meetings there
    again for ten years   50. 00
  From philanthropist to establish home for
    retired librarians on choice spot   75. 00
  From American Legion for contract not to
    hold state library meetings at same
    time of legion conventions   2. 98
                                                        ─────────

This unfortunately leaves a deficit in the
  treasury of   37. 59
                                                        ─────────

              Respectfully submitted,
                  Signed,

                     Treasurer.

A Library Report in Verse
(Berkshire [Mass.] Athenaeum and Museum Report,
1910-1911)

Harlan Hoge Ballard

From Library Journal 36:430-1, 1911. Reprinted by permission of the Berkshire Athenaeum.

I have the honor of presenting here
The report of the library for the year:
Books on hand when the year begun,
55,391;
Added to June 1, 1911,
2387;
Total number of books to date,
57,238;
The parts and the total will now be proved,
By noting 440 removed,
By reason of wear, or tear, or age.
Or the fatal defect of a missing page.

The circulation last year, I see,
Was 91,073;
We have added this year to the former score
8530 more.
The total number this year will be
99,603.
March has led for many a year
In the number of books delivered here;
But now, as we shall long remember,
The largest total was last November.
The weather was cold, the winds were shifty,
And the count was 9250.

The largest day was Feb. 8;
When we issued 938.
Memorial Day showed reason plenty
For closing on holidays; loaned but 20.
The new cards issued this year we fix

159

At 3626.
Of pamphlets, 12,023
Were reported in 1910 by me;
We have gained 642.
Of these but 71 were bought;
The others, presented, have cost us naught.

Of the volumes gained as the months have run,
We bought 1441.
One hundred are books or papers bound,
And two by means of exchange were found;
While generous gifts increased the store
By 744.
Miss Fannie S. Davis deserves a line;
She gave us 339.

The cost of rebinding our books has been spared.
For 15,000 have been repaired;
Miss Pierce has carefully planned this work,
Which none of the ladies have tried to shirk.

The quality sought in our literature
Has shown improvement, slow but sure,
There still are thousands of boys and girls
Who revel in stories of knights and earls,
There still are thousands of women too,
That borrow our novels and read them through;
But as nothing relieves the average mind
So quickly as these, I am half inclined
To believe that those writers have served us best
Who have brought to the weary the gift of rest.

And yet I am glad to report again
A growing use of our books by men;
To men of the factory, shop and farm,
The library calls with increasing charm.
There is high reward in the grateful look
On the face of the toiler who finds the book
That will teach him the better to use his tools;
Or give for his guidance the latest rules;
And many a man is rejoiced to learn
That the more he knows the more he can earn.
For every one, sooner or later, finds
That better books make better minds.

Conversely, the people's good taste will cure
The evils that trouble our literature.
The law of supply and demand is here

As potent in the commercial sphere.
Authors of readers must take good heed,
For folks must write what folks will read!

We note already a higher trend
(You know it is never too late to mend)
In fiction; the books show greater care,
A brighter sky, and a purer air;
For example, in "Molly-Make-Believe"
There's the merriest, sauciest child of Eve;
The story is bright, and the wit is keen;
And it loses no strength for being clean,
Another good tale is "The broad highway,"
As sweet as the flowers that bloom in May;
Yet, brimming with love, and with blood and fire,
It thrills with courage and strong desire.
A hero and heroine self-reliant
Are drawn by the pen of "Margaret Bryant;"
And many a heart has warmly glowed
For Anne's career, and Aston's road!

In "Flamsted Quarries," away down east,
Is the tale of a dear old parish priest;
It teaches the truth as few books can,
That he best serves God who best serves man,
While in Day's "King Spruce," and in "Nathan Burke,"
Are shown the rewards of faithful work.

But it isn't my purpose to burden you
With a catalog, or a rhymed review;
But only to prove that a book's not hurt,
By having it decent and free from dirt.

Outside of fiction the number is great
Of excellent books received of late;
But few will be read with more delight
Than "The great white north," by Helen Wright,
Though, strange as it seems, I cannot but fear
There are some don't know that she lives right here.

Miss Peck has charge of the catalog still,
And none could better the task fulfil;
Miss Axtell examines with patient care
Each book returned, for a blot or tear;
Miss Elizabeth Downs at the desk presides,
And verifies all our accounts besides;
The diligent hand of Miss Hawes is seen
In each reference-book and magazine;

161

She is questioned a hundred times a day;
And no one, unanswered, is turned away.
As first assistant, by every test,
Miss Waterman's excellence stands confessed;
Miss Lewis, Miss Feeley, Miss Mafred Rice,
Are faithful in service, in judgment, nice.

Not much has been done to the building; so
It's about the same as a year ago;
We have only done what we had to do.
The roof has been patched where the rain came
    through;
Some ceilings and walls have been kalsomined;
And the danger averted of being fined;
(The repair committee deserves the praise;)
For the doors have been hung so they swing both
    ways!
And among the minor improvements made
The lawn has been brought to a better grade.
The unfortunate state of the upper floor
Is not much worse than it was before;
The stairs are still crooked, and narrow and dark;
We still lack windows to face the park;
And congestion below is harder to bear.
On account of the wasted room up there!

It is not the conventional thing to do;
To present a report in rhyme, to you;
But I solemnly promise to break this pen,
And never do such a thing again:--
I offer no further excuse; for indeed it
Is written in hope that some people may read it!

P. S. --An important fact I forgot to mention;
Deserves a moment of your attention:--
A room-ful of things from the Athenaeum
Have been placed down stairs in the art museum;
Historical relics, that long have been
Neglected, and dusty, and all unseen.
New labelled and clean, have now their places
In twenty or more appropriate cases:
These are ribbons and laces, and beads that show
The fashions of Pittsfield, long ago;
There are belts and buckles and curly-cues
Of the style our ancestors used to use;
There are old-time scissors, and shears and fans,
And tables and chairs and warming pans;
Decanters and runlets with wooden cords;

There are lamps and lanterns and moulds for
   candles,
And quaint umbrellas with ivory handles;
Scales and steelyards, and keys, and rings,
And pistols and flintlocks, and lots of things;
Things of linen and things of yarn,
Things for the house and the shop and the barn;
Things for the use of the men that fight,
And things for the service of men that write;
Things of iron and brass and steel,
Things that belonged to the spinning-wheel;
Things that remind us of church and choir,
Things to light and put out a fire;
Things for city and village and farm,
Things for good and things for harm;
Things for the road and things for the stable,
Things for the hearth and things for the table,
Things of most every sort I think
With the single exception of things to drink!
And now they are there and the people know
We have them, it's pleasant to see them go,
And study the relics of long ago
Arranged in the cabinet down below;
Some go to see what their grandsires wore;
Some go to look at the arms they bore;
Some go to study a soldier's rig;
Some go to look at a doctor's gig;
Some go to behold an old plug hat,
Some go for this and some for that;
And some are most eager to scan the shelves
Where the things are kept they once owned them-
   selves!

Harmonious Numbers

An Average Librarian (L.J. M.)

From Northern Ireland Libraries 3:5, October 1962. Reprinted by permission of the author (Leslie J. Mitchell) and
the editor of Northern Ireland Libraries.

Statistics are they 301?
    Or 510 may be?
Or should we say they cast a spell
    At 133. 3?
At conjuring with statistics,
    Librarians win their fame,
So 795 perhaps,
    Should show their magic game.
Still studying figures is an art
    With which they're never done,
They know just where to draw the line
    At 741.
But at this very useful art,
    We engineer and build,
620 or 690
    For those who are so skilled.
And some will cook statistics,
    You know--for home consumption,
They'd put them 641. 5
    If only they'd the gumption.
The music of these gathered notes,
    The score I can affix;
I'll jazz 'em up and twist 'em round
    At 796.
The poetry and rhyme of it,
    The mystery and the motion,
I lisped in numbers--821,
    A literary notion.
With all these places dewey eyed,
    I try to avoid friction,
I add up my statistics
    And I put them under fiction.

As the High Priestess of Vers Libre
Might Have Reported

John C. Sickley

From Adriance Memorial Library, Poughkeepsie, N. Y.
Suggestions to Librarians for a More Literary Form of Report (2d ed. ; Poughkeepsie, N. Y. , 1918). Reprinted with the
permission of the Board of Trustees of the Adriance Memorial Library.

Ah, sweet!

Books, books, books, books.

How the heart cheers

With their very ~~looks~~* appearance.

Ennoble us? They do!

Libraries do lots of good;

Their reports show this.

Mamie Melton loaned

More books in 1917 from her library

Than ever before.

People read

More and are elevated thereby.

Something should be learned each day,

Something that will stick fast,

While the sun shines, make the ~~hay~~* dried grass

Do your work to ~~last~~* endure.

Let us exalt libraries!

A. Carnegie has spent

Much money for buildings to hold books;

165

His name is on many buildings.

His motto is, "Do good with wealth,

But never do your good by ~~stealth~~* secretiveness.

Let your right hand, and left one too,

Show to the world what you can ~~do~~* perform."

I love libraries

And hope they will increase

In usefulness.

*The author sometimes inadvertently drops into rhyme (as did Mr. Wegg into poetry) but at once makes the correction.

As the Spoon River Poet Might Have Written

John C. Sickley

From Adriance Memorial Library, Poughkeepsie, N. Y.
Suggestions to Librarians for a More Literary Form of Report. (2d ed. ; Poughkeepsie, N. Y. , 1918).   Reprinted with the permission of the Board of Trustees of the Adriance Memorial Library.

Old Huldah Simpkins
Gave out books
For forty-seven years at the library
In Fork River.
Boys and girls hated her,
And older people found her grumpy
And disagreeable:
But she did not care.
She was appointed librarian in 1870,
Because she was the widow of old Bill Simpkins.
Who was killed in the Civil War,
At the battle of Ball's Bluff.
Huldah died last July,
And the library is now closed
For repairs.
To be opened when the Trustees
Think best.

Questionnaire on Questionnaires

From Libraries 36:169-70, 1931.

Name (N. or M.)

Date of birth (if before January 1, 1900, you need not
answer).

When did you first hear of a questionnaire?
Give exact date.

Date of receipt of your first questionnaire.
What was it about?
Did you answer it?
Did you tell the truth?
How many questions did it ask for which you knew
the answer?
How many did it ask for which you did not know the
answer?
How much library time did you consume in searching
for correct answers?
How much did it cost the taxpayers?

What is your salary?
Do you earn it?
Are you overpaid?   Underpaid?

How many questionnaires have you received to date?
List below source and subject of each, giving approxi-
mate date in every case.
Average number of questionnaires per annum.

What was the date of your last questionnaire?
What was its subject?
How many times have you wanted to reply "None of
your business?"
Have you elegant manners?
Are you a reader of the writings of Lord Chester-
field?

Have you ever heard of him?

What is your nationality?
Are you an American citizen?
Are you a Republican?   Democrat?
Name of father.
Maiden name of mother.

Are you married or single?
If married, are you accustomed to questionnaires?
Check below what you consider the most used
questions:
Where are the keys to the car?   Why didn't you
meet me when you said you would?   Why don't
you sew on that button I told you about?   Where
are my clean clothes?   Who made this pie?   How
much money can I have today?   Add any others
you think of.

Do you like questionnaires?   Give reasons.

Have any of your ancestors ever suffered from insanity?
idiocy?

What is your I. Q. ?   (N. B.   This may be considered
to mean intelligence quotient or impertinent
quotient or impertinent question.)

Have you ever been called a moron?

Have you a questionnaire complex?

Have you been psychoanalyzed?   By whom?
Did the analyzer know anything about the subject?

Have you ever been in jail?

Do you use intoxicants?   tobacco?   drugs?

Do you believe in the eighteenth amendment?

Before going to bed do you eat cold mince pie?   pickled
pigs' feet?

Total number hours, weeks, months, spent in answering
questionnaires.

Total value in salary.

169

Do you belong to any society for the 1) promotion and
        2) suppression of questionnaires?
    Give name, address, and purpose of the society.

Do you believe that the U. S. government should forbid
    the mails to questionnaires?

Give names and addresses of 20 persons who will vouch
    for your identity and character.

In space below write not fewer than one word, nor more
    than 1,000 words, of your opinion of question-
    naires.

Date   Signed

                                  Position

                                  Address

The Questionnaire

Barbara Toohey

(To be sung to the tune of The Blue-Tailed Fly)

Our colleagues write prolifically.
For gold, fame, or advance degree,
And in their writing chores we share,
For they send us a questionnaire.

Chorus:

Fill in the blank-blank questionnaire,
Fill in the blank-blank questionnaire,
Fill in the blank-blank questionnaire,
And be professional.

Their subjects range from slight to small;
From little worth to none at all,
And riddles of the Sphinx compare
With questions on a questionnaire.

The authors add sad notes which say,
"I need these answers yesterday,
I'll sleep no sleep and breathe no air,
'Til you return my questionnaire."

Four members on our staff have we,
One does the work, the other three
Assume the far more heavy care
Of filling in each questionnaire.

LIBRARY ADMINISTRATION

Modern Methods in a University Library

Daphne R. Cloke and Sylvia M. Bishop

From The Assistant Librarian 50:193-4, 1957. Reprinted with permission of the authors and the editor of The Assistant Librarian.

It is felt by the writers that a brief review of the problems and methodology of one of the better-known university libraries may be of some interest to the readers of this journal. A description of the difficulties met and solved in special library work can occasionally assist libraries with bigger problems on a broader scale altogether; and it is hoped that this sketch of procedures followed by the staff of the library will arouse interest, if not imitation.

Staff

Library staff are selected only after rigorous examination as to fitness for the post. It is generally expected that candidates will have passed the preliminary examinations for the Metropolitan Police Force, and will be proficient in judo, hypnotism and elementary psychiatry; and they are encouraged to employ their spare time in pistol practice and fencing. It is one of the minor complaints of junior staff members that library schools and correspondence courses offer them little furtherance in their career, though a course in physical training would be much appreciated. Staff uniforms, consisting of a cowl and long gown, are provided.

Admission, General Duties and Issue Methods

Members of the library staff take it in turn to give an introductory talk to new students who propose to use the library, including a demonstration on how to fit leg-irons, and the most comfortable methods of adjusting handcuffs. After the initiation ceremony, during which readers are partially shaved and induced to recite aloud the time-honoured formula, "that ye shall ne brynge in, neyther fyre, nor termite, nor yette the dreded woodewyrme," they are required to sign a form devoting a portion of their annual income or grant to postal costs and possible loss of books. Before actual admission to full reading facilities, they are closely screened for undesirable tendencies, and if they satisfy the enquiry board, each is allotted an individual number and symbol which is branded upon the right hand. This symbol must be shown at the iron grill, which forms the entrance to the main library, and the password for the day is given to the reader who then is at liberty to enter the library. Immediately upon entry, he is conducted to a space upon one of the benches beside the library tables, and helped into the leg-irons and handcuffs by the assistant on duty. During library hours two members of staff walk up and down the aisles between tables, carrying the regulation issue dog-whips, and are summoned by a tug at the gown from readers desiring books or other material. No book can be issued unless the password for the day has been given by the reader. No material is ever removed from the library, except in the special case of finals students and research workers, which will be dealt with in a later paragraph.

Book Protection and Storage
    It may be of interest to university librarians who have suffered from damages and loss to publications, to know that, by virtue of the methods pursued here, protection of stock is almost 100 per cent effective. In the first place, as has already been mentioned, books are issued entirely by staff and are not allowed to leave the library. Both books and readers are chained to the desks during consultation, and are under constant supervision by the assistant on duty. No books are visible on the shelves, all of them, with the exception of necessary reference works such as Lombroso and the Police Gazette, shelved in the librarians' room, being kept in a large underground stack, whose doors are protected by selenium cell rays which set off a siren alarm when disturbed, unless the circuit is broken by a member of the staff or other accredited individual. Injury or defacement to book pages is almost unknown, readers are issued with rubber gloves for turning pages, and in cases where a reader desires to consult an old or valuable book, he is confined in a strait jacket and permitted the use of an automatic page-turner. With the object of minimizing all possible damage to property, readers are searched on entering and leaving the library, and all unexplained articles, such as watches, fountain pens, and signet rings, are confiscated.

Equipment and Fittings
    The library consists of two small rooms and a large rectangular hall, into which the smaller rooms open. One of the smaller rooms is used by the librarian, the other is that in which readers are searched and interrogated before entering or

leaving the library. The style of building and decoration is simple almost to austerity. After several experiments with various kinds of flooring and panelling material, the library subcommittee came to the conclusion that the most suitable of these were porcelain tiles, from which bloodstains and similar marks could be easily removed by the caretaking staff. Shelving presented no problems in the reading-room, as all books are shelved in the great basement stack, built into solid rock and running the full length of the building. In the main library each desk is fitted, as we have already stated, with leg-irons and handcuffs, allowing for six readers, side by side, to each bench. Readers are required to sign a form at the commencement of term stating how many candles they expect to use during the session; special permission must be received before this allowance can be exceeded. On the West Wall of the main reading-room an interesting and varied collection of ancient instruments of torture is permanently displayed.

Assistance to Readers

Readers of long standing and unblemished record ("trusties") are occasionally allowed in procession accompanied by two assistants, to consult co-operating libraries, when distance makes this possible. Otherwise full postal facilities are available, even for members of the teaching staff of the faculty. Finals students receive preferential treatment: books are taken to their cells, and they are allowed out during certain specified daylight hours for exercise.

Catalogues and Classification Schemes

The author and subject catalogues are for the use of staff only; students are not permitted to exercise the doubtful benefits of choice in reading, but study only works listed by their tutors. The classifiers, therefore, are free to employ Dewey's system to its fullest extent as typified in the British National Bibliography; with the geographical letter tables from Bliss. Cataloguers use the 1941 version of the A. L. A. Cataloguing Rules modified by some introductions from the Prussian Code. Maps before 1800 are arranged in order of papermakers' watermark.

Readers interested in the methods of procedure obtaining are cordially invited to approach the writers with a view to visiting the library.

How to Start a Library Without Ulcers

Albert Monheit

From Odds & Book Ends No. 47, p. 11-2, Winter 1965.
Reprinted by permission of the author and of the Nassau
County Library Association.

Starting a library is a simple process. There are
four requirements--aspirins, tranquilizers, complete ignorance of what the job entails and a Board of Trustees willing
to do all the work.

You have to learn to organize and administer. This
requires a desk, telephone, an efficient secretary, preferably
good looking, not sexy, not too young. It also requires an
ability to cadge free lunches from visiting salesmen--there
will be lots of these around during the planning phase of your
operation.

What to do first? Get hysterical. You might as well
get it out of your system. Sheer terror will follow later.
In order to cleanse yourself of any doubts about your ability
to handle the job say to yourself over and over again, "I
can't do it! I can't do it! I can't do it!" with real convic-
tion. Mean it. Convince yourself. Now that you know the
job is impossible what do you do next? Call Joe. Let him
do it. He's been through it. He has ulcers. He's sympa-
thetic and helpful. But don't listen. When he tells you
what's involved in starting a library it will leave you in a
state of shock and paralysis. Better to remain ignorant; not
know what's coming. Bumble around a bit. Look wise.
Sound impressive. Keep statistics at your finger tips. Murmur something about ALA standards--2.587 books per thousand population or 3.678 chairs per 9.6532 persons. Never
speak in whole numbers. Use only fractional figures. This
perpetuates an illusion of wisdom. Never let on that you
don't know what you're doing. This annoys Trustees. Pon-
tificate instead. Play the game. You're the Director. Direct! Issue orders, bustle about. Be busy--confuse everyone. Invent complicated forms. Become enmeshed with

civil service. This absorbs lots of time, appears impressive, and the resulting tangles are not your fault.

Buy lots of typewriters . . . All going at once, they create a terrific din. This has great publicity value. It makes visitors think that things are happening in your proposed library. To reinforce this illusion have the typists work on catalog cards. Look through catalogs of jobbers and suppliers. Buy only what you want, not what you need. This is the one time you'll be able to get all the toys you've always wanted--you'll need a bronze plaque with your name on it, a coffee pot, serving tray, lazy susan and cookies. Paper clips, pencils, erasers you can pick up by visiting other libraries and snitching a few at a time.

Consult with consultants. Listen to their advice. If anything goes wrong you're off the hook. It's their faulty information that started all the trouble. That's what you get for listening to experts. Do it yourself. After all babies are born that way. You can do it.

Starting a library is like being born. All you need is a slap on the rear to get started. After the initial pangs the rest is routine. You'll survive. Grab the ball and start to run. Don't drop it! Run faster than Sammy; preferably in circles. Agitate, cogitate; be aggressive and dynamic. Pretend you have leadership qualities. Don't just stand there. Do something! Never mind the other fellow, he's already built his library.

Begin with a table of organization. Draw a box. Put yourself in it. Now you need someone to administer. Draw another box under yours. Connect the two with a line. Put someone in the box under yours. Now you're a boss. The more boxes you can crowd on a sheet of paper the larger your staff. The more complicated you can make the connecting lines between boxes, the greater your administrative ability. Practice. This will help perfect your line drawing ability, a necessary adjunct to establishing a successful organization.

You need books. Try the Salvation Army and the Volunteers of America. Want shelving? Plant trees.

Now you're on your way. Things are going smoothly. The library is beginning to shape up. Opening day looms on the horizon, visible like doomsday or a day of execution. This is the most critical phase of your work. You know you've started something--you're not sure exactly what it is--perhaps an elephant? Sit back, relax. Let nature take its course. Don't interfere. You'll annoy the staff. Drop in from time to time just to say hello. Visit other libraries. Go to conventions. Take a vacation, you've earned it. Become a consultant. Misinform everyone about everything. To show that life agrees with you put on weight. Acquire status symbols--an onyx pen and pencil set that writes with real ink; a wooden desk with imitation wood grain plastic top; a rug for the office floor; curtains for the window. Don't forget to wash your car and press your suit. You've got prestige. Boy, you have arrived.

Get to know the community. Make speeches. Go to community affairs. Join a service club. Become a hero. Give free advice even when not asked. Tell everyone how wonderful you are. Cultivate a young executive appearance. Be certain your facial expression is grave and gentle. Make sure the hairs on your temples are properly gray. If not, dye them with a little aggravation--you'll have plenty of this.

By all means, start a library. It's lots of fun--if you survive.

The Efficiency Expert

Edmund Lester Pearson

From his column "The Librarian" in the Boston Transcript
July 1, 1914.

   It proves that I was in good humor that morning, for
I thought, when I let him come into my office, that he was
a book-agent. He was tall and he wore a brown beard, and
a frock-coat--beg pardon--a Prince Albert.

   "What of efficiency?" said he, standing over my
desk, and pointing a fountain pen at me.

   I made the sound that is usually written: "Eh?"

   "What of efficiency?" he repeated.

   I understood his question this time, but the only reply which occurred to me was: "Well--what of it?" I did
not say this, however, as it struck me he might be offend-
ed.

   He asked his question a third time, altering its form
a trifle.

   "What are you doing here for efficiency?"

   "We are trying to treat it respectfully," I said,
"we--"

   "Have you reorganized the library on a thoroughgoing
basis of business efficiency? Have you had someone prepare a plan, showing at a glance the exact relation, one to
another, of all the bodies, individuals, and officers concerned in the government of this institution? Have you had
blue-prints, and black-prints and brown-prints made, where-
on the mayor and City Council are represented by a series
of circles, transmitting their authority (represented by ar-

181

rows) through the board of trustees (or whatever the direct
governing bodies may be called) to you, as Chief Librarian, de-
noted by a single gold star? Are there rays, or arrows,
shooting out from all five points of this star, to other smaller stars (black or red) to signify the assistant librarian, the
chief of the cataloguing section, the head of the periodical
room, the grand commander of the order or purchase department, the Lord High Chemical Librarian, or whatever
he may be called, and all your other principal assistants of
Class Alpha, Grade A, Section I? Do arrows lead from
these to their assistants, in turn, all correctly grouped, classified, and placed? Are these assistants of the second rank
down on the plan as triangles, the sub or minor assistants
as squares, and those of inferior grade as dots? Does the
arrow system prevail throughout, leading in direct line from
the mayor down to that charwoman I saw out there scrub-
bing the steps? Are all these figures so arranged as to
show, clearly, the relation, the interrelation, the coöpera-
tion, the coördination, of all the units, of each microcosm
of the entire organism? Is it clear at a glance?"

"No," I replied, "I can't say it is."

"And why not?" he desired to know.

"Because no such plan has been made."

"What!" he exclaimed, "and why not?"

"Well," I told him, "we've all been too busy to make
it. I've no doubt it would be vastly amusing. Speaking for myself, nothing would delight me more than to be represented by
a Single Gold Star on any kind of a chart. But how do I know a-
bout the others? Perhaps Miss Carey, the chief cataloguer,
wouldn't at all care to be shown as a green triangle, or whatever it is. Perhaps green isn't her color."

"But--efficiency! Don't you know that the preparation
of such a chart as I have described is the First Step toward all
reorganizations on a basis of business efficiency? Haven't you
read Van Gobsutch? Are you unfamiliar with the Series published by the Battle Creek Correspondence School? Don't you
know what has been done in Wooster, Ohio, and Clawhammer,
Mich. ?"

"I am not altogether ignorant of it," I assured him,
"and I have examined a number of these efficiency charts.
Some of them are even better than the one you described. Some

182

of them have all the charm and seductiveness of the patterns which used to accompany Harper's Bazaar. But you see we were already organized and going when your efficiency game was invented. We make changes from time to time--too often for the comfort of some of my assistants. We have many faults. But I don't see how one of these picture-puzzles would help us. The Mayor and City Council are perfectly able to pare our estimates, and keep us all pegging along on beggarly salaries without being represented as circles on a blue-print. I don't believe they would be any more active in that direction even if we pictured them as paralellopipedons. It's quite clear to the newest assistant in the circulation department that if I want her to stand Mrs. Pomfret Smith's growls and complaints and not give her any sauce in return, I am to speak to Miss Hanway, the chief of the department, who will deliver my ukase in person. Gilt stars and arrows and purple triangles and pink spots wouldn't make it any plainer. If I thought charts would do that, if I believed they would patch up the historic feud between the catalogue and the order departments merely by showing people on them as triangles and curly-cues, and doo-dads--why, I'd order a dozen of 'em."

I had as well kept quiet. He had not heard a word I said. He was one of those persons whose idea of conversation is to deliver a lecture, pause to take breath--during which interval you may speak, if you like--and then begin again exactly where he left off. Your remarks, your own lecture, have been as inaudible as the music of the spheres. I have noticed that such persons are very successful, as a rule. They get their way, and come victors out of every discussion.

"Efficiency!" he cried, in a sort of lyric rapture. "It's the keystone of success. It's the very foundation of big business. Look at John D. Rockefeller! Look at American Steel! Look at Liggett's drug stores! Look at Mellen! Look at Brandeis!"

(I could not look at any of these personages and companies. None of them was in my office that morning. So I sat and twiddled a pencil.)

"Look at your desk!" he went on.

There I could obey him.

"I'm sorry, I murmured. I always tell Mrs. O'Hal-

183

loran not to dust it. She mixes up my papers so. I do it
myself--from time to time. I was just going to, when you
came in."

And I reached into a drawer for a dust-cloth.

"It's the distance between your telephone and your
hand I'm talking about. At least four inches too far to the
left. Do you realize how much time and effort, how much
efficiency, therefore, is lost by placing the telephone in the
wrong position? Here is a report on the subject, which
came in today. Bulletin No. 9, of the Sub-Committee on
the Arrangement of Desk Fittings of the National Efficiency
Congress in session all this week at Waukesha, Wis. They
estimate that the loss of time, money and efficiency to the
business men of the country by having the telephone too far
to the left was over three million dollars in 1910 alone. It
should stand eight inches from the left elbow--mark the
place on the desk with a Maltese cross."

"Suppose you move your elbow?"

He did not hear me.

"Now, the inside of the desk. The top drawer--yes,
just as I expected. All wrong, all wrong. Should be divided into twelve compartments--this has ten. First com-
partment: Rubber bands--this has postage stamps in it.
Next: pins--this has eyeglass case. All wrong. . . . I
will set it right."

He did so, and I have spent the rest of the week trying to find things.

The Old Ashmolean Doors

Edmund Lester Pearson

From his column "The Librarian" in the Boston Transcript
February 12, 1919.

However gloomy the weather, or however trying his
tasks, there is one bright day on every librarian's calendar.
This occurs when his library receives--as it usually does
about this season--the annual "Staff Manual" of the vener-
ated Bodleian Library at Oxford.

How agreeable to know what all the members of the
Bodleian staff will be doing on each day throughout the year!
It is like balm to read that on January 1 the order is "to go
for cleaning windows and wire blinds in New School basement."

On the same day the "dead cheques of 1911 to be destroyed" or the "Librarian will state what dead order-slips
are to be destroyed." The same official "can take Summary
Catalogue copy" on the same joyous holiday--if he chooses,
apparently.

On the 28th of the month is a notable anniversary:
"Sir Thomas Bodley died, 1613."

And on the 30th, the "Banking-book to be fetched."

There is an important action on Feb. 8--"Mr. G. A.
Bennett to recharge batteries in Old Clarendon Building and
at Fire Brigade station."

On March 2--"Sir Thomas Bodley born, 1545." And
on the 3rd--"Banking-book to be returned."

On the 7th--"Fire buckets to be inspected" and "Plac-
ards 'in case of fire' to be revised." The founder's fear of
fire has not been mitigated, nor his precautions against it.

185

On the 19th of March--"Dusting begins."

No one who was ever an undergraduate at any college
will misunderstand the meaning of the warning: "June 1.
All windows and ventilators to be closed at night. 'Eights'
celebrations to be watched for."

On July 7, again, "Dusting begins" and on the following day--though there may be no connection--"H. E. Maha-
raja Sir Chandra Shum Shere Jung born, 1863."

Oct. 14--"Bodleian Orator to be warned for Nov. 8."
Orators to be warned--surely they order these things better
in England!

Even disorders are fixed and foreseen, in this happy
library--thus on Nov. 5 (Guy Fawkes, we suppose) "Watch-
men to patrol from 5:30 till 12." From experience they
know that all will be clear by midnight!

The "Monthly, Weekly and Daily Routine" goes into
life of the Bodleian assistants and librarians even more
carefully. Here, as in the Calendar, the "Persons under-
taking" are designated, so we know exactly what person is
to fetch the bankbook, what official is to warn the Bodleian
Orator, and who are to watch out that the celebrants of
'Eights' Week do not work any harm to the library windows
or other property. On Monday the Bodley clocks are to be
wound and set. The Librarian's room is to be dusted. The
Old Ashmolean stairs and back and front areas are to be
cleaned. And so on. On Wednesday Mr. Wiblin is to send
books for binding. Orders for coke are to be sent.

The "Permanent Daily Routine for Week Days" is interesting. Furnaces are to be stoked, reading rooms are
to be dusted, the hygrometer to be read and "Boys' absence
sheets to be put ready." Certain minute symbols indicate
that these--and many other duties--are to be undertaken by
"Mr. Baker, Mr. Burborough, Mr. Wiblin, Mr. Miller, Mr.
Coppeck and Miss Pogson respectively."

We have searched the tables of the daily routine to
see what Miss Pogson's share might be, and find only one
entry, "stationery, etc., given out." Perhaps the fear that
women are displacing men, even in manual labor, is un-
grounded.

We wish we could visit the Bodleian just before closing time. There is something about the ceremony which appeals to the sense for the dramatic.

"5 min. before closing. . . . Bodley's Bell and Upper reading room bell to be rung."

"5 min. before closing. Bodley janitor to perambulate Upper reading room and H."

A little later:--

"Subway iron gate to be locked by trolley worker."

"The H to be dusted."

"Last trolley starts to Camera."

"Boy to take notes."

And finally (the great event is drawing to a close, and the shades of night are falling).

"Bodley janitor to lock up Library, inspect lift motor, and see that the doors in quad, are fastened."

"Old Ashmolean doors to be locked."

"Bodley furnaces to be banked up."

We could never, never, do it in this country. Not if the library were closing its gates forever, and the librarians, all old and gray, were being carried forth to die on the grass outside, could we arrange such a dignified final scene. Our janitors could not be taught to "perambulate" the reading-rooms, --somebody would forget to dust the "H," and the Boy would not be there to take notes. When it came to the Old Ashmolean doors, --but there--there are tears in these things, and we will not speak lightly about them.

Public Libraries and Department Stores

Edmund Lester Pearson

From his column "The Librarian" in the <u>Boston Transcript</u>
April 21, 1915.

If public libraries were managed like department
stores:--

An old gentleman enters.

Old Gentleman--I want to get Emerson's <u>Essays</u>,
please.

Librarian--Emerson's <u>Essays</u>? Second aisle to the
right, and take elevator, Fourth floor for essays.

The old gentleman finds the elevator and darts from
one car to the other for five minutes until he finds one that
is going up.

Elevator Man--Stand back, please. Going up! Yes'm,
going up. Religious books--no, they're in the basement.
Take the other car. Going up! Stand back, please. Yes'm;
tenth floor. Stand back. . . . Second floor--novels, short
stories, problem plays, sex fiction.

Eight women and two men get out.

Elevator Man--Stand back, please. . . . Third floor--
poetry, literary criticism, art and dramatic criticism,
Bacon-Shakspeare controversy! No'm, Shakspeare's plays
are on the fifth floor. . . . I don't know why; I didn't put
'em there. . . . Fourth floor! History and travel, jogra-
phy, atlasses and maps!

The old gentleman moves toward the door, saying:
"Essays? Emerson's <u>Essays</u> on this floor?"

Elevator Man--Essays? No; seventh floor. . . . Stand back, please. . . . Fifth floor! Political economy. Anybody for the fifth? . . . Sixth! Electric and civil engineering, telegraphy, wireless, sanitation, hydraulics. Yes, sir--far end of the room for turbines. . . . Seventh floor! Phylosophy, psychology, ethics, metaphysics. What ma'am? Special sale--philosophy marked down? That was on Monday, ma'am--guess they're all gone. This is yours--yes, sir.

The old gentleman gets out and the elevator shoots up.

The Old Gentleman--Emerson's Essays on this floor?

Librarian--Emerson's Essays? Right this way. . . . Miss Staltment, show this gentleman Emerson's Essays.

Miss S.--They're not here now. They're over in Mr. Gumphy's department. Second aisle to the left, and down at the end of the room.

The old gentleman walks to Mr. Gumphy's department and asks for Emerson's Essays. Mr. Gumphy smiles a superior smile.

Mr. Gumphy--Emerson's Essays? Oh, no. We don't carry those now. Nobody calls for 'em. No, sir. No demand at all. Haven't heard anybody asking for them in two years. Maybe . . . Joe, we haven't got any of those old Emerson's Essays left--down there under the counter, with all that old junk we were clearing up? What?

Joe--None. All trun out.

Mr. Gumphy--I thought not. No, sir. You see it wouldn't pay us to keep those things. All outer date. Now, here's something, Adventures of a Grass Widow. You ought to get it. By Hortense Risqué. Everybody's readin' it. Eighty copies of it went out yesterday. Up-to-date, you know. We keep it on every floor.

Old Gentleman--I'm afraid it won't do. You see I want Emerson. I don't think this is suitable for me. Too young and conspicuous.

Mr. Gumphy--Young and conspicuous? Not a bit. It suits you to a T. Snappy, and it's got some go to it--why we are furnishing lots of men twenty years older than you.

189

Just come over in front of this glass. . . . There--ain't
that neat? Turn round this way, and get the effect.

Old Gentleman--Do you know any place where I could
get Emerson?

Mr. Gumphy--No, sir. I don't believe you'd find it
anywhere. No call for it nowadays--absolutely none. If
you can get the effect--just let me fix this. There! You
look mighty well with this.

Old Gentleman--But it's such a dreadfully vivid yellow!

Mr. Gumphy--Yellow? That's the color this year.
Everybody's---what's that, sir? Oh, certainly, change it
if you don't like it. Certainly. But I'm sure you won't
want to change. You'll like it--the more you see of it, the
more you'll like it. Have it sent, or will you take it?
Send it? Sure! . . . Thank you, sir. . . . Yes, I know
you'll be pleased.

The old gentleman walks away.

Mr. Gumphy (to himself)--Well, I've stung another
one of 'em!

Latest Recent Advances in Current
Developmental Trends

Euphemia Z. Woodiwiss, Ph.D.
Library Consultant, Prof. of Alternate Alphabeting
(Letters A to E Only)

From The Australian Library Journal 2:57-60, 1953. Reprinted with permission of the author (Joan Ellard) and the
Library Association of Australia.

Have you ever been considered a responsible person
and been invited to organize a library and lay down, for the
layman, basic plans? This could happen to you. Therefore I advise you to study the ensuing notes for the occasion when you are asked for a professional opinion. I give
you this advice freely, in the hope that your organizational
paths will be smooth but not slippery.

Firstly required is a large building, preferably a dis-
used wash-house or potting shed no longer needed by a city
council; or perhaps a dressing room discarded by some local run-down cricket club. A new building designed as a
library by a qualified architect is definitely not done, as it
removes the necessary spirit of invention and improvization
in the incoming librarian.

Care should be taken that the roof leaks only in
places under which a bucket may be safely put; that the windows give the smallest possible light and that the bookshelves are designed for the special convenience of readers
with glandular disorders, such as pigmies, giants and other
visiting circus personnel.

The library's site is of utmost importance and should
be situated as far as is inconveniently possible from all public transport. One-room libraries will find they can best
achieve this desired end by selecting a position in their
building, up six flights of stairs, down the corridor to the
right, turn left, cross the ramp, move slowly along the

nearest parapet and then jump to the third left-hand window.

These sites should always be selected with appropriate landscape views in mind, such as morning sun rising over the gas-works and afternoon sun setting over the jam factory.

Closely following in importance is the selection of suitable persons to form the Board of Trustees, Library Council, Book Committee or whatever other designation is considered appropriate to this most august body. Control of the library will be vested in these gentlemen. Note that control is vested in and not given to the Trustees and therefore it is most desirable to become a Trustee.

They are of various sorts:

> Ordinary Trustees
> Extraordinary Trustees
> Elected Trustees
> Selected Trustees
> Absent Trustees
> And Distrustees.

Their function is most important, though rather vague. Their work is mainly thinking, and consequently they cannot work very long hours. A special word should be said about Chairmen of Library Committees. He usually knows the name of the Principal Librarian and what is the address of the library. . . . It is most essential, therefore, to have a Chairman of a Library Committee.

Sooner or later it becomes necessary to appoint Library Staff.

If the Library is a Branch Library, then the officer who is considered to be the most unpromising and mentally retarded person in the main library is automatically selected.

If, however, new ground is being broken, the choice is wider, ranging from the Mayor's wife's second cousin's next-door neighbour's half-witted sister to the Managing Director's semi-invalid aunt. Occasionally a librarian is appointed.

If the library is really thoroughly organized, the quantity of the staff personnel required presents no difficulties. Only in more primitive societies is it necessary to analyze the amount of work to be done, before any appointments are made.

A simple formula has been worked out. For every chief librarian, there must be two deputies. For two deputies, there should be four senior assistants. For four senior assistants there should be eight intermediate assistants. For eight intermediate assistants there should be sixteen junior assistants, and for sixteen junior assistants there should be thirty-two very junior assistants. This makes a small minimum of 63 persons.

Naturally three further appointments have to be made:

    (1)   a cleaner,
    (2)   a ratcatcher,
    (3)   a person to attend to the reading needs of the public.

In selecting staff, a psychologist should always be called in for the appointment conference. He will take the applicant and place before him an Unfamiliar Paragraph of Prose. If the applicant can read it, he isn't blind. If he cannot read it, he is either blind or he cannot read, in either of which cases he will probably not be suitable. The psychologist should be appointed in his place.

The Chief Librarian has some things in common with Trustees, in so far as he or she is likewise paid to think. He should remember this always, though occasionally he should rest by reading a recently-published newspaper, as he must conserve his greatest asset.

Secondly, he is paid to organize. It is obvious that the outstanding characteristic of a good organizer is that he never does anything himself. He should delegate his work so perfectly that there is nothing left to do. The whole science of organization is getting someone else to do your work for you. If the Chief Librarian finds himself doing anything he must stop immediately and start thinking.

He must never forget that his salary is higher than that of his very junior assistant and that he is actually saving the Library's money if he has a special buzzer installed in his office, so that he can summon a very junior assistant when he wants his fountain pen filled.

The Chief Librarian's main task is to take Visiting Experts on tours of selected parts of the library building. The more skilful the Chief Librarian becomes, the more selective are the parts inspected by the Visiting Expert. As this takes much experience and practice, care should be taken that the Chief Librarian should have a supply of at least three Visiting Experts a week.

A Visiting Expert is one who is sent to a library to be told what work is carried out in the library, so that he may write a report for the use of the library telling them what work they are carrying out.

The Deputy's duties are in the main:

(a) to be pleasant but firm with people who wish to sell cold drinks and frankfurters in the vestibule.

(b) To keep people away who wish to see the Chief Librarian.

(c) To control (by beating regularly) the rest of the staff.

(d) To take all the blame that cannot otherwise be disposed of.

A major part of the senior assistants' time is taken in calculating the approximate age and date of retirement of the Chief, the Deputy and other senior assistants. They also find work for the intermediate assistants. The intermediate assistants delegate this work, through the appropriate channels of junior assistants.

A major part of the junior assistants' day is taken in calculating the approximate time of their next holidays. They also find work for the very junior assistants. The very junior assistants do the work.

It is generally accepted that it is better to have gentlemen than ladies on the staff of the library, as ladies have a tendency either to leave the job or stay on, whereas gentlemen have a tendency either to depart from the job or to remain, which activity is regarded as preferable.

Ladies, however, are somewhat financially preferable and this may be said to outweigh their inadequacies of the intellect.   It is also most necessary to have ladies on the staff to buy the biscuits, make the tea and wash up the cups.

However, not too many ladies are required for this task and the Chief Librarian should be wary of too many ladies.   The very junior ladies have a tendency to be rather critical of traditional routine and the senior ladies often sleep after lunch.

The staff must be given a number of incentives.   The first and foremost incentive is a salary.   Salaries therefore should be paid regularly.   The team spirit should be encouraged.   Jolly group games such as card alphabeting and Hunt the Book should be organized daily.   Another necessary incentive is profit-sharing.   This should inspire even the very junior assistants to find new ways of levying fines, such as shortening the period of loan to ten minutes.

As variety is universally considered by advertising experts as a vital condiment, the hours during which the library is open should be changed without notice.   This will guarantee that readers who visit the library at the old hours will be surprised and will go away talking about the library, thus spreading its fame.

Time and motion studies should be made regularly of staff activities, though only of course of the junior and the very junior assistants.   It would be interesting to record the comparative time taken by a junior and a very junior assistant to read the best bits of "Down and Out in London and Paris" before letting the Chief Librarian get his hands on it.

Juniors should be taught that if you do a thing the right way, it doesn't take as long as it might to do a thing the wrong way.   It is not necessarily part of the experiment to discover whether the thing should be done at all.   On the whole, time and motion studies prove that it takes longer to finish a thing than if you leave off in the middle.

The properly organized library should be mechanized. The most important piece of mechanization is a late model American car in which the Chief Librarian can take out Visiting Experts.   Secondly, there should be handles on all the doors in the library, so they can be opened.   Thirdly, there should be a refrigerator in the Chief Librarian's office for the convenience of Visiting Experts.   Fourthly, there should be lifts in buildings over ten stories high.   Fifthly, there should be two-way wristwatches for the convenience of the Chief Librarian and the Visiting Experts.

Book trolleys should be designed and constructed and later books should be ordered to fit them. On the whole, book trolleys should have automatically removable tyres as it gives the very junior assistants something to do putting the tyres back on again.

Automatically removable wheels are not a great success as the trolley usually falls over when they are automatically removed. Only very junior assistants should be allowed to push trolleys as they are very heavy and the more valuable senior assistants might strain themselves.

Pedometers should be attached to the ankles of all assistants to record how far they walk. Chief Librarians of enthusiasm will probably calculate that two pedometers could be attached to the ankles of the more shapely members of the junior female staff. All relevant and irrelevant statistical data thus compiled should be recorded in triplicate and put in the archives.

There will be many other gadgets which University-trained salesmen will come and sell to the Chief Librarian in early spring. These should all be purchased and kept until a use can be found for them. Librarians all know that no matter how expensive a thing is, it should never be thrown away.

Eventually when the Building, the Board, the Staff, the Gadgets and the Readers are ready, the next step in organizing a library is to think about books.

It is the Chief Librarian's task then to inform the Accountant that the best way to acquire books is by buying them. This the accountant will be reluctant to believe, but may eventually agree to a temporary loan from the "Coloured Seats for Public Parks" Fund.

The Librarian then has two approaches in delegating authority. Assistants can be sent to the bookshops to buy a shelf or two, or can sit down and tick away with their coloured pencils through a publisher's catalogue. Both systems are recommended as they both guarantee a large collection of books which will last the library for years as they are sure not to be read.

In selecting books, readers should always be asked for their suggestions. These should be written, when they are proper suggestions, by a junior with a legible hand on a large piece of paper. This paper can then be cut up and used for scrap paper.

When the books are received they should be marked off, marked on, marked in, marked out, marked up and marked down. A very junior assistant should then shake them to see that the pages are stuck in and examine the pictures to see whether they are interesting.

The books are then put in a sack and dragged up and down the front steps and finally to the cataloguing department. This activity is most important because the weak books will break and can be thrown away, thus saving the cataloguer's time.

A cataloguer is a person who, between reading books, makes concise notes on a 5 x 3 card. Cataloguers consequently are very learned and are frequently classifiers.

Classifiers are people who think of a number, add two, divide by 3. 7 and write it in the book. This guarantees a decimal answer.

If a new library wishes to establish a reputation, it is recommended to use the classification evolved over years of research by readers. The classification is as follows:

Heavy Books
Light Books
Nice Books
Lovely Books
Pretty Poor Books
Tough Books
Rough Books
Good Books
And Hotstuff-Whacko Books.

It should always be remembered that it is not strictly necessary to purchase books for a library at all, provided there is another library in telephone distance. Two libraries sharing the one set of books is called Inter-Library-Loan. The library borrowing books should always be careful that the Lending Library never finds out it hasn't any books of its own.

This summary, brief though it be, contains everything a young organizing progressive librarian should know. Not all the librarian knows should be told, of course. The latter is the most important rule of all and should have general application.

THE LIBRARIAN AND THE USER

At the Information Desk

Ada A. Anderson

From Wilson Library Bulletin 16:25, 1941.   Reprinted by
permission from the September 1941 issue of the Wilson Library Bulletin.   Copyright (c)1941 by the H. W. Wilson Company.   Also with permission of the author.

They ask for	Astrology, Anthropology, Paleontology;
They search for	Arthritis, Phlebitis, Dermatitis;
They call for	Statistics, Ballistics, Pseudo-mystics;
They insist on	Dramatics, Quadratics, Numismatics;
They clamor for	Naziism, Bolshevism, Rosicrucianism;
They're in need of	Inflation, Irrigation, Predestination;
Their interest is in	Classicism, Positivism, Romanticism;
Their information must be	Alphabetical, Theoretical, Synthetical;

They depart with their "isms" and their
   "ologies"

But, in spite of their thanks and apologies,
   I am left with   Neurasthenia,
                           Demophobia,
                           Schizophrenia,
                           I-don't-know-bia.

After Dorothy Parker--a Long Way After

Louise Parks Banes

From Wilson Library Bulletin 16:555, 561, 1942. Reprinted by permission from the March 1942 issue of the Wilson Library Bulletin. Copyright (c)1942 by the H. W. Wilson Company. Also with permission of the author.

Of course it would happen to me. No one else would ever have to work on an afternoon like this, when the sun is as bright as bright, and all the flowers are in bloom. This was the day I had planned to go to the beach, too; much that matters to old Frozen Face.

No one will bother to come in for a book today; no one in his or her right senses will ever step into a dull old library on an afternoon like this. Maybe I can get caught up on my magazine reading, with the boss out of town.

"No, the Encyclopaedia Britannica does not circulate. You have to use it here."

The perfect goof; they will ask for the desk next. Miss, just let me borrow those shelves for the week-end. Of course it would have to be today I had to work. All kinds of time coming to me, and no one else could possibly work on a spring Saturday afternoon. There is that infernal telephone.

"Yes, the library is open."

Yes, indeed, it is open; come right on over. Sensible people are outdoors; intelligent people are gardening, or driving, or just loafing in the sunshine. I would choose to be a librarian, in a world full of interesting occupations, a world where some people can enjoy what they are doing, a world in which. . . .

"No, the fiction is arranged by author."

203

"Yes, you can find any book we have in the catalog. It is a card catalog; you look up things just as you would a word in a dictionary."

No, nothing would do but I had to work in a library. I wouldn't listen to reason; I could even look at an old librarian without flinching. What did I think? Did I think some extra-special providence would intervene and keep me different? Or maybe I didn't think at all. If I had taken just one single, tiny thought--well, that's that, I didn't think. I went on with my eyes shut, and here I am. Here I am on a Saturday afternoon when all the world except me is having a good time. Friends of mine are going on cruises; friends of mine are sitting in theaters; friends of mine are playing bridge. And what am I doing? I am sitting in a musty old library.

"No, madam, we did not buy Grapes of Wrath."

No wonder I am quietly going mad. Who am I to care what people read? They can read the Decameron all night if they want to, I don't mind. I don't care if they take Casanova's Memoirs in white calf to bed with them, but when the board says no Grapes of Wrath I have to bow my head. Who am I? A woman or a librarian? Great jumping catfish, I'm a librarian.

"There is the High School list. No, I don't know which one you would like. Try Adrift on an Icepan."

That's about his speed. He isn't going to read anything that will mean anything to him anyhow. He might as well concentrate on the sporting page of the Times.

"I'm sorry, Gone with the Wind is still out. Yes, we still have requests for it. No, I haven't seen the picture."

That's the type that would come in on a Saturday afternoon; the conversational type. No, I have no friends of my own; I just love to talk to the customers. How could I ever have a friend? Who wants to be a friend to a girl who has to work on Saturday afternoons in spring; a girl who works two nights a week, when things are happening in the world. Of course, I had to work the night the Ballet was here; other people can change their schedules when something important comes up; not me. Little Me--can always be found at the post of duty, a regular Casabianca. Just any night a good lecture is in town, or a good show, or a Saturday, here I am.

The next thing I know, some idiot will come in and ask me if I have a mission; yes, they still work that old gag. Just the other day an old woman asked me if I didn't feel I had a sacred mission as a librarian; indeed she did.

"No, if you borrow a book from this branch, it has to be returned to this branch. Yes, it would be nice if you could return it anywhere, but we can't do that."

"Pear Buck was born in Hillsboro, West Virginia. No, I can't say; that is in Who's Who."

"You owe forty cents. No, I don't decide what you owe. It is all calculated on this fine computer. No, we don't count Sundays. I couldn't say, I just work here."

I just work here; any Saturday afternoon at all you will find me here. Not the big boss, not old Frozen Face, but just little me. I can always be found here holding the fort. I would be a librarian.

Borrowers: their Cause and Cure

J. F. W. Bryon

From The Library Assistant 33:64-7, 1940. Reprinted with
permission of the author and the editor of The Assistant Librarian.

        Borrowers, those parasites that infest so many li-
brary systems to-day, are a menace to the profession, a
menace we should do well to face before it is too late. For
the disease they bring is infectious, and if not met with
stern measures, may take more virulent forms. Who does
not know the borrower-infested library, its counter pock-
marked with charges, its shelves riddled with readers?
Those so well known to us are warnings of what may happen
to our sturdy collections if we do not inoculate immediately.

        There was a time when Municipal Libraries were free
from infection--sound in wind and limb. They were noble
establishments, proud to preserve all that was best in English literature and learning, shrines dedicated to knowledge,
whose acolytes, awed by reverence, ministered silently.
That day, alas, has passed. Throughout the country libraries are succumbing to the malignant disease.

        History.--First signs of the complaint were not no-
ticed in this country until after the Act of 1850, but by the
turn of the century libraries in most of the large towns reported infection, despite the most elaborate precautions.
"Borrowers," as it came to be called, first took a firm hold
on the industrial areas, but since then it has extended its
grip to the rural districts, until no part of the country can
now claim complete immunity.

        Causes.--In attempting to prescribe, one must not be
like

        the Medico, whose aim before he goes is
        to make the illness fit the diagnosis.

206

It is necessary to make an examination of the root causes of the malady, so that the appropriate treatment may be administered. Like many complicated illnesses, its causes are simple, but are, in the main, contagious. Borrowers may be aggravated by a draught of new books, but this is no more than a contributory cause. The bacillus itself is an elusive microbe, the English equivalent for whose technical name is service-satisfaction. Borrowers, once it has obtained a foothold, is very hard to dislodge, because it is hereditary, infectious, and contagious. Large systems are among the greatest sufferers, while the leaner kind are less prone to infection.

Symptoms. --Librarians who are aware of the danger keep temperature charts of issues and registration. Borrowers makes itself evident in rises on both graphs, steep or gradual according to the gravity of the attack. Feverishness often accompanies, varying according to certain set periods of the year which correspond roughly with lengthened evenings, while minor weekly fluctuations are common. One result of the former has been an abnormal increase in the severity of attacks in many areas since the introduction of the black-out.

Treatment. --Excitement must be avoided at all costs. Under this head may be classed excessive provision of books in popular demand. With regard to these, a starvation diet is recommended, as over-indulgence in new publications leads to fatty degeneration of the issue.

Diet. --Sound, wholesome classics in standard bindings, long sets of uniform works, with an occasional O. P. technical work, are suggested. But too rapid a change is to be guarded against. The transition from one dietary to another should be effected gradually, if possible without the patient's knowledge. In the initial stages the system should be kept on an ordinary diet (except that sugar is to be replaced by saccharin) so that the daily output may be ascertained. Then the carbohydrates (biography, fiction, travel, etc.) are to be gradually withdrawn. No universal dietary has found general acceptance, the proportion being varied with the nature of the system, but it is a sound principle to avoid too fresh a supply of books, as those on the current market are sometimes quite unsuitable. Delay or postpone the purchase of suggestions by the Committee Process or any other of the recognized means. This policy will prove efficacious if pursued consistently, but any relaxing of the treatment will result in a relapse.

207

Fresh books are to be avoided, since they are liable to distend the issue. But obtain several copies of titles that are remaindered or otherwise obtainable cheaply, especially if in a large format. These will not impose too great a strain on the patient's resources, and are useful in placing the system on a healthy basis. Withdraw for binding or further examination such books as by their content cause increased interest.

A limb particularly prone to infection is the Children's Department. But it is here that treatment is easiest, the system not having hardened. The frame being more flexible, it is more amenable to alterations in regimen planned to combat an influx of borrowers. The same treatment as that prescribed generally may be applied, with modifications according to the seriousness of the attack. Here isolation is easier, and alterations in diet meet with less violent reactions. Another part of the library system which, though less susceptible, is subject to the more virulent forms when affected, is the Reference Department. Here the treatment is more direct, the diet remaining more or less constant. Borrowers is here replaced by its equally irritant counterpart--enquiries. Amenities, as being conducive to this, should be reduced to a minimum. A strict regimen, ruthlessly applied, is equally effective in any of the departments as a borrowers-deterrent, but here a bandage of red tape, the withdrawal of qualified assistants, the application of preventative brusqueness, and frequent notice-poultices in a small type-face, are considered advisable in addition. Enquiries in its most malignant aspect--that of students, which breeds rapidly--is sometimes encountered. In cases of this, reluctance, and an obvious unwillingness to pursue the matter further, will result in a diminishing.

Mention must be made of certain quacks in our profession whose claim it is that borrowers, in its milder forms, is to be encouraged in growing systems, as conducive to more rapid growth. But these smart people omit the sequel, seen in worn books, defaced pages, missing volumes, books out of order, queries, and a host of undesirable complications, necessitating duplication, rebinding, and other resource-draining expedients. These commercially minded practitioners who would like to administer our libraries for us are of just that type which does the most harm. Their prevention is best effected by the maintenance of low salary scales--a sovereign preventative which proves an encouragement to these undesirables to enter other walks of life.

Let us recognize in borrowers an evil whose eradication is a national necessity, and though our more dependable practitioners are facing it conscientiously, it is a menace that requires united efforts. Slackness in combating it in one region may result in an epidemic in contiguous areas, perhaps in a more malignant form. We may not have any compunction, even though in our case the attack be a mild one. Recurrences are common, and their repercussions cannot be calculated, and are often serious. It has yet to be recorded in any case of borrowers that amputation of the affected part has been necessitated, but this may perhaps be attributed to immediate precautions and treatment from the beginning of the outbreak. Nor is it to be assumed that extremes of age or youth in library systems renders them immune. All are liable to an attack. And, when it comes, we must be prepared to act without hesitation. It is a dire disease and demands a drastic remedy.

Hiawatha's Reading

Circus Maximus

From New York Public Library Staff News p. 47, April 24, 1930. Reprinted by permission of the New York Public Library.

Then the little Hiawatha
Turned his footsteps to the building,
Great and wondrous marble building,
Where the treasures of the ages
Neatly stand on miles of bookshelves:
Took at once the elevator
And alighted nearer heaven;
Walked along the gleaming hallways,
Brighly white and shining hallways,
To a room all square and awesome,
Lined with trays and trays of records.
    Then he asked of the attendant,
"Where, Oh please, are books on Cribbage?
For you know the old Nekomis
Ages daily and grows weaker,
And the Father of the Waters
Wants a game that will amuse her . . . "
But the harried, fast attendant
Didn't care for old Nekomis,
Told the waiting Hiawatha,
Patient quiet Hiawatha,
Where to find the cards for Cribbage.
    Finally in desperation
Hiawatha took the call slip,
Gave it to the "information,"
And was asked for name and address.
Hastily he then supplied it,
And at last the slip was taken,
(Banded with a brilliant color),
Dropped into a hissing maelstrom,
Where it vanished all completely.

Fifteen, twenty, thirty minutes,
Still the patient Hiawatha
Waits the flashing of his number,
Waits in humble pleading patience
For the brilliant wanted number.
Then at last the number flashes . . .
"Kindly verify" they tell him ! ! !
Back returns our Hiawatha,
Shows the tray to "information."
"Ah," they say, with smiles of evil,
"Change the classmark." Hiawatha,
Changes as he is directed.
And again the slip is taken.
Fifteen, twenty, thirty minutes
And the patient Hiawatha
Sees his number flash before him.
Once again he gets the paper,
And is told the book is missing.

    *   *   *   *   *   *   *   *

All the numbers swam before him,
All the chairs and tables wavered.
All was blackness; Hiawatha
Knew no more, for he had fainted.
Thus the little Hiawatha
Learned of all the books no meaning.
Found no book for old Nekomis.
And the Father of the Waters
Was excessive in his anger.
But the weary Hiawatha
Smiled and grimaced, but said nothing.

The Reference Desk Song
for
Voice, Bongo Drum and Telephone Bells

Catherine Colegrove

From Hawaii Library Association Journal Fall 1964, p. 11.
Reprinted with permission of the author and of the editor of
the Journal.

andante . . .　　How many miles to Babylon,
　　　　　　　　　　What's the time in New York?
　　　　　　　　How do you write to a Congressman--
　　　　　　　　　　Where, oh where is the Stork?
　　　　　　　　And how in heck should I vote this year?

maestoso . . .　Find the Gross National Product!
　　　　　　　　　　How is Dow-Jones today?
　　　　　　　　How can I make a sawbuck,
　　　　　　　　　　And what did Confucious say?
　　　　　　　　Show me "The Secrets of Selling and Buying,"
　　　　　　　　　　Or "How To Succeed Without Even Trying."

cantabile . . .　What shall I name my kitten?
　　　　　　　　　　What can I read tonight--
　　　　　　　　Great Book or Best Seller well written?
　　　　　　　　　　And is this quotation right?
　　　　　　　　Direct me to Etiquette, Health and Glamour,
　　　　　　　　I want to make speeches and tone up my
　　　　　　　　　　grammar.

so-so . . .　　Who said "Barkis is willing?"
　　　　　　　　　　Who said living is cheap!
　　　　　　　　How many pence in a shilling,
　　　　　　　　　　How many pounds in a jeep?
　　　　　　　　In the towns of Snohomish, Sequim or
　　　　　　　　　　Seattle,
　　　　　　　　Who manufactures a baby's rattle?

212

presto . . .   Translate a Latin motto,
                         Locate a firm in Hong Kong.
                 How can I fix up my auto?
                         The Library never is wrong.
                 What never? no never--well hardly ever,
                         And there goes the Closing Gong . . .

furioso . . .   But Lady, please show me the shelf for
                         O'Grady,
                         And Sir, my Assignment is due!
                 I live in Pearl City so kindly have pity
                         And read me a line from Who's Who.
                 Find "Real Estate Questions & Answers,"
                         please,
                 And data on Government Policies.

vibrato . . .   How many Supermarkets?
                         How many Millionaires?
                 Find me a Rating on Carpets,
                         And Television Repairs.
                 Where is your File of Famous Facts,
                 Where is the Law on Income Tax?

and resto . . .   Give 'em the axe, the axe, the axe,
                         My brain is folding in furrows . . .
                 The lights are out, the people are gone,
                 What shelf did I put my spectacles on,
                         And my novel by Edgar Rice Burroughs?
                 That's what I need to settle my head!
                         --And So To Bed . . .

Ballad of the Author and His Book

Great Scott

From Bedlam p. 28-9, April 26, 1930. Reprinted by permission of the New York Public Library.

I

A learned author gave to fame
    A lively treatise on "The Flea,"
Within the book inscribed his name
    And gave it to the library.

II

And every day he used to sit
    And con its pages lovingly--
It was a treasury of wit--
    He turned each leaf approvingly.

III

Until one day his book's denied--
    Now could the fates unkinder be?
They searched it far, they searched it wide--
    They said: "It's at the bindery."

IV

"Now this is but a month's delay"
    The page assured him smilingly,
The hapless author turned away
    The page, he winked beguilingly.

V

Three weary months he waits, and then
    With patience meritorious
The precious volume clasps again
    In new red binding glorious.

VI

What joy to pore each chapter o'er--
    What if his book's unsalable?

214

But envious fate persues once more,
 For now--'tis "Not available!"

VII

No more shall anxious readers wait
 With minds uncertain and befogged!!!??;
To bring our knowledge "up to date"
 His book must be recatalogued!

VIII

Spring passed, and opulent Summer
 Was garnered into Fall,
And wheeling stars and planets
 Time's leaden march recall,
And "tilted moons" have waxed and waned
 To see the slow weeks crawl.

IX

After eight months of hope deferred
 The happy author flew--
His book restored--the altered card
 With trembling haste to view.

X

His name--John Johnson used to be,
 But now they spelled it with a "t"--
His scholar's soul was thrilled anew
 To find it writ so accurately, --
So touched too--they even knew
 The date of his nativity!

XI

And 'tis time to end my rime,
 For after much abuse
The faithful author hears this time
 His precious book's "in use!"

XI

Ye winds of fate, still blow unkind,
 Nor think that he will fear it--
For now at least his anxious mind
 Has found a kindred spirit!

Psychology Course for Librarians

Barbara M. Hudgins

Reprinted from Doorway 6:6-8, January 1968.   Reprinted
with permission of the author and of the Co-operative Book
Centre of Canada Ltd.

A librarian who works with the public must be more
than a helper, a researcher and a detective; he must also be
a psychologist.   He must comprehend the motivation behind
the student's vague request for a book on "whatchamacallit."
He must probe the depths of a fuddled mind in order to as-
certain the meaning of a reference question.   Above all, he
must understand and sympathize with those eccentricities common to readers of books.

The following is a description of four of the most common behaviour patterns found among library users, along with
recommended treatment.   It is hoped this short course in
amateur psychology will be helpful.

The Time Warp
    Any librarian who has ever sat at a periodicals desk
has come in contact with the Time Warp.   In a typical case,
a reader may come to the desk and request the March issue
of Atlantic Monthly.   There is an article on psychiatry by
John Fromquist in that issue, he tells you, and he's quite
anxious to recheck it for certain information.   After you produce the issue he leaves the desk, only to return five minutes
later.   Something is wrong!   The article is missing!   You
check the table of contents and the pagination.   There are no
pages missing, and yet the article most certainly is not there.
Has the article entered a time warp?

No!   Actually the reader has entered a Time Warp, a
common manifestation of the Ego Supra Omnes complex.
Since the article had importance to him,   he remembers it as
being closer in time than it actually is.   Therefore, it is
useless for the librarian to run for the February or April

216

issue of the Atlantic. The desired essay most surely lies in the January issue of Harper's magazine.

It is interesting to note that the time warp enlarges in direct proportion to the distance of the desired object. The following chart will illustrate this axiom:

The reader saw it in:	It appeared in:
Sunday's newspaper	Friday's newspaper
Last week's Time	Time or Newsweek
	2 weeks ago
Atlantic, March issue	Harper's January issue
Life, one year ago	Life, Look or Reader's
	Digest
	2 to 3 years ago

As you can see, not only is the reader's sense of time warped, his remembrance of the exact periodical is pretty mixed too. This is because the Ego Supra Omnes complex disregards facts it deems to be of little consequence to itself.

The best treatment for victims of the Time Warp is to lead them over to The Readers' Guide to Periodical Literature immediately, and have them check it either under author or subject. The reader will recognize the author and title of the article quickly enough, although he'll be unable to understand the apparent switch. While he's pondering this mystery, you can initiate him into the use of the Guide. If you're lucky, he'll look there first the next time he walks into the periodicals section.

(N. B. The only person immune to the Time Warp is the author of the article himself. Authors always know the exact date and issue of their articles. This is another manifestation of the Ego Supra Omnes complex.)

The Switched Author Syndrome
You are sitting at the circulation desk when an irate patron puffs over with a catalogue drawer in his hand. "What's wrong with this library, anyway?" he demands. "I've been looking for Steinbeck's For Whom the Bell Tolls for an hour, and it isn't here!" He waves the "S" drawer at you belligerently. "Now don't tell me you don't have it!" he adds.

At this point you might assume a superior attitude

and smugly mention that the real author of the book is Hemingway and if he looked in the "H" drawer he would find the catalogue card complete with call number. However, unless it would save considerable time, do not take this tack. If you do, the reader will hate you for being smarter than he is, avoid your desk for the next five years, and end up writing nasty letters to your Library Board.

The Switched Author Syndrome is a symptom of the cultural pretension prevalent in the world today. The same people who switch authors also plague record shops for albums of Beethoven's Pathetique and tell their friends of the beauty of Verdi's Madame Butterfly! They are basically insecure about their education and status and try hard to compensate by cultural name-dropping. Unfortunately, they often drop the wrong name. Correcting them, however, will only unleash the hostility they secretly feel toward the cultural superstructure of society. Therefore, never put down a person who switches authors.

It is best to suggest to the patron that he check the catalogue under title. First of all, it makes him realize that there are alternative methods of searching the catalogue, and secondly, it allows him to find his own error. Chances are he will come over to you afterwards, all meek and apologetic, to tell you that Hemingway wrote For Whom the Bell Tolls, that this is the first time he's ever found a book he wanted, and that you are very nice.

The Switched Name Syndrome
When a librarian gets a request for On the Beach by Arnold Matthews, or The Old Wives Tale by Benedict Arnold, he is faced with one of the most perplexing problems of librarianship: the reader with the Switched Name Syndrome. Unlike the Switched Author Syndrome, which is primarily a cultural problem, the Switched Name Syndrome is a personality problem and has its roots deep in the childhood experience of the reader. Name switching can begin as early as ten years old and generally continues throughout adult life. There is no known cure, but habitual name-switchers often carry pads and pencils with them in order to jot down names, telephone numbers and so forth before their minds can perform the switch.

Since the victim of this syndrome may scramble the title as well as the author's name, it is useless to send him to the catalogue to search the title. If you know the correct author and title of the book you might as well tell it

to him. The name scrambler does not mind being cor-
rected. After all, his wife corrects him when he calls her
best friend Jeanne instead of Joan, his mother probably cor-
rected him all his life, and he's quite used to it. In fact
he may rather expect other people to unscramble his names
for him--he has definite infantile tendencies.

If he requests On the Beach by Arnold Matthews,
help him to find Dover Beach by Matthew Arnold and call it
a day. If you don't recognize the book he requests, check
any current bibliography under the author's first and last
name. If that doesn't help, try under subject--the reader
may recognize what he wants under the subject listing. Beyond that, there is little that can be done to help the name-
switcher until medical science learns more about his malady.

The Department of Utter Confusion
          The Department of Utter Confusion is peopled with
students--college students, high school students, any kind of
student. Occasionally a little old lady on her first trip to
the library may fall into this category, but she is a refresh-
ing rarity. No-one, it seems, can become quite so confused as a student.

We have all read of the communication gap between
the younger and the older generations, between the student
and the teacher. Nowhere is this gap more evident than in
the assignments the student thinks he has been given. I
have met students who assured me their teacher expected
them to read every book on the First World War before
Tuesday. They knew it was impossible, and I knew it was
impossible, but they acted as if their teacher existed only
to give them impossible assignments.

The crux of the problem is the Anti-Authority Complex. Almost all members of the student generation have
an anti-authority complex and it can work in very subtle
ways. For instance, when the teacher gives the homework
assignment, he has the power of vested authority behind
him. The student hears the assignment, but the anti-authority mechanism subconsciously garbles it for him. By the
time he has it down in his notes, it has metamorphized into
nonsense. Of course the student is not consciously aware of
this, and the librarian is only aware that the homework
sounds like nonsense.

My classic case in the Department of Utter Confusion

was the freshman girl who came over to the circulation desk of an American college library, practically in tears. "I have to read a book for English class," she said, "and I can't find it anywhere."

"What's the name of the book?" I asked.

"It's called "Short Stories" by Harper and Row. I've gone through all the Harpers in the catalogue and all the Rows," she sobbed. "And there are so many listings under Short Stories!"

It turned out her assigned reading was "Bliss" by Katherine Mansfield. How she could transform publisher into author, when the assignment was clearly printed in her class syllabus, I'll never know. But then the mind boggles when faced with manifestations of the Anti-Authority Complex. The best advice for librarians faced with students in the communication gap is to forget psychology, grab the student's notebook and translate his garbled homework for him. After all, the librarian is not only a helper, a researcher, a detective and a psychologist--he is also a translator.

The Normal Reader;
Some Observations on Branchmanship

Geoffrey Langley

From The Assistant Librarian 50:76-8, 1957.   Reprinted with
permission of the author and the editor of The Assistant Librarian.

All librarians who are in constant contact with the
public know that the reaction of an average citizen to a given
circumstance or situation can be forecast with some accuracy.   In so far as this applies to the borrowing and use of
the fiction stock the following reactions have been observed
in an urban branch library of moderate size over a period of
some years.

The Reactions

The Unusual Shape
Readers are very cautious in their approach towards
unusual shapes in books.   When confronted with a tall work
of fiction they pass it by.   This, it has been observed, does
not take the form of an appreciation followed by a considered
rejection, but a definite antipathy towards the accidental oddity presented to the eye; the seasoned reader acquires in
time a power of selective vision which automatically rejects
all but Crown Octavo without, apparently, being aware of it.
An exception must be made in cases where the large size retains the dust-jacket.   In such a case it is issued without any
difficulty, unless, of course, it happens to be published by
Gollancz.   Examples of this selective vision can be seen in
cases where the library possesses copies of the same work
in both Crown Octavo and a larger size: in such a case the
larger size will remain on the shelf while the normal one is
issued.   Is this due to the widespread impression that a large
book is a heavy book and, consequently, a dull book?

The Book Beautiful: Oddities in Binding
A corollary of the above is the reaction to unusual

colour combinations or unfamiliar spine designs. When these are combined with the Unusual Shape then the fate of the work is assured: only a drastic re-binding will ever get it off the shelf. When it is a standard Crown Octavo the result is in doubt: The Asiatics (Prokosch) is a good example. This book issued rapidly until the jacket was removed, revealing a pink-and-purple decor enriched with a curly panel on the spine. Two copies of this work have been in permanent residence on the shelves ever since. (There is some doubt here, of course, as to whether this illustrates a craving for normality on the part of the reader, or simply a sound artistic sense.)

Fine Printing
    The "Book Beautiful" tends to suffer a similar fate. These books, when their idiosyncracies are confined to their insides, are sometimes issued on their titles alone, but unless they have some especially powerful and compelling theme generally remain fresh and clean after about page six. They fall into several well-defined groups:--
    (a) Books using unusual type-faces (not necessarily exotic ones). Cheltenham is a good example, but there are many others. This also applies to type-faces which, though normal in most respects, have yet some marked eccentricity: the affected "st" ligature in many pre-war books (and at least one current professional journal) comes to mind at once, as does the lower-case "g" in Perpetua family. The verdict of the public is usually "there's something funny about this print."
    (b) Works of fiction with illustrations, other than the classics, are avoided: whether because their being illustrated savours of childishness, of oddity, or of artiness is in doubt. Decorations, head- and tail-borders and anything in the nature of floriated or decorative initials are also viewed with misgiving. It is true that such things tend to obtrude themselves between the reader and the story and provide a source of irritation: there may also be an instinctive realisation on the part of the reader that books treated in this manner are usually aggressively literary and often obstinately unreadable. For some reason, wood-cuts are easily the most unpopular. The observations made in (a) and (b) above apply, naturally, to marginal authors only. Collins' Romances would issue if they were printed in black letter in two folio volumes.
    (c) Books whose titles run vertically. Unless these happen to be the only form in which a very popular author is obtainable (as for instance Dorothy L. Sayers) they remain on the shelf. When re-bound, be the new horizontal

letter never so small, they issue well.

What To Do About It

This tendency of regular fiction readers to establish a groove, and thereafter automatically to follow it, may be used, together with an appreciation of their group psychology, to combat the above prejudices and to even out the use made of the stock. Some reliable methods are:--

The Shelf Switch
Most gratifying results may be obtained by exchanging the bay to which returned novels are taken with a less-used section of the fiction stock. This has been known to empty S-Z almost completely for months, during which time Zola, Zweig, Frances Brett Young and Hugh Walpole enjoyed unprecedented popularity.

The Duplicate Split
This is an extension of the Shelf Switch, and is to be used in the common events of duplicate copies coming together on the shelf. Often this will result in the issue of neither. If, however, one copy is removed and placed on the "returned books" shelves the probability is that both will go. This can also be applied to any work of fiction that sticks.

White Sepulchres
The attraction which piles of apparently forbidden books have for readers is widely known. Readers will ransack a pile of "sticking" fiction if it is mixed with one or two new books and left unattended for a few moments, and carry much of it off in triumph. Readers of Western novels will recognise the principle of "Salting" a gold-mine. A shelf near the counter with some such notice as "Books are not issued from these shelves" would be an even better ploy. Again, during a busy period, Branchmen may leave a pile of books on the counter instead of removing it (the pile) to the rear, works which it is desired to issue being infiltrated into it. Whether this conveys something of the atmosphere of the bargain basement or for some other reason books so left exercise a powerful fascination on readers. A less scrupulous method of issuing books, and one resorted to only by the desperate, is to present the urchin who asks for two murders and a love with something choice by Dostoevsky, or a couple of obscure Priestleys. Surprisingly enough, so strange are the ways of man, borrowers so treated have been known to send for more.

The Date-Label Gambit

An experiment which can produce very interesting results is this: take a persistently sticking novel and insert
upon the date-label a dozen or so date-stamps at intervals
of ten to fourteen days, marking these unobtrusively for your
own information. In many cases the book will then issue
regularly on the strength of this fictitious popularity.

Some books, naturally, fail to issue through sheer
lack of interest rather than through some defect in their presentation. The only thing to do with these is to get rid of
them as quickly as may be. If you don't, then you may experience the devastating reply given to the present writer by
a borrower invited to comment on certain outstanding books:
"My husband was tidying the house, and threw them out with
a lot of other rubbish."

Half a Dozen Ways to Increase Your Circulation

Ruth C. Miller

From Wilson Library Bulletin 23:72-3, 1948. Reprinted by permission from the September 1948 issue of the Wilson Library Bulletin. Copyright (c)1948 by the H. W. Wilson Company.

Would you like to get rid of that dull period in the average library day when business falls off almost to the vanishing point? Wouldn't you like to increase your circulation materially? It would be pleasant, wouldn't it, to be so busy all the time that the dread possibility of having the head librarian pop in for an entirely unexpected visit only to find the entire staff reading magazines, would vanish completely? You will be more than happy, then, to learn that there is a solution for your problem--a way to get rid of your trouble with a very negligible expenditure of time and trouble on your part. Years of research and practical experience have revealed several tried and tested methods, not one of which has failed when properly used. The first of these is most popular.

If your library is, at any given time, almost deserted, and the few patrons present show no indication of requiring any books checked--if they are all engrossed in newspapers, just decide that this would be an excellent time to begin filing the day's circulation. Cover every available space on the desk in front of you with book cards and go to work. You may not believe it, but in no time at all the entire population of the city will be crowding breathlessly in front of the desk with armloads of books to be checked out, or returned. Simple, isn't it? If you think it's a bit too early in the day to do the circulation, you may litter the desk with any other complicated task of filing--or try cutting out pictures for the information files. When you get right in the middle of a very intricate bit of work with the scissors, business will suddenly take a distinct turn for the better.

Then there is another clever little scheme: bring to work with you a bag of very sticky, very long-lived candy (caramels are good) and pass it around to the members of the staff. All your customers will ask questions requiring long and detailed answers. There is nothing like it. You will be rushed to death with reference questions.

If by chance you are not satisfied with either of these suggestions, try this: If there is a thrilling story in one of the late magazines, decide that inasmuch as there is nothing else to do, you might as well catch up on your reading. There is no doubt but that at the moment you reach the climax of the tale and feel that you cannot wait to discover the turn events are going to take, literally hundreds of people will be milling about requiring instant attention.

There's still another method which has never broken down under any sort of test. Whenever you are shorthanded for any reason--if one of the staff is taken ill and there isn't time to get a substitute--the busiest day in years will unfailingly result. If but one person is absent, the prospects are good but if two members of the staff are lying on beds of affliction, the circulation for the day will break all previous existing records.

There are also those who favor the "leaving-the-desk-to-powder-your-nose" method. Why not try it sometime? Making sure that everything is properly dull and quiet, slip into the back room and begin your repair work. Instantaneously the library will become a scene of hustling, bustling activity. When the avalanche has subsided somewhat your superior will look at you coldly, and remark that she thought she told you always to stay at the desk, especially when you are alone. This may be a bit humiliating, but think of your circulation!

Again, it is excellent to become involved in lengthy and tiresome arguments or discussions with persons who are either unreasonable or merely talkative. The line that will form behind these persons is almost unbelievable.

Although there are multitudes of other remedies for circulation trouble, it does not seem wise to bother going into them in detail here. Anyone with a spark of originality or ingenuity can easily evolve methods which will more readily serve their own particular local need. Of course there are always situations over which you have no control, such as having trouble with the electricity. Just as soon as the

lights go out, the entire neighborhood will become possessed
of an insatiable desire to come to the library for a book or
two.   There is bound to be great confusion with the candles
you have hurriedly produced dripping hot wax on all the new
books to say nothing of your customers, but the business you
will have will atone for everything.

These few simple remedies will, it is hoped, be properly followed and enlarged upon and used in such a manner
as to point the way to a new era: an era of larger and more
satisfactory circulation.

It Can't Happen Here

Nina Napier

From her Library Levity, Seattle, Dogwood Press, 1952.
p. 9-11.   Reprinted by permission of the Dogwood Press.

Once there was a man whose name was Mr.
    Theophilus Littlecherry,
Who wanted to borrow a book from the public
    library.

One morning he went to the library and told a
    young lady behind a desk he wanted to read
    a book by a man called Smith,
And she directed him to another young lady
    behind another desk who said he must register
    and gave him a pen to write with.

So Mr. Littlecherry wrote down his name and
    address and the young lady asked him how long
    he had lived here and he said he had just come
    here because his Aunt Ada had died of heart
    trouble but she had always been as strong as a
    mule and he didn't see how that could cause it,
And the young lady said that since he was a
    stranger he would have to pay a two dollar
    deposit.

Then she asked him where he worked and Mr.
    Littlecherry started to explain that he didn't
    work now because of his Aunt Ada but she
    looked rather annoyed,
And wrote down on a card "Unemployed."

Then she said she would like him to meet the
    readers' adviser,
And Mr. Littlecherry who was very polite said
    he would be charmed so he was introduced to
    another young lady behind another desk who

228

was just as nice as the first two only she
wore spectacles and nail polish and looked
wiser.

Mr. Littlecherry sat down and told her all about
his Aunt Ada and she asked him if he had a
hobby and if he had ever been to night school
and what books he had read lately,
But he said he hadn't read any books for a long
time because of his Aunt Ada's heart attack
that had ended fately.

And the young lady looked so disappointed she
reminded him of the late Mrs. Littlcherry when
he refused a second helping of pudding she had
taken a lot of trouble with,
So he had told her he wanted to read a book by
a man called Smith.

Mr. Littlecherry was directed back to the very
first of all the young ladies who asked him if
he had looked in the catalogue and he said no,
So she showed him a large cupboard with drawers
in it and he said thank you and looked in all
the drawers which took a long time because he
was rather slow.

But finally found a drawer marked Smith and he
read all the cards of Smith Albert and Smith
Charles and Smith Henry and Smith John
And Smith Moses and Smith Sydney and then he
found a card which the name of the book he
wanted was written on.

So he pulled out the card and took it back to the
first young lady who said he must never never
take cards out of the catalogue and she nearly
cried,
And Mr. Littlecherry hand't felt so bad since his
Aunt Ada died.

He said he was very very sorry and he would
never do it again and she said she was sure
he wouldn't,
Then she wrote down a number on a piece of
paper and told him all he had to do was find
a book with that number on it and Mr. Littlecherry hunted and hunted and still another lady

229

came and hunted and hunted but he couldn't
find it and she couldn't.

So she said wasn't there another book he would
like to read because the book by Smith couldn't
be found,
But Mr. Littlecherry said he didn't want any
other book thank you because he was very
tired with all this running around.

And he thought about his Aunt Ada and wondered
if there were heart trouble in the family and
if he were going to have an attack,
So he said good afternoon to all the charming
young ladies and he went home and Mr. Littlecherry never came back.

Question Box

Edmund Lester Pearson

From his column "The Librarian" in the <u>Boston Transcript</u>
January 17 & January 24, 1917.

Question Box

1.   Sir: Many years ago, when I was at school, we
used to sing a song which began with this line:
    "Oh, say can you see, by the dawn's early light."
I have tried in vain to locate this line.   Can you help me?
Newcastle.

(Have you tried these aids: Bartlett's "Familiar
Quotations;" "Tunes Every Child Should Forget;" the
City Directory?   If none of these help you, perhaps
some of our correspondents can solve your problem. --
The Librarian.)

2.   Dear Sir: I am in a great quandary.   There is a
rule in our library that every gentleman must remove his
hat, while he is in the building.   Everyone obeys except the
trustees.   They all keep their hats on.   Most of them wear
tall, silk hats.   It is very embarrassing, since I cannot ask
an ordinary "public" to take off his hat when the president
of the treasurer of the board of trustees is standing near,
with his hat firmly fixed on his head.   Yet, if the head librarian should see one of the public with his hat on, he
would reprove me for not enforcing the rule.   What can I
do?
                                            Desk Assistant.

(I am surprised to have you ask this question.   One
of the settled things about a public library is that a
trustee never removes his hat.   That is how you know--
when you are new--that he is a trustee. --The Librarian.)

231

3.   Dear Sir: Can you help me locate the poem containing the following lines:
The breaking waves dashed high,
On a stern and rock-bound coast.
I am about certain I heard this recited somewhere once--perhaps at school.   But I cannot recall the rest of the poem.
Estelle.

(Try these works of reference: Mulvaney's Dictionary of Statistics; the latest U.S. Census Reports; Blair's Encyclopedia of Classical Antiquities;   Miss Rorer's Cooking for a Family of Twenty-seven. --The Librarian.)

4.   Sir: Should small high school libraries omit author's initials on all catalogue cards?   A.D.D.

(It depends on how small the high school is.   For a school 10x14 or even 11x16, the initials should certainly be omitted.   But in one 14x18, or any size up to 24x32, put in the initials.   Make your measurements with care. --The Librarian.)

5.   Sir: How can I best prepare myself for library work?   Having done so, how can I secure a library position?
Anxious.

(Graduate from one of the leading universities. Graduate from one of the leading library schools. Spend two years in Europe--say at the University of Bologna, studying bibliography and paleography.   Acquire the degree of Doctor of Philosophy somewhere.   Spend several years working in important positions in American and European libraries.   Remember the last injunction--experience is essential.   Approach the chief librarian with your credentials.   Make out application blanks A221, B36 and D7.   File Character Reference 36H. Submit Physical Qualification Test 27K and Personality Examination M.   Attest these before a notary and add Diploma of Vaccination and Certificate of Marriage, if married.   The librarian will return these with the remark that your educational qualifications are hardly sufficient.   Study some more.   Have some more experience--especially in responsible executive positions in large libraries.   Try again, making out Blue Application Blank X10, and Yellow Form Y16.   You will then be informed that you have been put in Class Z, entitling you to be put on the Waiting List for vacancies in Sub-Class Q, for under assistants (without pay) in the Binding Department. This is what it seems like anyhow. --The Librarian.)

Last week, in looking at a number of publications from libraries and elsewhere, the writer happened to notice the increasing frequency of departments called "The Question Box" or "Answers to Correspondents," or something of the kind. To these departments anxious inquirers write to ask harmless questions about library administration, and to have their difficulties solved by some wiseacre who overflows with good advice on all sorts of subjects. These "Question Boxes" reminded him of other departments, in various publications, largely devoted to the capture of stray bits of forgotten verse. There is, in a New York newspaper, for instance, a patient editor who is desired every week to print "The Boy Stood on the Burning Deck" or "Curfew Shall Not Ring Tonight," and there are the thirty or forty correspondents--a resolute band--of another department of this paper, with their regular annual longing to see "The Blackberry Girl" in print.

There is something about certain phases of these departments and question boxes which is irresistably winsome to the writer of this--something which delights and pleases. Thinking that among his readers there might be some to whom these questions and answers appeal from the same angle--not altogether a serious one--he composed a series of similar questions, writing (it might have seened unnecessary to say) the answers as well as the questions. To make assurance doubly sure, and to cause nobody any inconvenience, either the question or the answer, or both, was purposely made absurd or preposterous.

This explanation is undoubtedly quite unnecessary to more than ninety-nine per cent of all the persons who happened to read the "Question Box" which was printed here last week.

Nevertheless, the "Question Box" has elicited these letters:

Dear Librarian--I see by the Transcript of this date "Newcastle" asks someone to locate the lines of an old song learned at school--

233

Oh, say, can you see by the dawn's early light.

Is it possible that anyone who went to school in these United States does not remember "The Star Spangled Banner!" Any book of national airs will give the words and music. Has "Librarian" forgotten, too?

Here is another letter:

The Boston Evening Transcript of Jan. 17, 1917, contains in its "Question Box" this request:
Sir, many years ago, when I was at school, we used to sing a song which began with this line:

Oh, say can you see, by the dawn's early light--

Can you help me?

Would it not be possible for a paper like the Boston Transcript to mention our National Hymn by Francis Scott Key, beginning with the line quoted without suggesting Bartlett's familiar quotations. Many of the old copies of Bartlett make it very difficult to find "The Star-Spangled Banner."
Mrs. Felicia D. Heman's poem on "The Landing of the Pilgrim Fathers in New England" is also asked for by giving the following lines:

The breaking waves dashed high
On a stern and rock-bound coast.

I should think that any library could refer one to several books that would contain "The Star-Spangled Banner, and "The Landing of the Pilgrim Fathers."

To these correspondents, who seem to have written more in sorrow than in anger, The Librarian desires to extend his thanks for their kindly-meant assistance, and his appreciation of their patience with his supposed ignorance.

One other correspondent, who writes from an attorney's office, seems, on the contrary, to have been more animated by anger than by sorrow. With admirable legal precision, he takes up a number of suppositions about the correspondent who asked "assistance in locating the poem beginning with "The breaking waves dashed high, etc." He supposes (1st) that the question may have been asked by "an elderly woman, whose memory is failing." In this case, he finds against The Librarian, and convicts him of "nothing short of an insult, and a cheap attempt at sarcasm." Or (2nd) it may have been written by "some person who attended school in a limited way in some other State where that famous poem is not so popular as it is in Massachusetts." On this count, also, he finds The Librarian guilty, and again he pronounces sentence. Toward the end of his letter, this correspondent admits that he has taken counsel of a friend, who seems to be possessed of a singularly penetrating mind, for he (the friend) suggests that "possibly the question was propounded by the person who wrote the answer."

In other words, perhaps our legal correspondent has made the curious mistake which he would never make in his profession of only half reading an article, and then going off at half-cock about it. Some thought of this kind seems to have struck him, and naturally to have made him angry, for he ends with an observation to the effect that even if no elderly ladies nor half-educated persons have really been insulted by the article, it was a very bad article, nevertheless.

The more than ninety-nine per cent of the readers of the "Question Box" to whom we have referred need, of course, no explanations about it. They read the trifling thing, and some of them were probably made to smile--not at any humor in the questions and answers themselves--but at the frequent unconscious humor of the real "Question Boxes" and "Answers to Correspondents" of which it may have served to remind them. It did not occur to them that the writer was ignorant of the national anthem, or that he was likely to engage in brutal insults to elderly persons. They have lost--this ninety-nine and a fraction per cent of our readers--they have lost, alas, their innocence, and when they hear a man asking for help in placing the first line of "The Star Spangled Banner," their hearts are filled with suspicion.

It may be almost impossible to convince this ninety-nine plus per cent that the three letters which have been quoted are really genuine. But genuine they are.

The incident has a certain significance for librarians, for writers, critics, and all who have to deal with the printed word. The peculiar twist of the mind which causes people to accept, in all gravity, statements which they would not think of accepting when spoken, is of everlasting interest. It partly explains the influence of yellow journalism, and it is at the bottom of many of the curious judgment of books,

235

passed by all of us. Some of us ignore the surroundings of a statement, an article or an essay, and hence arrive at false conclusions. Some of us place too much dependence upon the extraneous conditions, and do not judge enough by internal evidence. Thus we often fail to realize that men of sober demeanor often write or utter a good deal of foolishness: and we forget that a jester is occasionally wise.

Their Just Reward

Edmund Lester Pearson

From his The Librarian at Play Boston, Small, Maynard, & Co., 1911. p. 187-206.

I looked and beheld, and there were a vast number of girls standing in rows. Many of them wore pigtails, and most of them chewed gum.

"Who are they?" I asked my guide.

And he said: "They are the girls who wrote 'Lovely' or 'Perfectly sweet' or 'Horrid old thing!' on the fly-leaves of library books. Some of them used to put comments on the margins of the pages--such as 'Served him right!' or 'There! you mean old cat!' "

"What will happen to them?" I inquired.

"They are to stand up to the neck in a lake of ice cream soda for ten years," he answered.

"That will not be much of a punishment to them," I suggested.

But he told me that I had never tried it, and I could not dispute him.

"The ones over there," he remarked, pointing to a detachment of the girls who were chewing gum more vigorously than the others, "are sentenced for fifteen years in the ice cream soda lake, and moreover they will have hot molasses candy dropped on them at intervals. They are the ones who wrote:

If my name you wish to see
Look on page 93,

and then when you had turned to page 93, cursing yourself

237

for a fool as you did it, you only found:

> If my name you would discover
> Look upon the inside cover,

and so on, and so on, until you were ready to drop from
weariness and exasperation. Hang me!" he suddenly ex-
ploded, "if I had the say of it, I'd bury 'em alive in cocoa-
nut taffy--I told the Boss so, myself."

I agreed with him that they were getting off easy.

"A lot of them are named 'Gerty,' too," he added, as
though that made matters worse.

Then he showed me a great crowd of older people.
They were mostly men, though there were one or two women
here and there.

"These are the annotators," he said, "the people who
work off their idiotic opinions on the margins and fly-leaves
of books. They dispute the author's statements, call him a
liar and abuse him generally. The one on the end used to
get all the biographies of Shakspeare he could find and cover
every bit of blank paper in them with pencil-writing signed
'A Baconian.' He usually began with the statement: 'The
author of this book is a pig-headed fool.' The man next to
him believed that the earth is flat, and he aired that theory
so extensively with a fountain-pen that he ruined about two
hundred dollars' worth of books. They caught him and put
him in jail for six months, but he will have to take his medicine here just the same. There are two religious cranks
standing just behind him. At least, they were cranks about
religion. One of them was an atheist and he used to write
blasphemy all over religious books. The other suffered from
too much religion. He would jot down texts and pious mot-
toes in every book he got hold of. He would cross out, or
scratch out all the oaths and cuss words in a book; draw a
pencil line through any reference to wine, or strong drink,
and call especial attention to any passage or phrase he
thought improper by scrawling over it. He is tied to the
atheist, you notice. The woman in the second row used to
write 'How true!' after any passage or sentence that pleased
her. She gets only six years. Most of the others will have
to keep it up for eight."

"Keep what up?" I asked.

"Climbing barbed-wire fences," was the answer; "they don't have to hurry, but they must keep moving. They begin tomorrow at half-past seven."

We walked down the hill toward a group of infamous looking people. My guide stopped and pointed toward them.

"These are snippers, cutters, clippers, gougers and extra-illustrators. They vary all the way from men who cut 'want ads' out of the newspapers in the reading-rooms, to those who go into the alcoves and lift valuable plates by the wet-string method. You see they come from all classes of society--and there are men and women, girls and boys. You notice they are all a little round-shouldered, and they keep glancing suspiciously right and left. This is because they got into the habit of sinking down in their chairs to get behind a newspaper, and watching to see if anyone was looking. There is one man who was interested in heraldry. He extended his operations over five or six libraries, public and private. When they found him out and visited his room it looked like the College of Heralds. He had a couple of years in prison, but here he is now, just the same. The man next to him is--well, no need to mention names,--you recognize him. Famous millionaire and politician. Never went into a library but once in his life. Then he went to see an article in a London newspaper, decided he wanted to keep it, and tore out half the page. Library attendant saw him, called a policeman, and tried to have him arrested. You see, the attendant didn't know who he was."

"Did anything come of it?" I asked.

"Yes," replied the guide, "there did. The library attendant was discharged. Blank simply told the Board of Trustees that he had been insulted by a whipper-snapper who didn't look as if he had ever had a square meal in his life. One or two of the board wanted to investigate, but the majority would have jumped through hoops if Blank had told them to. He is in this section for five years, but he has over eight hundred to work off in other departments. The men on the end of the line, five or six dozen of them, used to cut plates out of the art magazines--a common habit. Woman standing next, used to steal sermons. Man next but one to her was a minister. He was writing a book on the Holy Land, and he cut maps out of every atlas in a library. Said he didn't mean to keep them long."

This group interested me, and I wondered what was

239

to be done with them.

"You will see in a minute," said the guide: "they are going to begin work right away."

As he spoke, a number of officials came down the hill with enormous sheets of sticky fly-paper. These were distributed among the "snippers, cutters, clippers, gougers and extra-illustrators," who thereupon set to work with penknives, cutting small bits out of the fly-paper. In a few minutes the wretched creatures were covered from head to foot with pieces of the horrible stuff; pulling it off one hand to have it stick on the other, getting it in their hair, on their eyebrows, and plastering themselves completely.

"That is not very painful," I observed.

"No," said my companion, "perhaps not. Gets somewhat monotonous after four years, though. Come over to the end of this valley. I want you to see a dinner party that is taking place."

We left the sticky fly-paper folks behind us, and proceeded through the valley. On the side of the hill I noticed a small body of people, mostly men.

The guide pointed over his shoulder at them, remarking: "Reformed Spellers."

They were busily engaged in clipping one another's ears off with large scissors. There was a sign on the hill beside them. It read:

Ears Are Unnecessary. Why Not Get Rid Of Them? Leave Enuf To Hear With. Don't Stop Til You Are Thru.

At the end of the valley there was a large level space. Something like a picnic was going on. People were eating at hundreds of little tables, and some were dancing, or strolling about on the grass. The guide stopped.

"The Boss is prouder of this than of anything else in the whole place," he said. "The people who are giving this party are the genealogists. Nearly all women, you notice. These are the folks who have driven librarians to profanity and gray hairs. Some of them wanted ancestors for public and social reasons; some of them for historical or financial

240

purposes; some merely to gratify personal pride or private curiosity. But they all wanted ancestors for one reason or another, and ancestors they would have. For years they charged into libraries demanding ancestors. Over there, you see that big crowd? They are the two hundred and fifty thousand lineal descendants of William Brester. Next to them are six thousand rightful Lords Baltimore. That vast mob beginning at the big tree, and extending for six miles to the northeast are the John Smith and Pocahontas crowd--some descended from one and some from the other--we haven't got them sorted out yet."

"How many of them are there?" I demanded.

"According to our best estimates," he replied, "in the neighborhood of eight million at present; but of course we are receiving fresh additions all the time. Thirty-five hundred came in last month. There is no time to count them, however."

I laughed at this.

"Time!" I exclaimed, "why, you've got eternity!"

But he merely waved his hand and went on.

"They are the largest crowd here, anyway, with the possible exception of the Mayflower descendants. They have a whole valley to themselves, beyond the second hill. Some say there are twelve million of them, but no one knows. Recently they applied for another valley, for theirs is full. You see it is so thickly planted with family trees that they have to live in deep shade all the time, and it is very damp and chilly. Then there are upwards of three hundred thousand tons of grandfather's clocks, brass warming-pans, cradles, chairs and tables, so they hardly can find standing room."

We walked down amongst the people who were giving the picnic. I wanted to see what was the object of this lawn party, for it struck me that it looked more like the Elysian Fields than any other place.

I soon discovered my mistake. Near the first group of tables was a sign with the inscription: "Grand Dames of the Pequot War," and at one of the tables sat Mrs. Cornelia Crumpet. I remembered the hours I had spent hunting up two ancestors to enable Mrs. Crumpet to join the Grand

Dames. I had found them at last, and so, apparently, had Mrs. Crumpet, for there could be no doubt that the pair of sorry-looking rascals whom she was entertaining at luncheon were the long-lost ancestors. One of them was the most completely soiled individual I have ever seen. He was eating something or other, and he did not waste time with forks or any other implements. The other had finished his meal, and was leaning negligently back in his chair. He was smoking a large pipe, and he had his feet on the table.

Mrs. Crumpet wore an expression that showed that her past desire to discover these ancestors was as a passing whim, compared with her present deep, overpowering anxiety to be rid of them. I felt sorry for the poor lady; but she was not alone in her misery. All about her were Grand Dames of the Pequot War, engaged in entertaining their ancestors. Some of the ancestors were more agreeable, some far more distasteful to their descendants than Mrs. Crumpet's pair. None of the Grand Dames seemed to be having what would be called a jolly time.

My guide at last led me through the maze of tables and out into the open.

"We have a good many Japanese visitors in this section," said he. "They come to get some points from the Americans on ancestor-worship."

"What do they say?" I asked him.

"They just giggle and go away," he replied.

Beyond the genealogists we found a large group of people, who, the guide said, were the persons who borrow books and never return them. The complainants, in their case, were mainly private individuals rather than public libraries.

"They are not particularly interesting," remarked the guide, "but their punishment will appeal to you."

As we passed them I shuddered to see that they were all engaged in filing catalogue cards in alphabetical order.

"How long do they have to keep that up?" was my question, and I was horrified to learn that the terms varied from twenty to thirty-five years.

"Why, that is the most damnable thing I ever heard,"
I said--"the sticky fly-paper folks were nothing to this!"

The guide shrugged his shoulders--"It's the rule," he
said.

The next lot of people we came on were curiously engaged. Long lines of bookshelves were set up about them,
and they wandered up and down, forever taking a book from
the shelf, only to sigh and put it back again. As we came
amongst them I could see the cause of their weariness. The
shelves seemed to be lined with the most brilliant looking
books in handsome bindings. They were lettered in gold:
"Complete Works of Charles Dickens," "Works of Dumas,
Edition de Luxe," "Works of Scott," and so on. Yet when
I took one of the books in my hand to look at it, it was no
book at all, but just a wooden dummy, painted on the back,
but absolutely blank everywhere else. They were like the
things used by furniture dealers to put in a bookcase to make
it look as if it were full of books, or those used on the
stage, when a library setting is required. There were many
cords of wood, but there was not a real book in any of the
cases.

I asked one of the sufferers why he was doing this,
and he stopped for a moment his patrol, and turned his
weary eyes upon me.

"We are all alike," he said, indicating his associ-
ates. "We are the literary bluffers. Most of us were rich
--I was, myself," and he groaned heavily. "We bought
books by the yard--expensive ones, always--editions de luxe,
limited editions--limited to ten thousand sets and each set
numbered, of which this is No. 94," he added in a dull,
mechanical fashion, as though he were repeating a lesson.
"We were easy marks for all the dealers and agents. Especially illustrated editions, with extra copies of the engravings in a portfolio; bindings in white kid, or any other tom-
fool nonsense was what we were always looking for. And
they saw that we got them. Whispered information that this
set of Paul de Kock or Balzac was complete and unexpur-
gated, and that if we would buy it for $125, the publishers
would throw in an extra volume, privately printed, and given
away to purchasers, since it was against the law to sell it--
this was the sort of bait we always bit at--cheerily! And
now here we are!"

And he began again his tramp up and down, taking

down the wooden dummies and putting them back again, with dolorous groans.

I could not stand this dismal spectacle very long, so we hurried on to a crowd of men bent nearly double over desks. They were pale and emaciated, which my guide told me was due to the fact that they had nothing to eat but paper.

"They are bibliomaniacs," he exclaimed, "collectors of unopened copies, seekers after misprints, measurers by the millimetre of the height of books. They are kept busy here reading the Seaside novels in paper covers. Next to them are the bibliographers--compilers of lists and counters of fly leaves. They cared more for a list of books than for books themselves, and they searched out unimportant errors in books and rejoiced mightily when they found one. Exactitude was their god, so here we let them split hairs with a razor and dissect the legs of fleas."

In a large troop of school children--a few hundred yeards beyond, I came across a boy about fifteen years old. I seemed to know him. When he came nearer he proved to have two books tied around his neck. The sickly, yellowish-brown covers of them were disgustingly familiar to me--somebody's geometry and somebody else's algebra. The boy was blubbering when he got up to me, and the sight of him with those noxious books around his neck made me sob aloud. I was still crying when I awoke.

The Birds of Academe;
a Natural History for Librarians

John Sherman and Robert S. Nugent

From Library Review 21:65-7, 1967.   Reprinted with permission of the authors and W. & R. Holmes.

        Nearly two decades of labour in what used to be called
'the groves of academe' affords one a familiarity with the
denizens of those misty woodlands.   One remembers well the
groves of yesteryear.   Perhaps, because of the general twentieth-century lack of conservation, time has not passed lightly
over the stretches of hoary deciduous and coniferous perenni-
als in this historic arboretum.

        Alas, the groves of academe have suffered much de-
foliation and resemble in many ways the old rotogravure
scenes of the Meuse-Argonne or Belleau Wood, where great
armies once clashed.   Considering this state of the natural
habitat, it may be that environment has influenced the ornitho-
logical species which live in the grove.

        There are several libraries, in various parts of the
grove, in which the authors have toiled.   These often re-
sembled dilapidated summer villas and were literally overrun
with numerous species of wild life.   Being ornithologically
inclined, we were naturally attracted to the wondrous species
of bird life.   We say naturally, because we have often over-
heard students say, 'Those librarians are for the birds.'
As is characteristic of most bird watchers, we have been as-
siduous in our observations and have made careful notes in
our journals over the years.

        We have selected a choice descriptive list of distin-
guishable species of bird life which we present below in the
hope that this brief contribution to natural history will prove
enlightening to our bibliographic colleagues who also labour
in the grove.   Certainly, nothing is more disheartening, to
those of us who labour to plant and nurture the seeds of

245

knowledge, than the depredations of the omnivorous Biblio-
praedatores who infest academe's grove.

The first species we will describe is the Blue Beaked
Library Opener (Glaucorhynchus Bibliothecae Aperitor).   This
bird is an exceptionally early riser.   Experienced bird
watchers have suggested that the bird may have eccentric
nocturnal habits.   Others believe that he just can't sleep.
In any case, he is usually flitting about when the librarians
arrive and is easily recognized by his rumpled feathers and
the piercing cries he utters as he dances about awaiting the
opening of the front doors.   He often frightens the clerical
staff with his tonal range of angry sounds.   However, he is
quite harmless, and once the doors are open he will flit into the stacks and will not be seen or heard again all day.
Or perhaps he may not enter the library at all--once the
doors are open.

By contrast the Red Breasted Late Flitter (Pyrrhor-
hynchus-Sero-Volitator) does not make his gaudy appearance
until it is almost time for the library to close.   He habitual-
ly swoops in, nests in a prominent area, and hops to the
catalogue.   He picks and chooses at length and with great deliberation then flies to a remote stack area to peck about.
This bird has been known to get himself locked in the library overnight.   When this happens, he squawks loudly in
protest, turns on all the lights, and beats his wings against
the front doors with great vigour.   Experienced bird watchers
advise handling this bird deftly as soon as he is spotted.
Shoo him out of the library before he can nest comfortably.
Once settled he is hard to dislodge, and his shrieks of out-
rage attract much attention and often frighten timid folk there-
about.   This bird is rather a bully, but will fly out at closing time if confronted courageously.

The Purple Vested Book Snatcher (Porphyreo-Sterni-
cus-Biblio-Surreptor) is often thought to be a predator, but
actually it isn't.   It has some characteristics of the Whoop-
ing Crane in that it likes to wade into library cataloguing
and processing areas and plunge into depths of unclassified
materials.   Of voracious appetite this bird soon balloons with
fresh acquisitions and waddles out loaded with new books
which are often unmarked, or in early stages of processing.
Ultimately this bird will disgorge and bring up materials long
sequestered.   The usual bird frightening devices such as
signs and mobiles bearing such alarms as No Admittance,
Keep Out, or Staff Only, have no effect.   Because of its at-
tractive plumage and pleasant chirruping, one hesitates to

use buckshot in discouraging its depredations. Careful observation indicates the depredations of this bird are seasonal
and usually correspond to periods of heavy acquisition. A
true bird lover will be keenly observant during the bird's
visitation and force disgorgement at a convenient time, rather
than resort to drastic action.

The Razor Bill Page Slasher (Oxyrhyncus Pagincida-
tor), on the other hand is indeed a predator of the most obnoxious kind. Since it is nocturnal and extremely secretive,
few librarians have ever learned enough about this bird to
recognize it. Its ordinary colouration is a perfect camouflage and its lack of identifying characteristics fails to differ-
entiate this species from other more harmless birds. When
observed in predatory action, one quickly recognizes large
digital claws, and the presence of claws in modern birds
must be regarded as primitive remnants. One species carries saliva-soaked string in its beak. This emulsed string
is surreptiously applied to the inner margin of a book page
to soften the page for extraction. When apprehended in action by librarians this bird is usually netted and plucked.

The Six-Clawed Reserve Hoarder (Sexungulatus Libror-
um Reservatorum Conquirator) is easily identified by its distinct habits. It is a slow flier that hunts in enclosed areas,
usually the stack areas. The bird has great stamina and
will spend hours pecking away at titles on reading lists which
it then regularly carries to the Reserve Reading desk and
adds to its already burgeoning collection. The bird appears
to evolve a sense of security by placing untold numbers of
books on limited reserve status. However, the bird never
returns to observe if its hoard is being visited by student
fledglings, and never indicates whether it has further interest in keeping its hoard on reserve after its initial action has
been taken. Some Six-Clawed Reserve Hoarders have been
known to hold books on reserve for as long as two decades.

Akin to the bird just described is the Puffle-Necked
Office Hoarder (Physo-Trachelasimus Archi-Thesauristes).
The differentiation between these two is largely one of habit.
This bird flits in and out of the library with great frequency.
After meticulously pecking about he flits out again with various finds which he adds to the shelves of his office nest.
Any effort to get a book away from this bird causes a spas-
modic ruffling of his feathers creating the puffle-necked appearance from which the species derives its name. Its cries
may be piercing and its spur-winged buffeting of anyone attempting to raid its office hoard may discourage librarians

from attempting to cope with members of this species.

The Tattle Bird (Ornis Polylogus) is a distant relative of the Horned Rumour Monger and is undistinguished in
appearance. Being a common singing bird it often falls victim by yielding to the temptation to chirrup to decoys which
are often set to entrap this lively fowl. The Tattle Bird
perches in the library and watches and listens. Since most
people talk softly in the library the Tattle Bird does not often hear the whole story, or any part of it accurately.
Snatching wisps of conversation, or any general information,
the bird will flit away to find a perch in the faculty dining
room, or the President's Office, from whence it proceeds
to crow its misinformation: 'Caw, caw, the library opened
late today! Caw, caw, the librarian had a hangover! Caw,
caw, Mr. Gore hates Dewey!'

The White Vested Fine Beater (Leukosternicus Multa-
victor) is easily recognized by the sounds it makes. This
begins with bill-rattling, producing a noise like that of a nut-
meg-grater. This bird usually flies into the library and
perches on the circulation desk. Instinctively, it arrives
just before lunch, at closing time, or conveniently to interrupt one's departure for a needed coffee break. A bevy of
these birds can literally ruin a circulation librarian's day.
This species indulges in bill clappering, bill snapping, and
defensive threatening sounds which rise in crescendo as one
attempts to deal with it. The general angry squabbling and
raising and flapping of wings reveals the nasty disposition of
this fowl. It is always open season on this bird and a wise
librarian will net it immediately and thoroughly pluck it in
spite of its noise. Its pin feathers are usually collected in
fine drawers.

Our next feathered visitor is the Addlepated Book
Loser (Malaco-Cephalico-Biblio-Perditor). This ungamely
bird has an omnivorous appetite and an irrascible disposition. It is not strictly a bird of prey. However, its failure
to remember where it has deposited borrowed library books,
leads this bird to make dangerous inroads in a collection.
When confronted this feathered creature resorts at first to
song-flights of explanation which soon deteriorate into snapping and squabbling. After much bill clappering the fowl will
usually disgorge payment for lost books, but not usually
without confrontration by a threat of a general plucking.

The Rainy-Day Visitor (Ombrico-Hemerico-Visitator)--
of ordinary coloration this bird is not recognizably different

from most other birds in academe's groves.   It is given to
song-flights, bill-clappering and is generally omnivorous.
Its one great failing, which places it in great disfavour with
librarians, is its behaviour pattern in regard to returning
library books.   It is a great borrower, hence the name of
the species.   This bird will emerge from its nest carrying
large numbers of unshielded books under its wings.   In
transit the books become thoroughly soaked, but of this fact
the Rainy Day Visitor is serenely oblivious.   Most librarians,
upon spotting this fowl in action, will extract several large
feathers in payment for the damaged books.

The last species in our list, the Wet-Eared Whipper
Snapper (Ornis Hygroto-Mastigo-Fractor) is perhaps one of
the most objectionable of all.   This cocky little bird hops into the library and chirrups loudly, disturbing all who are
within earshot.   His bill clappering indicates that he thinks
he knows more than most birds, and certainly more than
those incompetent librarians who make stupid rules about not
taking away reference books, and who annoy people about returning things to the library.   This bird is always a fledgling, its habits and coloration change with maturity and it often grows up to resemble other species noted above.   However, in its fledgling stages it is a holy terror to librarians
and their helpers.

(The authors are indebted to their colleague Dr. James W.
Pugsley in genera describere.)

Alice's Adventures in Libraryland

John C. Sickley

Separately published Poughkeepsie, N. Y. , 1919. Reprinted
with permission of the Adriance Memorial Library Board of
Trustees, Poughkeepsie, N. Y.

A little nonsense now and then
Is relished e'en by a librarian.
(Adopted from Anonymous.)

Preface

Alice in Libraryland, may appeal to those who at
times have struggled with card catalogues, schemes of classification and other forms of library technic which although
sometimes puzzling and vexatious, are really designed as an
aid in developing the resources of a library, and without
which it would merely be a vast storehouse of books, scattered and disorganized, and about as useless as a storage
warehouse with its contents unarranged. That some librarians
have carried their various schemes to an excess which makes
it extremely difficult for the reader to get what he wants
without the aid of an expert, goes without saying. In this respect they resemble the so-called efficiency experts, who in
many instances have so tied up business management with
their peculiar fads, that the facility for work is rather retarded than advanced.

J. C. S.

Adriance Memorial Library,
    Poughkeepsie, N. Y. ,
        February, 1919.

CONTENTS

CHAPTER I

Alice Comes to the Library

"Do you have books in a library?" asked Alice of the Desk Attendant.

The Attendant was about to annihilate Alice with a crushing retort, but seeing she was a nice appearing little girl relented, and told her that there were many books, and asked her what kind of a book she wanted.

"I want a book that tells me about everything," replied Alice.

"Then you had better go to the reference room and look at the encyclopedia," said the Desk Attendant.

"The en--en--sigh,--what do you call it?" asked Alice, hesitatingly.

"Encyclopedia. There is a Reference Librarian over there; ask her."

So Alice went to the reference room and asked the Reference Librarian for the encyclopedia.

"What is it you want to read about?" asked the Reference Librarian.

"I want to read about everything. I want to know everything," replied Alice.

"In that case you will have to read the encyclopedia through," the Reference Librarian informed her.

"Well, give it to me please, and I will sit down and read," said Alice.

"But it is more than one book; some of the encyclopedias have twenty books or more, like those big books up there," said the Reference Librarian, pointing to the Encyclopaedia Britannica on the shelves.

"Oh, my," said Alice, "I won't have time to read all those this morning. Have you a book called Jack and the Bean Stalk?"

"That book is in the children's room; and I think you could not have the encyclopedia, you are not old enough. You had better go to the children's room."

So Alice left the reference room and wandered over to the children's room.

CHAPTER II

"Is this the children's room?" asked Alice of the Attendant.

"Yes," replied the Children's Librarian, "and do you know it is the hottest room in the building?"

"No," replied Alice, "and why is it so hot?"

"Because it is the coldest in winter."

"But--but--I--I--don't understand," said Alice.

"You would if you were here," said the Children's Librarian; "but I never speak of it. I never mention it to anyone."

"Oh," said Alice.

"And what do you want to read?" asked the Children's Librarian.

"Jack and the Bean Stalk," replied Alice.

"You will find it over there with the books on children's gardens," said the Children's Librarian.

"Why do you put it there? I thought it would be with the Fairy stories and such books," said Alice.

"Oh no, the bean stalk is a plant, and the child might see some other plant books and become interested in gardening."

Alice was unable to find Jack and the Bean Stalk, and went back and so told the Children's Librarian.

"Well," said she, "go look in the card catalogue-- that case over there with the little drawers; you may find something else."

Alice pulled out one drawer after another, and seeing nothing but cards with writing or printing on them, went back and told the Children's Librarian there were no books in the drawers, only cards.

"Oh," said the Children's Librarian, "the cards just give the names of the books. You will not find the books there, only the cards."

"Yes," said Alice, "but I don't want the names of books, I want the books. Please tell me where I can find the books."

"You must get the name of the book from the catalogue before I can get the book. It would break the library rules if I get a book before you look in the catalogue," said the Children's Librarian.

"But the cat--cat--log, is too hard. Haven't you a kitten log for little girls?" asked Alice. But the Children's Librarian was now busy with several school children and paid no attention to Alice.

So Alice turned to a Big Girl standing near and asked her if she had read all the books in the children's room.

"Why no, goosie," said the Big Girl, "I am only in the eighth grade."

"How many have you read?" asked Alice.

"Well," replied the Big Girl, "I have read seven history books and six nature books and nine story books, and Little Women and Old Fashioned Girl, that makes eleven."

"Why," said Alice, who was good at mental arithmetic, "it is more than that. Seven and six and nine and two make twenty-four."

"Oh," replied the Big Girl, "you must not count the improving books. Of course I never count them. I only count the books to read."

"But--but--" began Alice, and seeing a look of displeasure on the Big Girl's face said nothing.

CHAPTER III

Efforts to teach Alice library technic.

When Alice turned to the Children's Librarian, she found that lady had gone out, and the Reference Librarian was in charge. Alice approached the desk and asked if she had a life of Mother Goose."

"Look in the catalogue under Poultry, said the Reference Librarian.

"Y-e-s, y-e-s," said Alice in a puzzled voice, "but it is a book about Mother Goose, I want, not about a goose."

"Well," said the Reference Librarian, "a goose is certainly poultry, and you must look under that subject to find it; and you will probably find another card, marked, See also, Mother."

But Alice was afraid of the card catalogue, and asked, "Is rhyme and poetry just the same? The name of Mrs. Goose's book is 'Rhymes of Mother Goose',"

"No," said the Reference Librarian, who here saw an opportunity to impart some useful knowledge to Alice's youthful mind and reaching for a Webster's Unabridged, continued, "I will read you the etymological definitions of the two words, so that you can at once understand the difference. Listen! Rhyme is defined as 'a correspondence of sounds between two or more words, especially at the ends of lines, as in poetry.' Poetry is 'the form of literature that embodies beautiful thought, feeling or action, in rythmical and (usually) metrical language.' Now you see there is quite a difference between rhyme and poetry, do you not?"

254

"No," said Alice, in a hopeless tone, "such big words only make my head ache. I don't think I understand at all."

"Well you will understand if you repeat what I have read over and over," said the Reference Librarian.

"My grandpa says he used to read some books called the Franconia Stories. Have you any of them?" asked Alice.

"Heavens no!" replied the Reference Librarian, "Why, the idea! Such books are entirely obsolete. What a strange child you are." And the Reference Librarian looked at Alice in amazement.

"And my papa says he used to read Oliver Optic books, and Alger books; have you any of them?" asked Alice.

"Why, no indeed, such books have long been discarded from libraries. We could not permit such publications to contaminate the minds of children," said the Reference Librarian.

"Was my papa taminated by Optics and Algers?" asked Alice.

The Reference Librarian was confused for a moment, but finally said, "The books of these days are quite different from the old time books which interested your father, but such books would not interest the boys of today."

CHAPTER IV

Further efforts to instruct Alice.

Seeing a book on the desk, Alice asked what it was.

"That is a book which shows us how to classify, "but seeing a puzzled look on Alice's face added: "It tells us whether a book is a story book or a history, or just what kind of a book it is. It is called, Dewey's Decimal Classification."

Alice could only associate decimals with her arithmetic and began to repeat to herself:

"Ten mills make one cent.
Ten cents make one dime.

255

Ten dimes make one dollar--"

But catching a glimpse of some of the words in the Decimal Classification, asked, "Didn't Mr. Dewey write more arithmetics than class--class--cations?"

"I don't know that he ever wrote any arithmetics or mathematical works of any kind. But why do you ask me?" said the Reference Librarian.

"Why he don't spell very well," said Alice, pointing to some words, which either by abbreviation or alteration had as much resemblance to the original word, as the music for Yankee Doodle has to a poem in the Greek language.

"Oh," said the Reference Librarian, laughing, "that is simplified spelling; we all understand that now."

"I wish he would make a simple-fied classication, I think that would be better," said Alice.

Seeing another book on the desk, a smaller book bound in blue, Alice opened it and asked what it was.

"That is the Library Primer. It tells us about the simpler methods of library work," replied the Reference Librarian.

"Gracious," said Alice, who had been looking through the book, "if this is a Library Primer, what must a Library Fourth Reader be? I believe I don't want to study to be a library lady."

"Oh," said the Reference Librarian, "when you are older and have perused the Library Primer thoroughly, and mastered the intricacies of the Dewey Decimal Classification, and acquired a thorough knowledge of all the poets, historians, scientists, discoverers, artists and novelists, and attained a general knowledge of literature, ancient and modern, and are able to classify and catalogue books properly, and," but the Reference Librarian, who with uplifted eyes had been so eloquently descanting on her theme, suddenly paused in her rhapsody as she saw Alice stretched unconscious on the floor before her.

When Alice recovered, she found herself seated on a chair and the Cataloguer was giving her some water to drink, the Reference Librarian having left Alice in her care as she was obliged to go out to lunch.

"If you please," said Alice, "I think I will not try to learn any more about libraries today. I will come some other time."

"But you must let me explain about the card catalogue," said the Cataloguer, "The Children's Librarian tells me you apparently know nothing about it, and if you use the library you must understand the card catalogue."

"Very well, if I must, but I don't want to make my head ache any more" said Alice.

So the Cataloguer took Alice by the hand and led her to the card catalogue.

"Now," began the Cataloguer, "of course you know your alphabet?"

Alice began indignantly to assert that she did, but the Cataloguer soothed her and said: "You see all those little drawers there. They are full of cards which contain the names of the books."

"Yes," said Alice drawing back a little, "but I don't care about the cards or the names of the books; I want the books."

"The cards," continued the Cataloguer, not heeding Alice's assertion--but just then she was called away for something and left Alice alone.

CHAPTER V

Alice's library instruction ended.

In a moment a boy whom Alice had observed about the library, putting up books and working or pretending to work, more or less, approached her and said,

"Say, was she givin' you her song and dance about that old cat log?"

Alice did not understand slang very well and looked inquiringly at the boy and said nothing.

"Say, are you goin' to learn libry work?" asked the boy.

"Oh no," replied Alice, "I just came in to get a book."

"Well, I wouldn't if I was you. I'm sorry I learned. I've been here two weeks and am goin' to quit. I'm goin' to be one of them radiators."

"Aviators, you mean, do you not?" asked Alice.

"Yes, that's it. I don't like her nor none of these libry girls. They're always pickin' on me."

Alice inferred by the boy's somewhat indefinite use of the pronoun he referred to the Cataloguer, but before she could ask the reason for his dislike to the library staff, he said,

"Say, come over here, I've got somethin' to show you," and he led Alice to a secluded place in one of the alcoves.

"Say, do you know I make up poultry sometimes?" he asked looking at Alice as if he expected an exclamation of admiration from her.

"You mean poetry, do you not?" asked Alice.

"It's all the same," said the boy. "You write a line which ends with potato, and you write another line which ends with tomato, or something like that you know."

"Yes," said Alice, "I like nice poems. What kind of a poem did you write?"

"It's about her and all the rest of 'em. I'll read it to you," he said taking a very soiled sheet of paper from his pocket. "It's like this. I call it,

The Libry Ginks

them libry girls they think there boss
They think they own the plase
they make me tired by always askin
wen did you wash your fase.

258

        mi fase duz sumtimes nead a bath
            But then o mi o lands
        thyd say nothin' about fases
            if they cud see mi hands.

"Hows that sound?" asked the boy, looking at Alice to
see how she appreciated his effort.

"Why--why--" replied Alice, who did not wish to be
severely critical, "it certainly rhymes."

"Sure," said the boy "I told you poultry, poetry I
mean, always does."

"But you haven't said much about the librarians, it is
more about your dirty face," said Alice.

"Yes, but I've got more.   I've got somethin' about
'em.   Listen."

        i sez to them you think yure smart
            Tellin' me mi fase aint clene
        and makin out to every boddy
            that i aint fit to be sean.
        i no mi fase has sumtimes smut
            i no i aint no dandy
        for i dont use no powder puffs
            nor such stuff as girls has handy.

When he finished he again looked at Alice inquiringly,
as though expecting some favorable remarks.

"Have you read it to the librarians?" asked Alice.

"I read it to the whole gang," replied the boy.   "You
see it was like this.   She caught me writin' one day and took
me to the liberrian, and told him I was always skinnin' out
of work, and he ast me what I was doin', and I told him just
writin'.   So he ast me to read it, and all the bunch was
standin' round grinnin', and so I read it and you ought to
heard 'em laugh."

"What did the librarian say?" asked Alice.

"Why he sez, George Augustus--that's my name you
know--George Augustus, as you think you'd rather be one of
them radiators--I mean avyators, in the future you'd better
devote your energies to the modern horse of the air, rather

than the ancient Peg Asses."

Just then a voice called, "George Augustus, George Augustus."

"That's her now. I've got to go," said the boy. "Say, if you want to skin out without havin' her give you any more dope about that old card catalogue, slip out that way. Good by."

Alice took the way suggested by the boy, and hastily opening the door, ran home as fast as possible.

Imagism in the Cleveland Public Library

William F. Smyth

Reprinted from Edmund Lester Pearson's column "The Librarian" in the Boston Transcript April 25, 1917.

Sunday
In the Library.
Ah!
What bliss!
What opportunities to form
The minds
Of Infants!
And to reform
The minds
Of Adults!
All of which we,
The Staff,
Have done
Today.

Debaters
For multitude
Like unto grasshoppers
Swarmed around
Desk 2.
And lo.
It survived their swarmfest!
And their wants
Were satisfied,
We trust.

Also,
And moreover,
Each of the other
Departments
Sure done noble.
They made glad
The hearts

261

Of the many seekers
For information
In their respective
Lines.

On the whole
It
Has been
A large day.
Selah.

A Cry from the Corner

A. B. Stables

From The Assistant Librarian 55:48-9, 1962.   Reprinted by
permission of the author and of the editor of The Assistant
Librarian.

" . . . and somewhere in a corner there may be a reference
librarian who is obviously under-employed. " -- S. H. Barlow,
F. L. A. , in the Library Association Record, December, 1961.

The reference librarians of England--how under-
employed a band!
As the clairvoyant chief of Nuneaton would have us
to understand.
They sit in their cosy corners with nothing whatever
to do
But cope with a query a minute, and answer a 'phone
every two.
And ransack the Bookseller weekly, and skim through
that old B. N. B. ,
And make sure their selections are ordered before
there's a risk of "o. p. ,"
And frisk all the local newspapers for plums for
their vertical file,
And their index of local societies (which has taken
them years to compile),
And besides all these simple employments they may
well have to catalogue lots
Of ref. books, maps, pamphlets and pictures, to be
shelved in appropriate spots. . .
The reference librarian of England, in the small or
the middle-sized town,
Though he's no registration of readers, or dealings
with Kodak or Browne,
Has a thing called a Local Collection he's supposed
to know something about;
It may have its own classification, and its own dingy
patches, no doubt,

263

And its newspaper files may be micro'd, and its
    readers be some of them cracked,
But the ref. man must master the former and
    handle the latter with tact.
There's a Reading Room, too, in most places,
    though we've cancelled or modified some,
And it's usually left to the ref. man to make things
    (not nasally) hum!
. . . What shall I say more, Mr. Barlow? for my
    time and your patience would fail
If I went on to mention time-tables, be they road,
    airline, steamer or rail,
Quick-ref., Hansard, Keesing's and What's On?,
    trade catalogues, Which? and Who's Who?
Who Owns Whom? Who Makes That? Where? and
    what not . . . well, it may appear little to you,
But I know that my job keeps me busy, and you as
    a chief surely shine:
So you beaver away in your corner, while I sit and
    idle in mine!

Ballad of the Reference Desk
(To be sung to the tune of "Streets of Laredo")

Barbara Toohey

From Wilson Library Bulletin 37:410, 1963.   Reprinted by
permission from the January 1963 issue of the Wilson Library Bulletin.   Copyright (c)1963 by the H. W. Wilson Company.   Also with permission of the author.

As I go out on the desk to do reference,
As I go out to do reference each day,
I'm ready and eager and have the resources,
To answer all questions that might come my way.

A woman approaches, eyes bright with a
     passionate
Fever to learn of two-hundred degrees,
I'll help her to find the great truth she is
     seeking . . .
She says, "Tell me where is the ladies' room
     please."

Next to my desk comes a man of importance,
Exuding authority, Homburg to shoes,
I'll give him some facts and he'll make empires
     tremble . . .
He asks me, "Do you have a phone I can use?"

Now, horn-rimmed and tweedy, here comes a
     great scholar,
I'm sure that his question will be recondite,
Perhaps he's in quest of obscure Greek quota-
     tions . . .
His words are, "What time do you close here
     tonight?"

Oh why did I spend all those long years in college,
Learning the answers, when everyone knows

That all they will ask you is, "Where is the restroom?"
"Is there a phone here?" "What time do you close?"

the readers' advisor explains modern poetry to a patron
(in the manner of e. e. cummings)

Barbara Toohey

> modern poetry is like a perhaps nothing
> maybe looking at itself
> in an almost mirror (which
> not quite shows
> something to anyone) carelessly

> modern poetry is like a perhaps nothing
> in a mirror
> which reflecting probable
> emptiness looks like something to (maybe
> guessing) somebodies
> (who think they nearly see a definite
> next to
> Something so important that
> it's close to nothing in
> maybeness)

> modern poetry is so
> much probably the most not
> quite perhaps nearly nothing in
> a world
> full of almost complete
> certainly Nothings that everyone surely
> doubting his nobodyness
> should read (just about considering
> to think about) it
> not

> modern poetry might be a--listen

there's a hell of an edgar guest book
in the stacks; go read that

Somebody's Mother

Barbara Toohey

Excuse me, but I'm in a hurry,
Are you the librarian here?
I'm looking for something on Milton . . .
Or Hilton . . . or Walton--Oh dear!
Well, you must know, it's the assignment
For eleventh grade English this week,
My daughter is taking that course now
And she's writing some kind of critique,
So since I was going right by here,
I thought I would drop in to see
If you had a book that might help her--
She must get an A or a B,
Her father and I are quite worried,
Just next year she has to apply
To the college of his and my choice which
Requires a grade-average that's high,
But the poor girl has no time to study,
She has something to do every day,
You know she's the head baton twirler
And she's taking both tap and ballet,
Then her social life, too, is important
A girl of her age should have fun
And there's always some party or movie
Or dance to keep her on the run.
But she needs a career to fall back on,
Her father and I just insist
That she study for some nice profession . . .
Maybe lawyer or psychiatrist . . .
Oh, look at the time! I must run now,
My bridge club is meeting today,
But do be a dear and find something

And just sort of hide it away,
Her father can get it this evening,
He'll be glad to help out--he agrees
That parents should <u>always</u> encourage
Worthwhile research <u>projects</u> like these.

Sonnet to a Student Standing in the Library
in Front of the Reference Desk With Tears
in His Eyes Because His Teacher Has Assigned Him to Do a Report on a Book Which
Cannot Be Found in Masterplots, Thesaurus
of Book Digests, Reader's Digest of Books, or
The Book Review Digest.

Barbara Toohey

From Wilson Library Bulletin 36:751, 1962. Reprinted by
permission from the May 1962 issue of the Wilson Library
Bulletin. Copyright (c)1962 by the H. W. Wilson Company.
Also with permission of the author.

I see the etchéd brief upon your brow,
And experience its painful counterpart
In every throb of my empathic heart,
Oh, would that it were mine to thee endow
With miriad précis to gently plow
Into the barren mental wastes and start
A germination of the critic's art.
But cruel gods of dearth exact my bow.
Yet stay, one way remains to fleet assay
The contents of the book, although I vow
The method is considered quite passé,
In fact almost bizarre, so seldom now
Is it employed among your happy breed--it
Is to open up the book and read it.

At Examination Time

Carleton Vonnell

From <u>Minnesota Daily News</u> February 2, 1928.   Reprinted
with permission of the editor of the <u>Minnesota Daily</u>.

I went into the library,
As is my custom during
Midquarters, and said I to
The pretty lady at the desk,
"I want a copy of Orlando Furioso; that is,
If it isn't at the binders,
Is not on reserve,
Is not set aside for graduate students,
Is not in the 'Z' collection,
Is not in some professor's library,
Is not in the Arthur Upson room,
Is expurgated enough for minors to read,
Is not in the reference room."
Said she, after rummaging thru
The catalogs, fixing her hair,
Powdering her nose, and adjusting her
Delta Gamma pin,
"The book fulfills all your requirements;
It is not on reserve, in the 'Z' collection,
In the Arthur Upson room, or anything."
"Wonder of wonders," I exclaimed.
"Then might I have the book?"
"You might if we had it," spake she,
"But we haven't bought it."
Of course, I fainted.

Nothing Further to Adler

Sarah L. Wallace

From Wilson Library Bulletin 18:152-3, 1943.   Reprinted by
permission from the October 1943 issue of the Wilson Library Bulletin.   Copyright (c)1943 by the H. W. Wilson Company.   Also with permission of the author.

I found my friend Peter sitting with a closed book before him.   He looked tired.   I told him so.

"I am tired," he admitted.   "I just finished not reading this book.   It's a long one, too, 790 pages," he said,
holding it up.

"Not reading it," I repeated.   It's a habit of mine to
repeat the other person's sentences.   It saves depreciation of
brain cells and they like it anyway.   "That shouldn't be tiring."

"Just one, no," Peter said, "But not reading a hundred is quite a task.   Especially when you're working against
time.   It's all very well not to read a hundred books a year,
but to not read a hundred books in a couple of weeks takes
effort.   And I'm a busy man."

"But who would want to not read a hundred books!"
I said.

"Hundreds of people, thousands of people, millions of
people," Peter waved his arms excitedly.   "Ever since I got
the idea I've had letters pouring in demanding that I finish
it."

"It, it!" I said, "What's it?"

"My list."

Peter sat down again, more calm.   He lit a cigarette.

"It all began some time ago during some Book Week, or Author Week, or Press Week, or Laundry Week. I asked several famous people for lists of ten books they would not like to be left with on a desert island." He looked thoughtful. "Though why anyone would want to be left on a desert island with or without ten books has always been beyond me. But anyway, I got such a good response--"

"What were the lists like?" I broke in. You have to keep Peter primed.

"Oh, the usual thing. The same ones people always say they want to be left with on an island. Probably wouldn't be caught dead reading them any other place," he added. "Shakespeare, Plato, Bacon's Essays, Euripides, stuff like that."

"I don't see anything very original there," I protested.

"No," said Peter. "But that's when I got my idea."

"Idea for what?" I demanded. Peter loves to drag things out.

"For my list," he pulled a long sheet of paper out of his pocket. "I had just finished it when you came."

He unfolded it and read the title.

" 'One Hundred Books Not Worth Reading: a selected list of books you can afford to miss.' "

" 'One Hundred Books Not Worth Reading'?" I echoed. "Don't you mean worth reading?"

"No, I don't! No, I don't!" cried Peter. "How many lists of a hundred books worth reading have you seen?"

"Too many," I said. "I'm always going to dinner and having the lady on the other side ask, 'Have you read The Moon Is Down over the White Cliffs?' Then I say 'No.' Then she looks at me the way a dietitian looks at a fried egg and says, 'But you must, you simply must. It's at the head of Quimby Mortimer Whatsit's list.' "

"That's precisely it," Peter said, triumphant. "It came over me all of a sudden that no one could keep abreast

274

with the tide of books being published today. And the war
has made it worse with everybody learning first aid and collecting waste paper. The average person doesn't have time
to read at all. Does he want a list of books he must read
or be damned? No. As long as he's not reading he wants
to know what books not to read first. And that's where this
comes in," and Peter tapped the list.

"How did you go about compiling it?" I asked.

"First I had to have a board of experts, critics, you
know," said Peter. "They add tone. They had to be entirely biased, prejudiced and susceptible to outside influence.
They conscientiously did not read a hundred books and then
submitted their selections to me. I went over them and
picked the titles most frequently mentioned. You'd be surprised how many were on last week's list of books to be
read at all costs."

"Not really!" I exclaimed.

"But that was last week," he said. "And of course,
they're old now."

"What's on this list of yours?" I was curious.

"Almost all the books that are on the 'What Everybody's Reading in Boston' list," he said.

"But if they're actually reading them there--" I protested.

"Oh, Boston!" Peter tossed it off. "It's different.
Besides, think how nice for you the next time you sit beside
one of these Great Readers at dinner."

"How so?" I humor Peter.

"She says to you, 'Have you read The Moon Is Down
over the White Cliffs; it's at the head of Quimby Mortimer
Whatsit's list, you know.' Don't say 'No' and leave it at
that. Look at her as if she were a fried egg with a broken
yolk at that and say, 'I've just finished not reading it. It's
at the head of Peter's "One Hundred Books Not Worth Reading." I never miss not reading every book on his list. And
that one's starred!' She'll wilt, you see if she doesn't."

"What do you mean it's starred?"

"That's a little added service," Peter said. "I starred those most worth not reading a second time."

"But," I leered at him. "Wait until the librarians get wind of it. The A. L. A. will polish you off in short order. Those lists will hit them right where they live."

"That's what you think," crowed Peter. "My board of experts was made up mostly of librarians."

"How come?" I asked.

"Simple," explained Peter. "According to their own admission librarians don't read more books than anybody. They're going to be my biggest supporters."

"It doesn't seem right to me," I protested.

"That's because you haven't thought it out," said Peter. "Circulation is falling off in all libraries. That means fewer readers, doesn't it?"

"Ye-es," I admitted slowly.

"That means that a larger percentage of the population is not reading and that those who do read are reading less."

"Ye-es," I said again.

Peter sat back smugly.

"There you are," he said. "Those people who are not reading are taxpayers. The library is largely tax-supported. The library wants to serve its supporters. So, if the taxpayers are not reading it's the library's duty to help them. The librarian is the one to whom they turn to find out what not to read."

"I suppose you're right," I admitted again.

"Sure, I'm right," Peter said. "I'm so right that the American Library Association is backing me while I do research on a new bibliography."

"What will it be?" I asked, interested.

"A standard catalog of books not for a public library,"

Peter rattled off. "It will be a guide of what not to order."

"But how are you going to launch the scheme, Peter?"
I asked.

"Oh, easy," smiled Peter. "It's going to be published as part of the No-Book-of-the-Month Club."

"What!" I exclaimed. "Is there more to this?"

"It's just another little idea I had for busy people who
don't want to be left out of things," Peter explained. "Members simply agree not to read four books a year. In return
the Club guarantees not to send them any books, even at
regular rates, and of course, offers absolutely no dividends.
There's just one difficulty I have to iron out yet," he admitted.

"What's that?" I asked.

"I'm having a little trouble persuading the publishers
not to publish the books the Club selects."

"Not the progressive companies," I said.

"Oh, I'll persuade them." Peter tossed off a couple
of perfect smoke rings. He looked pleased.

"Well," I conceded, "you may have something there
at that."

"I have." Peter was confident. "I plan to follow
this with a selected list of books not to give for Christmas.
It will be classified: 'Books Grandmother Won't Want for
Christmas,' 'Books Father Won't Want for Christmas,'
'Books Mother Won't Want for Christmas'--you know. And
for Children's Book Week I'm planning a two-color job, 'Ten
Books Every Child Should Not Know.' "

"I wish you luck," I said, not taking my hat and not
opening the door.

"Thanks," said Peter. "I'm not worried. It's got
the Good Housekeeping seal and the approval of the American
Medical Association Committee on Foods already."

Information

Robert Wilberforce

From The Landmark 13:213, 1931. Reprinted by permission of The English-Speaking Union of the Commonwealth.

(In 1920 the Foreign Office established in New York a
British Library of Information.)

The Library of Information
Has this congenial occupation,
To gather for the recreation,
Close study and examination
Of U. S. A. (a near relation)
Facts all about the British Nation.
It has arranged in due rotation
For every mood a publication,
Or shall we say a balanced ration,
Of Blue Books for your consultation,
From Zululand to Aviation,
On Law and Art and Education,
On Shipping and on Navigation,
And naval tonnage tabulation,
And charts of cruiser elevation,
And long reports on Arbitration,
And figures of Intoxication,
And recent rules on Vaccination,
And many another regulation,
And late Lord Balfour's Declaration,
And last, not least, our high taxation.
I could continue this narration,
But won't so that's a consolation
I'll only add for due notation
That should a future generation
Indulge in any agitation,
Or should an unforeseen sensation
Too greatly tax imagination,
The Library of Information
Will always give elucidation.

278

In moments of exasperation,
E. G.   If statesmen in each nation,
Without sufficient meditation,
Express ideas in wild oration
Which to the general consternation
Create a world-wide perturbation,
And even the mildest man (quotation)
Asks, "what the hell is meant damnation,"
And here we aptly close quotation,
Merely with this brief observation;
At times like that 'tis information
Alone will meet the situation.
So if there's never a cessation
In friendship and communication
Between the U. S. A. and our nation,
In spite of every irritation
You'll know the cause is Information,
Which helps restore the gravitation
When danger threatens the foundation;
It's really not a bad creation,
This Library of Information.

CATALOGING AND CLASSIFICATION

En Garde, B. N. B.

G. Dixon

From The Assistant Librarian 50:24, 1957.   Reprinted by
permission of the author and of the editor of The Assistant
Librarian.

It's happened! as I knew it must!   I   hadn't any doubt,
    But I wondered whether I should live to see
The cataloguing gaffe that we are always warned about,
    And perpetrated by the B. N. B. !

"St. Mary's Abbey, York," was what I hunted for, and hence
    I started off by looking under S,
I was not at all surprised therefore when re-directed thence
    To . . . "York. St. Mary's Abbey," How'd you guess?

I quickly turned the pages of the Cumulated thing,
    My eager eye sought Y out like a hawk,
I found it, paused, and stared, transfixed, my head
        began to sing,
    It stated "See St. Mary's Abbey, York."

Nor is this all (once started, I must criticize some more)
    And just in case you should search on and on
For "Candlelight in Avalon" by Muir in '54,
    It's indexed but class entry there is none!

One other thing that baffles me, I've tried and given up
    To understand the difference between
The bibliogs, that lurk in B. N. B., at O-one-two,
    And those that flaunt themselves in O-sixteen.

Perhaps I'm just a crazy mixed-up kid, or just plain dumb,
    But I cannot see what Oscar Wilde has done,
That he should go at O-one-two while Rupert Brooke
        should come
    At O-one-six-point-eight-two-one-nine-one.

Aha! thought I, perhaps it's "books about" at O-sixteen,
    Whilst O-twelve takes "books by" (though whence
    precision?),
But further study has not enabled me to glean,
    A sound characteristic of division

Just one more moan; again in '54 I searched because
    A Forestry Commission Guide I sought,
For Queen Elizabeth Forest Park, but the only entry was
    For subject, which when looked up, came to nought.

There are points which I've not noticed, I am sure,
    and yet still more
    Which escape me though my memory I prod,
But it's nice to know, and comforting when at the
    daily chore
    That Mr. Wells, like Homer, can still nod.

Cool for Cataloguers

Peter Gann

From The Assistant Librarian 53:227, 1960.   Reprinted with permission of the author and of the editor of The Assistant Librarian.

Let there be no derision;
A cataloguer's job is decision, decision, decision
As with each problem he grapples,
It's just like sorting apples.

Should it be under Tante Marie?
But Marie, Tante is used by B. N. B.
On the other hand, from the forename entry slant
It should be Marie, Aunt.

Classifiers are a race apart;
They practice a mysterious, hidden art;
And as their positions get stronger --
Their classification numbers get longer and longer.

Mr. Coates,
I imagine, sits and gloats
And says "This will make W. Howard Phillips writhe:
Travel agents: 338.477965."

The lending library staff
Greet the cataloguer's efforts with a laugh
Or mutterings or fierce fanatical stares --
But they're just a bunch of squares.

A Cataloging Aptitude Test;
or, Do You Really Know the Difference Between
an Entry and an Imprint?

Lenore S. Gribbin

From Library Resources & Technical Services 8:151-2,
1964. Reprinted with permission of the author and of the
American Library Association.

Now that you have completed a few courses in library
school, including one in cataloging, you are probably wondering: should I or shouldn't I (go into cataloging, that is)?
Sometimes the answer is so obvious you need not ruminate
further. If, for example, your coordination is too poor to
get the tray rod through all those little holes, you'd better
go into administration. Or, if, at your tender years, you
already show a marked tendency toward alopecia, consider
another specialization--you can't afford to tear out your hair
over details. On the other hand some affinity for cataloging may be noted early in life, as in the case of a child who
enjoys counting the beans in his bean bag, or grouping his
yellow, red, green, and black gum drops.

Aside from obvious indications, the following questions
are presented to help predict your success in this specialized field. You have a choice of three answers to each question. (Did you really think there could be only one correct
answer to a cataloging problem?) Select the answer which
most closely describes what you would do.

1. You have a book by John Smith. You need to establish
    your entry. In the catalog you find five other John
    Smith's--one born in 1817, one who died in 1900, one
    plain, one from Screeching Halt, Minn., and one desig-
    nated as "astronomer." How do you handle your entry?

    (1) Write John Smith to get his middle name or date
        of birth.
    (2) Pretend your John Smith is one of those already
        in the catalog.

(3) Put it on the desk of the cataloger in front of you when she is away. Let her worry about it.

2. Your book gives no place of publication; however, you know that the author's residence is in New York, the printer in Chicago, and the bookseller in London. What do you use in your imprint?

    (1) Heads, New York. Tails, Chicago. London if it stands on the rim.
    (2) Scour the bibliographic sources for three hours. Then tails, Chicago, heads, New York, etc.
    (3) Use n. p. and don't forget the brackets.

3. You are holding volume 2 of a set. According to four excellent bibliographic sources, volume 1 was the only volume ever published. How do you treat your volume?

    (1) Prepare a card for the set, giving both vol. 1 and vol. 2 in contents.
    (2) Ignore vol. 1 and catalog the set as if only vol. 2 had been published.
    (3) Throw away your vol. 2. You have found sufficient evidence that it doesn't exist.

4. A husband and wife write singly and jointly under the same pseudonym. Their real names are unknown. How do you enter his, her, and their titles?

    (1) Under pseudonym regardless of authorship.
    (2) Under title.
    (3) Establish practice of community property cataloging.

5. John Henry Methuselah published his first book in 1868 at the age of 48. Seven years later he published a second book. Nine years later a revised edition of his first book. Six years later another revised edition of his first book was combined with a revision of his second book. Ten years later a condensation combining the two titles appeared. Twelve years later a new title was based on the expanded abridgement of the two previous books. What is your main problem?

    (1) To give a clear picture of the bibliographic relationships.
    (2) To establish Methuselah's dates.
    (3) Your problem is nothing compared to Methuselah's.

He just couldn't make up his mind in all those years.

6. You have a serial which changed its title six times. Three of the titles are almost identical. How many cross references do you need?

    (1) 4
    (2) 6
    (3) None, if you can make it sound so complicated they decide to delay cataloging until publication ceases.

7. The title on your title-page appears in Swahili, Telugu, and English. How do you transcribe it?

    (1) Use just the English. Those other things are obviously meant to be decoration.
    (2) Put the book aside until someone who knows Swahili and Telugu can help.
    (3) Put it on the desk of the cataloger behind you when she is away. After all, didn't she slip you that nasty John Smith problem?

Diagnosis of answers. Are your answers predominantly (1)? The cataloging field needs you. You unimaginative types are the backbone of the profession. Are your answers predominantly (2)? The cataloging field needs you, too. And anyone else willing to go into it. Are your answers predominantly (3)? You'll go far. Possibly to another field.

Cataloger at Large

Edward J. Humeston, Jr.

Reprinted from ALA Bulletin 48:134-5, 1954. Reprinted
with permission of the author and of the American Library
Association.

Enumerative documentation has since its inception
subsumed a pluralistic development. Where cataloging and
classification are concerned, we are able to reduce the matter to relatively simple terms. "How did Dewey do it?"
One more problem is basic, too, --"Why did Dewey do it?"
Although we may never have the full answers to these questions, it is undeniable that the great man imbued countless
generations of librarians with new force and determination,
with the true Dewey-die spirit.

The history of cataloging is characterized by something of this same courage. Take one of the types of added
entry. Book writing in ancient times was a dangerous calling, in which secrecy was essential. Here and there writers
would find some cranny, or nook, or room in the home of a
friend, in which to work out their ideas. No matter where
it was, the authors were very close to their works. The
Latin word to express this relationship was junctus or
joined, that is inseparable from the works. Here is the
origin of the term joint author. Today by extension and an-
ology the word joint applies as well to any small room,
beer parlor, or hole in the wall.

A second example of our debt to Rome is seen in one
of the items of collation. Early catalogers made use of a
phrase that appears today in abbreviated form on catalog
cards. When describing a book with pictures or drawings
cut from wooden blocks, they wrote on the outside of the
manuscript; in libro legis umbras scissas. Umbra meant
shade but stood for black and white (shaded) drawings. In
other words, the book contained illustrations. The initial
letters of the Latin phrase (the i l l u s) are the same illus

that we type on cards today.

Mathematics, too, has counted for something in cataloging and classification. For the extension card came as a result of the invention and development of the slide rule. Here was a device, like the classification, capable of indefinite expansion. Why not apply the same idea to library cards, on which there was often enough not room for the material on the title page? Careful and exhaustive research brought results, and today we have the extension card, able to provide for the longest title. Since the first users of slide rules in libraries had been accustomed to asking, "If a slide rule extends, why not a card, too?" (or sometimes "card two") the term Card 2 became synonymous with the words extension card.

Dewey, it is said, was given to rather frequent arguments, especially with persons close to his immediate family: cousins, aunts, uncles, and the like. Knowing him thus troubled by controversies real or imagined on the part of his kinfolk, we are hardly surprised to learn that we owe him the first really comprehensive and successful relative classification. Once the initial step had been taken, other classifications were bound to follow. After Dewey comes Bliss, and then the Brussels sprouts.

One of the spatial problems that vexed Dewey and his contemporaries is still with us, the parallelism of the tracing. We are confronted not only with the problem of spacing the tracing but also the equally knotty task of tracing the spacing. Today perhaps the former is more important. The demand for more facts requires that the tracing be spaced with utmost care. If economy of spacing is rigorously practiced, there will be room for other material on the card. Important and valuable items such as telephone numbers of board members and friends of the library, circulation statistics, or brief annotations could easily be included. Whole forests' wood be spared! The second phase of the problem, the matter of tracing the spacing, is not without real significance, but the limited scope of this paper does not permit the discussion it deserves.

In some quarters it is held that analytics constitute another fertile field for study and stand in some need of streamlining. Possibly one or two practical suggestions here will be of value. Do you forget the indentions to which succeeding lines in author and title analytics should return? A good rule is: Don't analyze for any title that runs to more

than one line in length. The same type of reasoning holds
where a collection is entered under title. Space and time
can be conserved by remembering not to make added entries
or trace for editors, especially those with two or more fore-
names. Carrying this to its logical conclusion, many if not
all books can be handled most expeditiously by never being
analyzed at all.

As progress is possible in the areas noted above, so
is there room for improvement where classification is concerned. For the average public library the Dewey classification is unnecessary and outmoded. In the place of the Dewey
system libraries might well adopt the Bookolorguide or (Col-
orbookide), a system based on the intensity span of ten different colors. Since the Japanese can distinguish up to
10,000 shades of a given color, it is obvious that ten colors
would suffice for a library collection of 100,000 books. The
administrator need only purchase strips of gummed cloth in
various shades. When a book comes in, the fifth assistant
librarian pastes a small strip of cloth on the spine, and the
seventh assistant librarian puts smaller strips on the main
card and added entries. Gone the need for bookmarks and
hours of tedious typing! The user looking for a book finds
the card in its regular place in the dictionary catalog. Removing the card, he walks to the stacks, matches the strip
on the card with the strip on the back of the book, and is
ready to check the book out. What could be more simple?
And the reader who says, "I'd like the dark reddish book
Mrs. Van Clobney had out last week," is no longer a problem. Turn him loose in the stacks."

For the few color blind persons found in the community there has been developed the Kwikoloradjustor. This
neat, compact machine weighing slightly over thirty-four
pounds fits over the head and within seventeen minutes con-
verts the color the reader thinks he has in mind to one in
which the library has the largest stock of books. An electric pump supplies extra air for those whose minds cannot be
made up for them in the regularly allotted period.

In conclusion we would return to and remind our readers of the potential of the Dewey differential. "Forward and
downward" is the watchword. Keep your eyes on those cards.
The highway to the Elysian Fields, to the heaven for catalogers, is paved--need I say it?--with good indentions.

Unfrequented Paths in Classification

Manor G. North

From The Library World 9:437-40, 1907.   Reprinted with
permission of W. H. Smith and Son, Ltd.

Classification, in common with other branches of library administration, is in a state of evolution.   The old order, that of a jumbled, or occasionally alphabetical sequence
under a general class heading, is gradually giving way to the
new order, or classification by subject.   The word gradually
is used advisedly, for not only is subject classification unknown in many libraries, but even in those libraries where it
has been adopted it is only used in a greater or lesser degree.

This state of affairs is largely due to a weakness on
the part of librarians, who, in order to make themselves popular, pander to the convenience of the public, instead of en-
deavouring to inculcate in the minds of the people a love for
strict classification, which, though perhaps not so obvious to
the uneducated mind, is perfectly logical (when understood),
and is quite scientific.

By way of illustration let us take three important
classes of literature: Biography, Fiction, and Poetry.   In
nine thousand nine hundred and ninety-nine cases out of ten
thousand, there is no attempt to classify these divisions other than an alphabetical sequence under a general class heading.   This is not to be wondered at, when no less an authority than Mr. Brown, in the introduction to his "Subject Classification," says: "To distribute the individual biography at
subjects [is] a very inconvenient and frequently impossible
task. . . The main difficulty in the way of distributing biography throughout subjects is the impossibility, in numerous
cases, of determining in which class a man is most known.
Buckingham, who 'was chemist, fiddler, statesman and buf-
foon' is just the type of man who cannot be classified, and
there are thousands like him."   But surely Mr. Brown must

be aware that such difficulty could be overcome by a series of references, or better still, by purchasing in this case five copies, and classifying this particular book under Chemistry, Violins, History, Government, and Folly.   There is no reason, except perhaps the low monetary one, why this principle should not be applied throughout the biographical class.

Turning now to the class known as Fiction, there is much to be said in favour of distributing it according to its subject.   One of the greatest benefits of such a course is that the "fiction percentage," which is identical with our old friend "Aunt Sally," entirely disappears.   The works of Ainsworth, Dumas, and Weyman, instead of being registered as fiction, would increase the issue of History.   Kingsley's "Alton Locke" would find a place in Sociology, "John Inglesant" in Philosophy and Religion, and so on.   Think of the advantages of fiction classification to the educated man, who would immediately spot "The Strange case of Dr. Jekyll and Mr. Hyde" under "Human Personality," while his illiterate brother would be wading through the books on Medicine. Some difficulty might be experienced in locating certain of the problem novels, and in some cases it would be advisable to apply the rule, which, if not originated by the "Pseudonyms," is at least worthy of them: "If you can't classify a book, don't buy it."

Compared with the foregoing, the classification of Poetry according to subject is complicated, for here we may have, in one volume, the collected works of an author, which deal with almost every topic under the sun.   It is necessary, therefore, in treating this branch of our subject, to bring to bear upon it that originality and ingenuity for which the librarian is deservedly famous, and to devise a code of rules in keeping with the standard set before us by the most progressive librarians in this respect.

1.   Buy all poems, essays, and other collected works in the sheets.
2.   Carefully read each individual work or poem, and classify it according to its subject-matter, not its author.
3.   Arrange the works thus classified in groups according to their respective topics.   Put like with like, in volume form, and bind.
4.   Destroy all works that you cannot classify.   (Do this neatly so as to leave no trace of any such works.)

By this means we secure the advantage of having all
the written matter connected with a particular subject gathered together in one place, instead of having a great deal of
it practically lost in an alphabetical author arrangement.
Take for instance the Battle of Flodden. Numerous poems
have been written on this subject, but what use are they to
the student of Scottish history who lacks the time and inclina-
tion to wade through the collected works of Scott, Aytoun and
others? Consider for a moment the immense value of a
subject classification to the student. All works relative to
his particular study, whether in prose or verse, romantic,
biographic or other dress, are to his hand.

To pass on from books to reading-room periodicals.
It is unnecessary here to touch on the question of the classification of the newspaper. This has already been done in
these columns by one more qualified to deal with the subject
than the present writer. There is no reason, however, why
the general magazine, and the technical journal covering a
very wide field, should not be put into line with the newspaper, and to do this it will be necessary to draw up definite
working rules. The following will serve as a basis, and
may be altered to suit individual requirements:

1. Carefully read each article, and classify it according to its subject.
2. Separate one article from another. (We have
   found a pair of shears of use in this respect.)
3. Attach a strip of manilla to the back edge of
   each leaf, taking care that no part of the print
   is covered in the process.
4. Arrange the articles according to a definite
   scheme of subject classification, thus: HISTORY
   --Egypt. Guerville. The situation in Egypt;
   CONSTITUTIONAL HISTORY. Wallace. A new
   House of Lords.
5. Take the several articles relating to one subject,
   and fasten the pages together by sewing through
   the manilla strips. A fold should be made in
   the manilla to enable each leaf to turn over easily.

6. Affix a cover of manilla or stiff paper to each
   unit, and place on the reading-room table.

The benefits that would accrue from such a scheme
of classification are many. There are a number of articles
on technical matters which appear from time to time in the
general magazines. By collecting these articles and placing

them side by side with relative matter in the technical magazines, they are at once brought to the notice of readers likely to appreciate them. Another advantage, perhaps not so evident, is that articles which in the opinion of the librarian are heterodox, could easily disappear, and few readers be any the wiser.

The writer is not aware that the schemes outlined above have been put into practice. If any librarian possessing an abnormal amount of courage is led through this article to experiment on the lines suggested, his labour will find its own reward. Criticism is not invited, and any communication sent c/o the Editor of the Journal will be promptly despatched, according to Jast, to 5329.

A Proposal of Marriage

Edmund Lester Pearson

From his column "The Librarian" in the <u>Boston Transcript</u>
May 31, 1916.

They were in a canoe together. That is, he was
seated on the stern seat, looking down at her where she re-
clined amidst cushions.   She looked up at him, her blue eyes
wide open, frank, fearless, questioning. He realized that he
was looking well--it had been a happy thought to get that
sport-shirt.

The sunset light was fading from the sky.   From the
borders of the lake came the faint fragrance of the apple
blossoms.   The last cadences of the song of a Blackburnian
warbler (or it may have been Wilson's No. 2 Flycatcher--or
even No. 3) were heard rising and falling in the distance.
They did not hear them however--so the problem naturally
arises: how do we know anything about the bird at all, since
we were not there?   Let that pass.   The bird sang, unheed-
ed by the two happy creatures in the canoe.   They had eyes
and ears only for each other.

The hour, the minute, had come for him to speak.
He realized that his fate hung upon what he said now.   Never
again would there be so favorable an opportunity.   She must
listen, and listening, grant his prayer.   He spoke.   Thinking
that there is nothing like a poetical quotation to lead up to a
proposal of marriage, he said:

"Miss Umlaut, do you know that little thing of Raphael
Berry's, the--"

"Do you mean," she interrupted, " 'Callicanthus Buds, '
the new book of free verse?"

"Yes," he replied, "that is the name."

"Oh, yes," said she.   "I remember it perfectly.   I

catalogued it at the library only last week."

He winced at the word "catalogue." It seemed to introduce a mechanical element into what he intended to be a
romantic conversation.

"Raphael Berry," he began again--but she interposed
a suggestion.

"Pardon me--his full name is Jonas Azarias Raphael
Berry, or rather, to put it in inverted form: Berry, Jonas
Azarias Raphael Dooley," and she added, under her breath
"1882"--in order to give the poet the date of his birth and
set him in order, just as she would at the head of a catalogue card.

"Oh, yes," said the young man, a little confused:
"well, his book is quite new, I think, and--"

"There is no date on the title-page," said the beautiful, blue-eyed cataloguer, "but it was copyrighted in 1913,
and although that isn't conclusive evidence of the date of the
separate poems, it may safely be assumed as the date of
publication of the book."

Her eyes wandered far over the lake--she was visual-
izing the date, neatly typed, and surrounded by two small
brackets, to indicate its omission from the title-page. It
should also be preceded by a small letter "c," she recalled.

"I wonder," the young man persisted, "if you noticed
one of the poems, one that seemed to me--"

"Let me see," the lovely girl ruminated, "it was published by Small Badger & Co., and it had ix., 7, 131 pages,
a frontispiece, and two plates. It was either 22 or 23 centimetres high--22, I am sure. Yes--but what do you want?"

"My sweater, if you please. Would you mind hand-
ing it over? I am rather chilled--I think if I paddle hard
we can just catch that car."

And so, you think she lost her chance of a proposal?
Well, she did from this particular man. But a few months
later she met a librarian to whom she is most happily wedded. And they have a daughter, date of publication 1916,
with a frontispiece, and 64 centimetres high, and all her
books, poor thing, are picked out in advance for her up to

the age of eleven and one-quarter and after that there is a dispute of authorities as to just what a girl should read till she is twelve and one-sixth. And she may be clad in buckram, as that is a good, stout, serviceable material, and wears better than morocco.

Library Lunchroom - Dewey System

Edwin E. Slosson

From his column "A Number of Things" in The Independent
81:440, 1915.

I had been working all the afternoon in the big reading
room of the city library until the daylight had become so dim
that I could not read another word. I snapped the electric
lamp over the table, but evidently the time had not come, according to calendar and clock, to turn on the juice.[1] My
eyes were weary, anyway, so I stacked up my books, stuck
a reserve card on them and went out to get something to eat.
As I came out between the stony lions I saw across the street
the sign

LIBRARY LUNCHROOM
DEWEY SYSTEM

"Just the thing," I thought, and entering took my seat
at a vacant table. In the course of human events a waiter
came around and asked for my "order slip." "You haven't
given me anything to order from," I replied indignantly. He
looked down at me with the cold contempt always felt for the
uninitiate and said, "Menu catalog room on the right of the
entrance."

Meekly I crost the hall and found myself in a room
surrounded by cases of little drawers neatly numbered. I
saw I was in for something new, but under such circumstances he who hesitates is lost, so I walked with a firm and
confident step to one of the cases and pulled out the first
drawer to hand. It was labeled "11400 Articulata," and I
found myself among the lobsters and shrimps and a lot of
things that I did not know that anybody ever ate. I exchanged
it for the drawer above, marked "11300 Mollusca," and ran
over the cards "Ostrea edulis," "Venus mercenaria, pseud.
quahaug," "Helix pomatia, pseud. escargots." No, not this
time. I peeked into the text above, "11200 Radiata;" mostly

guide cards, the rest not appetizing. Catching sight of "Béche de mer, see Mott St. branch," I hastily closed the drawer and started to leave.

But as I passed the desk marked "Reference" the little lady playing solitaire with catalog cards looked up and asked, "Did you want something?"

"Yes, I want something to eat," I said shortly.

"What do you want to eat?" asked the patient, tired voice.

I thought this was a time to follow the advice of Emma McChesney, so I said, "Roast beef, plain."

"You will not be apt to find that under Invertebrata," said the attendant, turning to another case and pulling out a drawer without looking. "It is a very simple system when you understand it. Here it is, you see; 10000 Animal Foods, 12000 Vertebrata, 12471 Mammalia, Family Bovidae, Genus Bos." And I looked on with awe while she wrote out the order slip and added the specifications in decimals, .2 mature, .07 sirloin, .004 roast, .0009 well done, S21 with brown gravy.

"Oh, yes, I see. Thank you," I replied eagerly, and to prove it I took another slip out of the tray on top and began digging potatoes out of the index. It was easy, Phanerogamia, Dicotyledonae, Sympetalae, Solanum tuberosum (here I narrowly missed getting a cigar instead, for it was on the next card), 23259.6FF, i.e. French fried. Elated at my success and interested in the game, I added mushrooms, Cryptogamia, Hymenomycetacae, Agaricus, 21347.24Z, and a pot of 23714.5B9, or in plain English, Camelia theifera, leaves, dried, English Breakfast, infusion, not decoction. Then returning to the dining room, filled with self-satisfaction in default of anything better, I handed my order slips to the waiter.

Fifteen minutes later he came back and said: "Head waiter wants to see you."

"Why doesn't he come then?" I asked.

"He don't come. You go to him," was the reply.

I went. The head waiter was an imposing personage

300

with a long gray beard.   As I approached his desk he looked
at me as a floorwalker looks at a suspected shoplifter, then
put me thru a catechism: "What's your name? Address?
Profession? Are you a church member? Can you produce
a certificate of character from your pastor? Have you a
physician's prescription?"

Here I rebelled. "Why do you ask all these questions?" I demanded.

"Because you have ordered a Z dish," he answered.
"All the dishes marked Z are poisonous and we have to be
very careful to whom we give them."

"But I did not order poison," I said. He held up my
slip and pointed out the last item. "This calls for the
Deadly Amanita. If you meant it for Agaricus campestris
you should have written 21346.57."

I meekly made the correction, but I could not help
inquiring: "Why do you keep poisonous foods at all?"

"Because we must have a complete stock. Such things
exist. They can be eaten and if any one really wants them
we must serve them. But we try to see to it that the im-
mature and weakminded do not get hold of them. We should
have served it to you if you had insisted, but we would have
watched to see that you did not eat too much and did not enjoy it."

I thanked him for saving me from dying of a mis-
placed decimal and returned to my seat, where in about
twenty minutes the meal arrived. All went well until I came
to pour out my tea when I discovered that the waiter had not
brought any sugar. Calling his attention to the omission he
said: "No slip for it."

I acknowledged the fault and asked him for the number.

"Menu catalog room on right of the entrance," he replied as before.

I made a dash for the vegetable section and soon was
hot upon the trail as follows:

20000 Vegetable Kingdom
26000 Carbohydrates

26100 Monosaccharides
26200 Disaccharides
 26250 Pentoses
 26260 Hexoses
  26264 Sucrose $C_{12}H_{22}O_{11}$
      d-glucose +d-fructose
.1 pulverized
.2 granulated
.3 domino
.4 cube
.5 loaf
.01 brown
.02 yellow
.03 white

   This led directly to 26264.33, which I jotted down with a pencil, pens being barred, and then, with the providence born of experience, I took down the single drawer marked "Mineral Kingdom" and made out slips for 327.3 which is NaCl, fine, and for 314.7, which is H_2O, Croton, iced.

   I got back to my table before the tea was quite cold and finished the meal without a mistake unless my omission at the end to hand the waiter any 384.6Ag might be counted such. As I settled my order slips at the desk by the door I noticed that an extra item, 26904.2.Mx, had been added. It evidently stood for some polysaccharide, which I was sure I had not eaten. There was no charge for it, but I had the curiosity to look up the card in the catalog. It read: "Toothpick, orange wood, round, double pointed, sealed in paper."

Notes

1. Yes, that's all right. Brander Matthews said we should say "juice" and he is a member of the Academy.

GADGETS AND INVENTIONS

The Famous Cherokee Charging System

Joseph Eisner

From Wilson Library Bulletin 25:60, 64, 1960.   Reprinted by permission from the September 1960 issue of the Wilson Library Bulletin.   Copyright (c)1960 by the H. W. Wilson Company.   Also with permission of the author.

The past few years have seen the development of many new library charging systems.   Much has been written about the merits of the IBM system, Shaw's Photographic Charging System and its various modifications, and the Audio Charging System, to name a few.   However, a diligent search of the records has failed to reveal any mention of the Cherokee Charging System.

The Cherokee Charging System was developed to meet the needs of the large number of libraries which collect and circulate Egyptian papyrus rolls, Babylonian cuneiform tablets, and prehistoric rock carvings, as well as those which have a large lost and found.   A radical departure from any other previously known system, it embodies the best features of the Scotch Tape System and the FBI Fingerprint and Photograph System.   Certain features of the Black Hand have also been incorporated.

The chief feature of the Cherokee Charging System is its extreme simplicity.   It needs no trained personnel, except three or four people who are sufficiently able to speak Choctaw, Chicasaw, and Cherokee (a knowledge of Chinese is helpful, but not necessary); it can easily be understood by even the most illiterate reader or by the library patron who is barely conversant in Sanskrit.   Branches communicate by Indian smoke signal.

Early History

The Cherokee Charging System was developed by the American Library Association, Indian Division, after years of research, and was first put into operation at the Alaska Indian Reservation Library by Egtxz Shrdlu in either 1842 or 1942. The system needs no involved equipment, except three or four tepees easily and cheapily purchased from Laygora Brothers' Yokahama, Japan, branch. Identification cards are not needed; instead, the borrowers' ear, left or right as the library chooses, is carefully notched with a coded geometric pattern. This system is undergoing revision, since it has been discovered that a large number of overdues result from the bleeding to death of borrowers in the loan interval.

An upstate library reports that by substituting branding upon an essential part of the patrons' anatomy for notching of the ear, it has practically eliminated the problem of a limited reading room capacity which it formerly had, as well as done away with the need for using a call slip.

Call slips are made of genuine birch bark or scraped otter skin (some libraries prefer mink); illegible handwriting is eliminated by having the borrower sign his name in standard Sumerian picture symbols. The problem of maintaining a separate shelf list or card file for purposes of inventory is easily circumvented by stocking only one book in the library. Once the book is borrowed, the library closes until it is returned; this cuts down on operating costs and overhead appreciably, and results in a saving of a considerable sum of money--one library reported a saving of 96.2 per cent.

Nothing Simpler

The Cherokee Charging System is particularly adaptable for use in any antiquated library setup, chiefly because it embodies certain features of the medieval library, although in a slightly different manner. Whereas, in medieval libraries books were chained to desks, in the Cherokee System the reader is chained to the desk, thus eliminating tiresome records and statistics concerning reading room use. This method also forestalls any inadvertent desire on the part of the patron to remove books from the library without proper authority.

The Cherokee System needs no complicated machinery, extensive records, nor does it entail a great amount of intelligence on the part of the patron, thereby making it very practicable for all libraries which have patrons of this type.

It is easily adaptable to any other system now in use.   Its
many users attest to its great popularity:

"Banned in Boston! . . . "   Library Bulletin,
March 1901.

"Ugh!"   Chief Lonesome Polecat, Curator,
Fearless Fosdick Library.

"I don't know what we'd do without it, but
we'd sure like to try." C. U. Soon, Director,
Chunking Chopstick Library, Chunking, China.

Further information about the Cherokee Charging System can be obtained by writing to the firm, which is located
at Little America Base Camp Number 3, South Pole.   (We
are informed that the town is at present closed for the duration of the penguin hunting season.) Installation of the system, as well as upkeep, can be financed through FHA, RFC,
or the Marshall Plan.   The system is offered at a discount
when purchased in dozen lots.

Patents Impending

Martin Erlich

From Odds & Book Ends No. 47, p 22-5, Winter 1965. Reprinted by permission of the author and of the Nassau County Library Association.

With the invention of various devices to detect book theft from the library (see Sentronic and The Book Detective) it was only a matter of time before I hit upon my new invention.   It really should be considered as a mere extension of the above mentioned devices, a refinement let us say. These gadgets, we are told, prevent a person from making off with the bulk of your book collection.   They operate upon magnetic principles the salient features of which have been detailed in Time Magazine, Oct. 2, 1964, p. 98 and Odds & Bookends, No. 46, p. 3-5.   In order to appreciate my refinement, a thorough knowledge of how these inventions work is mandatory.   This is how they work:

1.   A book is treated by inserting a magnetic strip in its spine.   This renders the book "active" or magnetized.

2.   In order to leave the building you should then bring the book to the charge-out desk where it is demagnetized by means of a special machine.   It takes but a second to demagnetize the book and the patron may now leave the library without setting off red lights or alarms.

3.   All persons must leave the building through two magnetic columns.   If a thief attempts to remove magnetized books without first charging (demagnetizing) them out, the magnet in the book reacts to the two magnetic columns at the exit causing lights to light, bells to peal, turnstiles to lock, and Ippolito to toss a fit. The person in question then must offer his apology for forgetting to charge-out the reference book which

308

doesn't circulate anyway--and all is forgiven.   But--
the book is not lost!

A Patent is Pending

It is now obvious that once we learn to screen our
staff, only two sticky book problems remain.   How to stop
the mutilator, and how to get back books properly charged
out.   As for the mutilator, Al Monheit, Director of the Wan-
tagh Library, has pointed the way.   He will photostat the
material requested for free (number of pages within reason).
So that leaves us with the thorny problem of how to get back
the books which have been properly charged out without going
to court, Rothraids, nasty letters and phone calls, in fact
the elimination of overdue notices!!   My invention is designed to do all these things.

In my initial disclosure to the patent attorney, I described my invention as a combination mechanical-chemical
device to encourage the return of books properly charged out
within 2 months from the time the books leave the building.
The device works like this: At the time that a metallic strip
is inserted into the spine of the book to prepare it for protection against theft, at the base of this magnetic strip a
small explosive, transistorized mechanism is attached. (see
diagram)   Now get this--when the book is properly charged
out, the device which deactivates the metallic strip, Activates My Device For the Encouragement of Returning Books
on Time.   What happens now.   The patron at the charge out
desk is informed by the clerk that unless the book is returned within a 2 month period (give or take a day) the book
will explode--probably in the person's home, maybe in his
hands.

Patron Reaction

Patron reaction to the invention varies: (I know we
should get up a questionnaire in the interests of science.)
Most are good sports; they realize how difficult it must be
to get back overdue books and in general support the experiments.   Some patrons, after engaging in a theoretical joust
on the merits of the device (in other words, is it worth
blowing up a book and possibly a human just to insure the
return of a book which costs a few dollars) are willing to go
along with some form of trial period to see if the benefits
outweigh the risks.   A decent attitude I think you will agree.

Then, there is the hard-core who will oppose progress whether it be in the library or in the laboratory. You know the type, they were against the invention of the wheel. They insist that the device is barbaric; they would rather see hundreds of books lost before seeing a single human go up in smoke. When they argue for a reduction in the intensity of the blast, it is useless to explain that we mean business and half measures are as futile as overdue notices. A lunatic fringe that will never be placated.

We have made every effort to inform our citizenry that the new invention is in effect. (Radio, T. V. News Media, Handbills, Posters, Flyers, Airplane smoke writing, Word of Mouth.) The back page of each protected book contains this printed notice:

Dear Patron: In order to insure a proper return of books on time (see explosive date) as well as to effect a savings in clerical time--(you will receive no overdue notices*) we urge you to return this book on time. Failure to do so will result in a serious explosion of the book on or about explosion date, for which the Library is not liable. You will be responsible for paying for the cost of the book, if you survive the blast. Therefore, we urge your cooperation--get that book back on time. Failure to do so could prove disastrous to you and your loved ones.

Your Friendly Library

*The public relations feature is obvious: The public is no longer antagonized with nasty notices and they can't receive notices which they shouldn't have if they never took the books out--and they can't claim that they have returned the books already--can they!

A device for the encouragement of the return of books within a two month period.

I. $CH(NO_2)_3$ (trinitro methane) is a stable compound. In the presence of air and iron it nitrates to form $C(NO_2)_4$ (tetra nitro methane), an unstable compound.

II. $CH(NO_2)_3$ is stored in section A of diagram. When magnetic strip D is demagnetized the connection C between D and B is broken. This permits the iron filings in B to drop into section A and combine with $CH(NO_2)_3$ and form $C(NO_2)_4$.

III. The chemical formula is as follows:

$$CH(NO_2)_3 \xrightarrow[\text{Air}]{\text{Fe}} C(NO_2)_4$$

When $C(NO_2)_4$ decomposes, it gives off:

N_2 (Nitrogen) CO_2 (carbon dioxide)

O_2 (oxygen) H_2O (water)

IV. If the book is returned before the explosion date, the magnetic strip is remagnetized. This removes the iron filings from the $CH(NO_2)_3$ in chamber A. The book is now rendered harmless until charged out properly again.

Three Fingers Smith, who was on vacation and never learned of our unique method of insuring book returns (there is always someone who never gets the message from Garcia to Smith) is in shock at the State Hospital. Doctors said that his physical condition is good considering the loss of several fingers. However, it is the mental attitude of the patient that has the medics worried. He refuses to be in a room which contains a book (or even a periodical) keeps mumbling that he didn't know the book was loaded, and his lawyers have served us with papers. Our lawyers feel that they haven't got a case at all, that once the judge learns all the facts he will dismiss the charges. Great inventions and inventors have ever thus been persecuted throughout the ages. It is the price of progress.

Summary Conclusions

1. When a book containing a magnetic strip is properly charged out--while the book becomes demagnetized--my device becomes activated and will explode in a two month period. (Patent Pending.)

2. If the book is returned on time, the device which activates, or magnetizes the book, deactivates the explosive mechanism. It now returns to neutral and the next time it is charged out it is good for the entire two month period before it explodes. (Patent Pending.)

3. Overdues have been eliminated. Savings in clerical time has enabled us to send clerks to visit hospitals, with books, to service delinquent or just plain unlucky library patrons. Our clerks have not been permitted to visit Three Fingers. We are willing to forgive and forget, but he continues to sulk and be a poor loser.

4. The Case of Three Fingers Smith vs. The Friendly Library comes up in Superior Court late in June 1969 (Heavy Docket). The publicity from this case has been simply marvelous and boy do the books come back on time. Do our patrons look a little nervous when handling our books? No more than anyone engaged in a hazardous occupation--you get used to it after a while. Part of living in a nuclear age I like to tell our patrons. The circulation statistics? I have noticed a precipitous drop in circulation figures, but I think it is only a seasonal thing--Christmas, New Years, people with Direct Access Cards going to better libraries, and to be perfectly honest--some patrons are just plain chicken. They won't even set foot in our library anymore. How can you reason with this type of spoil-sport?

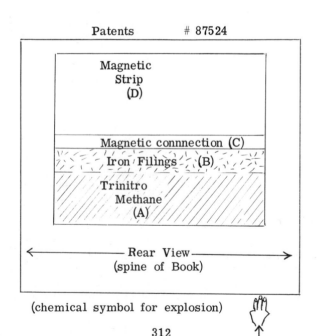

Patents   # 87524

Magnetic
Strip
(D)

Magnetic connnection (C)

Iron Filings (B)

Trinitro
Methane
(A)

← —————— Rear View —————— →
(spine of Book)

(chemical symbol for explosion)

A Baker's Half-Dozen

Rube Goldberg

From an article by Verner W. Clapp "The Future" in Library Resources & Technical Services 4:288-91, 1960. Reprinted with permission of Mr. Goldberg, Mr. Clapp, and the American Library Association.

. . . I would not have you think that the library world is without assistance in these and others of its problems. In the Council on Library Resources we get many offers of assistance. Let me read you a letter I received just the other day:

Council on Library Resources,
Washington, D. C.

Gentlemen:

I was for many years the chief engineer of a well-known firm engaged in the development of mechanical devices. Although now retired, I would like to continue to apply my talents in the interest of human welfare, and feel that I can be useful in your program. I have a baker's half-dozen of ideas which may interest you, and believe that working models could be produced comparatively inexpensively. I have listed them below, with the amounts needed for development. I hope to hear from you.

1. The Librarian's General-Purpose Uplifter. This would be very simple to develop. It would consist of a pair of jacks, concealed in the librarian's shoes. These would be actuated by small electric motors which could be plugged into any available outlet and would enable the wearer to raise himself at will up to approximately a foot above his natural height. Two principal purposes are envisaged. (a) The device would make it possible for short librarians to reach books easily on the upper shelves. (Indeed, the device might result in a new standard height for book-stacks, producing

313

enormous savings in building costs.) (b) It would enable librarians who have to meet the public to achieve a commanding stature, conducive to high morale and very useful for staring down obstreperous customers. etc.

Estimated cost, $1,500.

2. Pocket MicroBraille(R) Library. Although it is well known that the hand is quicker than the eye, libraries for some reason prefer the slower organ. Nevertheless, I believe that they might benefit from the possibilities of tactual communication.

Just as Microcards(R) contain a great deal of information in condensed form which can be read by the eye through the use of a suitable magnifier, so I believe it will be possible to develop a suitable magnifier to enable the fingers to read a kind of MicroBraille(R). This would enable the reference librarian to keep quite a library in his pocket, and while the customer was asking a question he could be feeling for the answer. (He might, for example, keep the catalog of his library in one pocket, Familiar Quotations in another, and the Dictionary of American Biography in a third. He would rapidly get the reputation for being quite a knowledgeable person.) It is easy to extend the principle. Female reference librarians could keep a MicroBraille(R) library tucked in their hair; then, while seeming to be patting their locks or thoughtfully scratching their heads they would be really finding the answers.

Estimated cost, $100,000.

3. Librarian's Bond-Issuer. It has come to my attention that one of the great difficulties of promoting library work consists in persuading municipal authorities to authorize bond-issues on behalf of the library. I propose to provide each librarian with a device with which he could issue his own bonds as needed. This would solve most library problems.

Estimated cost, $50 (the price of a second-hand mimeograph machine).

4. Library Recruiting-Kit. In all the libraries I visit there is a shortage of page-boys. This amazes me because libraries usually have the staff facilities as well as the incentive for producing and rearing their own page-boys; but a certain old-fashioned prudery--perhaps understandable in the circumstances--seems to stand in the way. I propose to get around these taboos by developing a special test-tube for library use by which libraries could produce their own

regular crops of page-boys, not only without offending any of the mores, but actually providing an attraction which should prove useful in community relations.

More recently, it has come to my attention that the recruitment of catalogers also constitutes a problem. If this indeed is the case, the proposed development would be simplified, because we wouldn't have to work out methods for restricting the test-tube librarians to boys.

Estimated cost, $27 billion (less than the national debt).

5. The Librarian's X-Ray. I am also informed that hunting through books for elusive quotations and other stray facts is a great burden in libraries. I propose to construct an X-ray machine which would do this automatically. In use, the sought reference would be displayed in the machine as a target; the machine would then see right through the pages of the book till it found the match to the target. By a process of zeroing-in the particular page would be found in a jiffy.

6. The Librarian's Weed-Killer. This is a spray which would be sprinkled over the catalog from time to time. It would immediately extirpate the entries for all unwanted books--unneeded extra copies, unbindables, obsolete works, etc., in accordance with a formula which would be adjusted according to the need. By a process of osmosis, the powerful hormone contained in this spray would proceed to the shelf-list and to the shelves, and would obliterate all traces of the undesired books. It is obvious that this spray will have to be kept from the knowledge of various groups who are aprowl in our land, and I leave it to you whether it had perhaps better not be developed.

7. The Cataloger's Dream. From what I know of catalogers, there's not much that can be done to assist them; they are doing everything possible already. But it seems to me that something can be devised to give them the sense of accomplishment and achievement which their work merits, instead of (as seems to be too often the case) a feeling of frustration. For this I propose the Cataloger's Dream.

This is a pill which all catalogers would take each night upon retiring. It would assure sweet, restful, and beauty-preserving sleep; but it would also produce an enchanting vision: a neat, bright, and flowery cataloging room in which every day's work is finished a quarter of an hour before closing time and in which there are never any arrears;

315

in which a perfect system of cataloging is applied, and every book fits the system; in which there develop no conflicts in the catalog, no jams of filing or of confusing or obsolescent entries to be unsnarled, no recataloging and certainly no re-classification to be done, and in which authors, organizations, and serials never change their names or designations; where all the books are perfect, and all the necessary bibliographic data can be secured from one authoritative reference work right there on the desk; where all the unexpected questions (including unknown foreign languages) can be answered by the cataloger at the next desk; where all the books are interest-ing and there is time to browse through them; and where--finally--the administration fully recognizes the real impor-tance of cataloging and rewards the catalogers accordingly. What a place to work!

But the vision might change. It might show a room in which the cataloger does not have to go grubbing around in various places for bits and pieces with which to catalog the collections--information which can be better provided by others and which should be right at hand. This information would come in as part of the book; for books and the biblio-graphical data which incorporate them into a bibliographical system of library organization are equally products of the mind, and can equally and simultaneously be mass-produced and disseminated so that the two are always together. The role of the cataloger in this room is not so much to create the bits and pieces as to create and supervise the catalog it-self--the all-important tool by whose excellence or deficiency the excellence or deficiency of the library is to a large de-gree measured, and without which the greatest collection is a dead thing. More than this: the cataloger in this room, having delegated to others, who are closer to the manufac-ture of the books, the job of incorporating the books into a bibliographic system, now automatically takes her place as a member of the board of directors which supervises the sys-tem--a national bibliographic authority charged with develop-ing a first class mode of library organization for a first class country--a system in which her library would be the local representative of a nation-wide movement which has for its purpose the putting of books to their maximum use for the welfare of mankind.

If these pills were taken nightly by catalogers, and oc-casionally by administrators also, who knows but that the vi-sion might really come true!

316

Estimated cost, the value of one good cataloger!

Sincerely,

(signed) R. Goldberg

Recent Inventions and Gadgets
to Lighten Library Labor

Dorothy Heiderstadt

After a severe study of library conditions in libraries
all over the United States, we have come to the conclusion
that what librarians need is gadgets which will lighten their
labors. We herewith submit a catalog of inventions, thought
up by ourselves, and for sale at moderate prices, strictly
cash.

Automatic Nose-Wiper for Children.   Standard size, $150.
          Double action attachment, which can take care of
          two noses at once, $200.

This machine fills a long felt need and is guaranteed
to give satisfaction. The child drops his penny into the slot
and the operation is performed by a mechanical arm and
hand holding a clean paper handkerchief which does the job
as painlessly and effectively as though propelled by his own
mother.

Rarely does this machine get out of order. One time
Andrew Zlomsowitsch (a patron whom we have mentioned
before) was having his nose wiped when suddenly the hand
clamped down on his nose and refused to let go. After we
were finally able to locate the janitor, Andrew yelling all
this time, it took him only about an hour to discover the
trouble. Andrew, long acquainted with the candy slot machines, thought he could put one over on our Automatic Nose-
Wiper. He had dropped a button into its midst. The Nose-
Wiper good naturedly started to wipe his nose, but suddenly

318

feeling a foreign substance within, indignantly clamped down on Andrew's proboscis.

> Advantages of the Automatic Nose-Wiper:
> 1. Slot machine characteristic enables it to pay for itself.
>
> 2. Does away with nerve-wracking and unsightly sniffling.

> Disadvantages:
> In the winter time, the Children's Librarian is out about 10c a day because of having to lend pennies to children who are taken unexpectedly and who forget to pay her back. Pennies may be hooked out of the fines, but this sort of thing is always a risk.

Automatic Hand-Smacker and No-No Mustn't Touch Sayer.
> Standard size, $300, and is it worth it! This machine satisfies the urge of countless harassed librarians when they see customers flatly disregarding the "Please Do Not Touch These Books" sign, pawing over the unslipped books on the desk, and making off with them.

The librarian who is the fortunate possessor of our Automatic Hand-Smacker needs only to slip her penny into the slot, and a gentle but firm voice speaks to the customer, saying "No, No." A pause of five minutes follows, during which the customer goes right on handling the books. The voice then says, a little more sharply, "Mustn't Touch!" At this point, the customer sneers and reaches for another book, whereupon a hand emerges from the machine and gives the customer a hearty rap on the knuckles.

One time a pugnacious customer resented this and smacked the machine right back again. The machine retaliated by biffing the customer in the eye and producing a jackpot for the fortunate librarian. Send for your Automatic Hand-Smacker today.

Automatic Hat and Cigar Remover From Customers Who
> Keep Their Hats on and Lean Cozily on the Desk,
> Resting the Cigar Just Below the Librarian's Nose.
> This gadget is $50, and worth it at twice the

price. When the patron leans on the desk, an arm reaches up silently and unobtrusively and plucks off his hat, and at the same instant a foot kicks the cigar out of his hand. If he acts indignant, the arm tosses the hat playfully into another corner of the room and the foot, after taking a puff at the cigar, hands it back to him.

This machine is worked by a foot lever, operated and controlled by the librarian. Since the workings of this machine do not give the librarian the moral satisfaction afforded by the Automatic Hand-Smacker, she is not required to put any pennies in any slots in order to work it. Besides, the machine is so inexpensive that many boards of trustees will probably be willing to give it to their libraries as gifts.

Automatic Dog Chaser-Outer. This is a little daisy. Or, rather, a little kitty. Only $150, and worth every cent.

Everyone knows how difficult it is to convince a dog-owner that His dog, or Her dog is meant by the sign which says "No Dogs Allowed." Our Automatic Dog-Chaser-Outer eliminates the dog without hurting the owner's Feelings. While the owner is checking in her books, and just as the dog begins to look around him interestedly and to sniff at things, a little kitty (automatically controlled by neon lights) runs out from under the library desk, and makes for the door.

Of course, the dog immediately follows, barking with wild delight. The little kitty doubles on its tracks once or twice, and acts confused, in order to lead the dog on, and work him up into an anticipatory mood. Then, when the dog is Just Sure that he is going to catch the kitty and tear it limb from limb, the kitty gives a despairing wail and runs straight for the front door, which opens automatically (also controlled by neon lights).

The dog shoots through the door with the velocity of a cannon ball, thinking that the kitty has preceded him, whereas in reality the kitty has run straight up the door frame and is proceeding peacefully across the ceiling and back down by a special pole to the library desk. An automatic amplifier above the door broadcasts the following words to the dog outside: "Meow! Meow!" Whereupon, the dog stops in his tracks and sits down outside the front door wait-

ing for the kitty to come down out of the amplifier. There
the dog remains, suitably amused and entertained until his
owner leaves the library.

Electric Scooter With Special Book Rack for Reference Librarians. Standard size $600, but it makes its
own batteries, so in the long run you lose nothing.

All reference librarians know how tiring it is to run
back and forth all day long, hunting up books and pamphlets
for patrons. With the Electric Scooter With Special Book
Rack, the task is many times simplified. Not only that, the
Reference Librarian can ride it home at night if she has no
car. One of our specially constructed Headlights (Price
$6.00) will light her on her way.

The sight of the Reference Librarian rolling gaily
down the street on her Electric Scooter cannot help attract
attention. "There goes Miss McNutt, the Reference Librarian at the Public Library on her Electric Scooter!" people
will say, and this will be good publicity for the library.

Special Phonograph Record Which Repeats the Rules About
How Long the Patrons May Keep Their Books, Information About Fines and Renewals, Etc. $500
for phonograph and record. Most of the money is,
of course, for the phonograph, which can be attached to any radio and made to play other records
as well as the Special Phonograph Record but not
(we hope) at the same time.

This Special Phonograph Record fills a vital need and
will add years to the voices of countless librarians, especially Children's Librarians. Adult patrons can read the instructions on their library cards, but children have to be told.
How many a weary Children's Librarian looks forward to the
day when she can press a little lever and a nice phonograph
record will say, "You may keep your library books for two
weeks. The date is stamped on the slip of paper in the back
of the book. That is the date on which the book must be returned, and you must not keep it any longer than that, Or
Else," and so on, ad nauseam. Head Librarians who are
looking around for something to give their Children's Librarians as a reward for good behavior, good circulation, or the
like, cannot do better than to purchase one of our Special
Phonographs With Special Record at this amazing price.

Special Pages' Helper for the Shelves. $5.00 per dozen.

This little gadget can be put up by your janitor, if he
is a clever one with electrical gadgets. It is intended to
help in keeping books in their correct places on the shelves.
When a customer takes a book down and then starts to put it
back in the wrong place, a little light flashes to warn him
that something is wrong. Most patrons will then search a-
round for the correct place to put the book. If, however,
some stubborn one persists in trying to put the book back in
the wrong place anyhow, a little bell rings to warn them a-
gain. If he disregards this, a good stiff electric shock runs
down his arm. The customer will then be in no condition to
proceed farther in his infringement of library procedure.

Special Calendar Providing More Holiday for Librarians.
        $25.00, but worth more.

This Calendar should rest on the Head Librarian's
desk, and should show all the holidays for the month. For
instance, in January:

        Jan. 4--Utah admitted to the Union. Holiday.
        Jan. 17--Battle of the Cowpens, 1781. Holiday.
    February:
        Feb. 10--Marriage of Queen Victoria and Prince
                 Albert. Holiday.
        Feb. 28--Upper Mississippi River exploration by
                 Hennepin begun, 1680. Holiday.

All this, besides the regular holidays like Christmas and the
Fourth of July, and the like.

The Head Librarian will be completely taken in by it.
On the morning of January 17, for instance, he will read on
his Calendar, "Battle of the Cowpens, 1781. Holiday." "Oh
good," he will say aimlessly, "a holiday." And then he will
go out to tell the staff that they can all take the day off.

All librarians need more holidays. It is terribly discouraging to have to sit at a desk and work when all the bank
clerks and school teachers are running around town having a
holiday, and coming to the library to complain about their
overdue fines, just so they can see the poor librarians
chained to their desks working.

Nothing will be more pleasant than to own this Special

Calendar and to wander into the bank in the middle of a busy morning and say casually, "What? You working? We don't have to work today. This is the day that Hennepin started to explore the Mississippi River. A holiday for us, you know!"

Book Opener and Digester, $500. This will fill a definite need in the library field, as it is an attractive little gadget like a phonograph in appearance, run by a can opener instead of a needle, and it tells people what the books are about.

All good librarians know that it is very wrong even to open a book while at the desk except for mechanical purposes such as slipping or stamping. Our Automatic Book Opener and Digester finds out what the books are about, thus leaving the desk attendant free to sort cards and do the thousand and one little routine things known as "busy work," which really matter.

Miss Heiderstadt and Miss Feldman will sail for Bermuda immediately, for a much-needed vacation. Orders for these little library gadgets may be sent to them at any time prior to that date.

The Lamentations of a Librarian; or,
The Evolution of a Book Wrapper

Sister M. Paula, O. S. F.

From The Catholic Library World 33:358-9, 1962. Reprinted with permission of the author and Catholic Library World.

I'm an assistant librarian and as such have been opening boxes and packages of books for the past seven years. Either my technique needs a revision or the book publishers and dealers are vying with one another to see who can ship books in the most "unopenable" packages.

The simple, old-fashioned string around the box posed no problem at all. I simply cut the string and the books were before me. Once in a while the Post Office would have to wire a faulty wrapping job. I'd get the wire snips (usually kept in the top drawer but subject to change without notice) and cut away the wire.

Then brown sticky paper was used liberally over the box or wrapper of corrugated paper. I was always afraid to stick my scissors in for fear of damaging the book binding. Carefully I'd tear open an end and shake out the contents. This resulted, more than once, in throwing away the bill which was skillfully concealed between the layers of corrugated paper.

With the advent of the second half of the 20th century they have invented new devices to make it even more difficult to bring the newly received books to light. This new wire-like-tar-paper on boxes has me. I size up the package. I shake it a little, hoping for a loose corner of the flap. But the flap is embedded at least three inches in the box and doesn't even show a sign of giving. I grip the corner and try to tear the box just enough to get my fingers under the flap. By this time I have the box between my knees, my feet braced against the shelf under the desk. Finally, after I have gotten a good paper cut across the index finger, the flap yields.

Then there are the quickie wrappings like the folded piece of corrugated paper stapled at both ends. This is simple. I yank the ends open and reach for the book, pulling it out with a slight twinge of pain to discover blood dripping from the back of my hand. I guess I should have removed the staples first.

All of us harbor regrets concerning lost opportunities of childhood. Why, oh why didn't I pay more attention to my Mother when she ripped open the sugar sacks. You remember the kind, the sack which would eventually be converted into a dish towel was presently sewed across the top with a mysterious stitch. If you pulled the right thread-- presto the sack was open. If you didn't, Mom would say, "This way, now watch." The idea is a good one, I admit it. You don't need scissors; no staples scratch your fingers; no wire bands snap back at you. Mom, please show me once more.

I know what you're saying. Yes, I too have received books via the new padded envelopes. They are neat and I say a prayer for their inventor every time I open one. But (yes, there is a but) being a Franciscan and realizing that these envelopes come in very handy for sending books out again, I take my nail file. This is a handy gadget for removing staples. I wriggle it in and pull out the staples. Some publishing firms have staple-happy clerks. After pulling out 11 staples my nail file looks more like a hair pin (which is also a handy gadget but not for nuns). Carefully depositing the staples in the waste basket I proceed to investigate the contents of the envelope. In a puff of grey dust and cotton balls out comes the book. I blow off the residue to see what the title can be. I might as well have pulled the little tab that states, "Pull Tab to Open" for I can't salvage the bag anyhow.

Today the mailman brought something that not only startled but downright frightened me. My first impulse was to say, "O, Lord, deliver us." The corrugated wrapping, about six inches longer than the book, is open at both ends. Two horizontal steel bands about a half inch wide bind the package and close the ends to prevent the book from escaping forever and forever. Amen.

Somewhere on the face of the globe I must have some fellow sufferers. If this is any consolation to them to know that they are not alone then my writing has not been in vain. If, on the other hand, they have found any solutions to the problem I'd appreciate hearing from them. I can answer letters now, the blood poisoning in my hand is quite well healed.

P. S.   Lacquer thinner is good for removing tar from the scissors' blade.

AUTOMATION AND THE WORLD OF THE FUTURE

It's Right Here Somewhere

Robert L. Dean

From America 108:404-5, 1963.   Reprinted with permission
from America, March 23, 1963.   All rights reserved.   (c)
America Press, Inc.   Also with permission of the author.

How do the experts on data processing index and file
those Important Articles--and retrieve them when they want
them? With the literature in every field growing daily, have
the research scientists created some refinements on the clip-
and-save system? some tips to help you put your hand on
the one article you need, when you need it for that talk before the women's club? or that special report to the faculty?
or maybe just for clinching that political argument with your
wife?

To find out, we visited the modern laboratories of the
man whose professional life is largely devoted to the filing
and retrieving of data. We talked to Dr. B. Willder, co-
developer of the Hamilton 1010101. While we talked, I could
hear the not unpleasant whirring sound of ten thousand
punched cards riffling through a dozen impressive machines
outside his modest office.

We first asked Dr. Willder how his Documentation
Group stores and retrieves articles.

"Usually by name," he said. "I just say to my secretary: 'I'm trying to find an article I saw last year, and
I'm certain it was written by somebody named Lewis'."

"Well, what does she do?" I asked a little puzzled.

"She just goes over to the library and they find it--
under Clarke. If I seem to recall it was written by Abbott,
it will turn out to be by Costello. It's a good system, almost always works!"

"Almost always?"

"Well, yes. Sometimes, I say 'It was written by somebody named Perkins.' Then it will turn up, only written by somebody named McGuggin. You see, that's because, to me, the name Perkins sounds something like McGuggin. And when I tell my girl that I think it was written by somebody whose name begins with 'R,' it will usually be by somebody whose name begins with 'D.' See how it works?"

"I see," I said, very much impressed. "Any other modern techniques?"

"Sure; we've worked out several ingenious devices based on color, shape, position."

"Color? Shape? How do they work?"

"Simple. I just tell my girl that what I'm trying to find was in a green book, about 9" x 12", about this thick, and on the right side of the page down near the bottom. With the directions like that, how can she fail?"

"How indeed!" I exclaimed. "Tell me, sir, have your retrieval techniques been accepted by the documentation fraternity?"

"They certainly have! I discussed them all in a paper at the recent International Symposium on Something-or-Other. In the discussion that followed, I was deeply touched to see how universal my techniques had already become in government labs, colleges and industry. The whole thing was then published somewhere--I think in that journal that has the shiny pages, the one with the sort of greenish cover."

"Dr. Willder, when you see an article you want to save, do you save the whole journal, or do you cut the article out?"

"I do both," he said. "In January, I might cut three or four articles out of a certain journal, then I'll save the whole February and March issues, but cut up the April and May issues. So, on my library shelves, the journals are all arranged shredded-solid-shredded-solid. Helps me place things."

"How about indexes?" I asked.

"I've created many," he said. "For example, I've got a foolproof file-card system, with all articles arranged alphabetically by subject. Let me see, it's right here somewhere." He was rummaging furiously in the litter under his desk. "Well, anyway, it's in a brown wooden box here . . . somewhere. Dark brown, about 5" x 7", with a lid on it."

I helped him up from the floor, and he went briskly to a huge cardboard carton over in the corner. He continued: "Of course, handwritten notes right on the article are the important thing. When you write, you reinforce the memory with physical action--you make it indelible."

His "indelible" was almost inaudible; he was head and shoulders into the carton, and papers and shredded journals were flying about. But finally he emerged, with a sheaf of papers, obviously roughly torn from some journal. He handed them to me and said: "Here read the note I made in the margin when I decided to save this important article."

The paper was called "Whether Existentialism?" I read the marginal note aloud: "Ask Al Blank if the lawn mower's fixed yet!"

"What's that mean?" Dr. Willder asked, a little vexed. "Let me see that thing. I wonder why I saved that article. Mm. . . . Al Blank? Who's Al Blank?"

"Sir," I said, changing the subject. "I think our readers would like to know how you got started in the field of data processing and retrieval."

"Oh, my interest goes back a good many years. It began one day when my son Harry came home from the third grade and said he had to have a picture of an aardvark."

"Were you able to find one?"

"No; so I decided then and there that we'd build a collection of pictures of everything. And we have. We've got ships and trees, dams, buildings, flowers, Presidents, trains, trucks, bridges and a whole scrabble of animals from aardvarks to zebras. We've got the National Geographic going back to 1919, a stack of Life four feet high, and 89 pounds of Holiday."

"How do you ever find what you want when you want it?" I asked.

331

"Well, the other day my youngest son, Chris, came home from the first grade and said he had to make a scrapbook with pictures to illustrate the ABC's. So my mind, which as you have discovered is like a precise electronic retriever, began to recall the magazine ads I had seen: big apples from Oregon, beer ads, cows in the Wisconsin cheese ads. . ."

"Were you able to find one for each letter?"

"You know, while I was looking, I ran across the darndest thing. I found an article in an old Saturday Evening Post about this man who actually rides sharks. He can free-dive 90 feet and stay under water for three minutes! You can bet I saved that article. Never can tell when I might need it."

"Do you have it handy?" Somehow, I felt I ought to ask.

"It's right here somewhere," he cried over his shoulder as he dived out of sight beneath the desk.

Computers and a Paradox for Librarians

S. N. Gaño*

From Bulletin of the Medical Library Association 51:499-
500, 1963. Reprinted with permission of the author and of
the Bulletin of the Medical Library Association.

Medical libraries nowadays are confronted by a paradox, which through the advent of computers is likely to attain menacing dimensions.

The paradox has two simple components: (1) doctors
read less and less, and (2) doctors write more and more.

The thoughtful librarian will at once perceive that this
paradoxical state of affairs is certain to produce seismic up-
heavals in the quiet world of library science.

In the first place the increasing disparity between
medical writings and medical reading will at once impress
our vigilant Marxist critics as a disparity between production and consumption and hence will be used by them as yet
another alleged example of Western decadence. This can
readily be employed as propaganda against us and will be especially effective among the habitual addicts of Marxism.
We may disregard this aspect, however, since persons susceptible to such arguments have few books anyway--at least
they have few books that get into our libraries--and such
books are written in unintelligible languages.

What concerns us more closely is the fact that the
aforementioned paradox will greatly increase in its malevo-
lent effects when the impending Invasion by Computers becomes a reality.

*Dr. S. N. Gaño describes himself as "a retired oudenog-
rapher now interested in poliorcetics and querciculture."

Surely every librarian now recognizes that this invasion has begun. Card catalogs will become obsolete, we are told. They are headed for the junk heap of disprized obsolescence, along with the expert skills and specialized knowledge of superior librarians. All these are about to become passé.

Such being admittedly the case, what has our paradox to do with computers? We can already foresee several ways in which these components will interact.

Since everybody writes but nobody reads, why must a computer have an output mechanism? Would not an input mechanism be sufficient? The saving in money would be huge, and the expression "IBM" could be reinterpreted to mean Input Bibliographic Morass.

But a reform of this kind will have to cope with the objection that the output mechanism of computers will be needed for the compilation of bibliographies, since bibliographies are indispensable in giving prestige to books and articles.

This difficulty must not be underestimated. One of our best librarians has told me that a physician requested her to furnish a bibliography for an article he had just written. An editor had rejected the manuscript because a bibliography was lacking. It is obvious that in situations of this kind the computer will render excellent service. The machine could be instructed ("programmed") to print out whatever kind of bibliography the author requires; e. g., a list of twenty-seven references all less than five years old (suitable for surgeons), or a list containing x references per page of text (for quantitative thinkers), or a list containing 20 percent of its items in foreign languages and 30 percent anterior to the eighteenth century (for the learned journals).

In such cases it will be necessary to admit the computer to coauthorship. Thus: Jones, Smith, and Medlars, 1970. But this reform is not certain to be adopted. Since librarians are often omitted from the partnership of the byline, it is likely that computers will make the grade?

These considerations do not exhaust the complexities of our problem. If nobody reads articles any more, why print them? Would it not be sufficient merely to print the title? Thus a complete article might be written as follows, in the ultramodern manner:

334

Effect of Desiccation on the Soul

By J. Jones, W. Smith, and Honeywell 2004

Test filed in Library X and to be transferred (on microfilm) to Depository Y. Research supported by NIH Grant No. P3.1416.

Obviously this system is superior to the tedious German method of printing the facts and encumbering them with footnotes.

Thesaurus

John O'Connor[1]

From American Documentation 15:226-7, 1964. Reprinted with permission of the author and of the American Society for Information Science.

An underwater archaeology team from the Museum of the University of Pennsylvania has for several years been exploring the Eastern Mediterranean. During the summer of 1962, in a sunken Greek Ship of the first century B. C., they found an amphora containing microfilm of the library of Alexandria. This microfilm has restored to us many ancient documents previously lost. Among them are some concerning what we now call "documentation." There are, for example, parts of Plato's Thesaurus, and some fragments of Thales on automatic extracting. A translation of the former follows.

Socrates:	Good morning, Thesaurus.
Thesaurus:	Greetings, Socrates. Is it morning?
Soc:	I cannot say with certainty. But the sky appears bright. Tell me, good Thesaurus, why are you sitting here under a plane tree, by all appearances, for all of the night through.
Thes:	I have been thinking.
Soc:	A noble activity, most blessed by the gods. Of what have you been thinking?
Thes:	Of retrieval. And especially of the theory of information retrieval.
Soc:	By the dog, those are most resounding words. I have not heard the like since Protagoras last visited Athens. But pray enlighten me, dear Thesaurus, for I am ignorant of such high matters, what are the meanings of these excellent words?
Thes:	It is of that that I have been thinking Socrates.
Soc:	Forgive me, for I am very stupid, Thesaurus.

	Pray tell me how you can discourse with your-self (for that is what thinking is) without know-ing what it is you are discoursing of.
Thes:	You <u>will</u> not catch me in that trap, Socrates. I shall show you how I can both know and not-know the subject of my thoughts. Let me do so by examples, as I have often heard you do in the Agora.
Soc:	Very good.
Thes:	You know Simmias, the astronomer, who pays traders, sailors, and other travelers for de-scriptions of the night sky as it appears in oth-er lands. And you know that he also pays for records from afar of how the night sky looked at earlier times. It is even rumored that he has paid for the theft of temple records in Per-sia and Egypt and elsewhere.
Soc:	I know that he is an excellent mathematician, and that he seeks to understand the motions of the celestial bodies. But of what avail this strange collecting habit is, I do not understand.
Thes:	He has studied with Hippias the Eleatic. But, excuse me Socrates, I cannot stop for the ques-tion now. I speak of Simmias because he has very many different parchments on which are inscribed various descriptions of the appear-ances of the night sky. I heard him say once that the number of records he has is already more than five multiplied by itself the number of times of which it is a measure. [2]
Soc:	I have seen his collection of documents. He keeps them all in a disordered heap, a very democracy of documents. And in that democ-racy, there is no respect for elders. The very newest parchment is thrown atop the others, and straightway has higher place than all that preceded it. Tell me why, gentle Thesaurus, he does not arrange them in some order. Even a kitchen slave knows enough to keep her cooking utensils in some order, in accordance with their functions.
Thes:	It is worse than that, Socrates. Simmias never forgets any mathematics he has ever heard or thought of. But he told me once that, as for his sky records, each morning it is as though during his sleep he had been bathed in Lethe. He remembers nothing. I think he exaggerates, for he never forgets what he paid for a parch-

	ment. But even though he reads each report when he receives it, he does appear to forget most of what it said.
Soc:	All the more reason for arranging his documents in some rational way. Why does he not do so, Thesaurus?
Thes:	Tell me, Socrates, what is the function of a knife?
Soc:	Why, to cut.
Thes:	And of a grinder?
Soc:	To grind.
Thes:	Does not a kitchen slave know that her knife is for cutting, and her grinder for grinding?
Soc:	She does.
Thes:	And does she not also know the proper function of each of her utensils?
Soc:	Certainly, Thesaurus.
Thes:	So that she can arrange them all according to their functions?
Soc:	Yes.
Thes:	Now tell me, gentle Socrates, what is the function of a document?
Soc:	Most wise Thesaurus, noble son of an illustrious father, you honor me greatly by asking such a question. But I am completely ignorant of these matters. Let me therefore rather question you. For I believe that you have in mind some answer to this question.
Thes:	I do, Socrates.
Soc:	Tell me, then, Thesaurus, what is the function of a document?
Thes:	To document, or to inform.
Soc:	And is this function one or many?
Thes:	Each document has its own special function. Socrates, to inform concerning that which is its subject.
Soc:	Does a document which a sailor carries to Simmias inform the sailor as it informs Simmias?
	[Here part of the dialogue is missing]
. . . .	. . . . both one and not-one. But is this not a contradiction, Thesaurus?
Thes:	It would appear so, Socrates.
Soc:	A general may take a city by attacking it not at a weak point where he is expected, but at a strong point where the blow is a surprise. Let us therefore attack the subject at its strongest point and seek to overcome it by surprise in its stronghold.

338

Thes: What do you mean?

             [The remainder of the dialogue is missing.]

Notes

1. The author's work on information retrieval is supported
   by the Information Systems Branch, Office of Naval
   Research [Contract Nonr 4183 (00)] and the Information Sciences Directorate. Air Force Office of Scientific Research [Contract No. AF 49 (638)--1300].
   The present example of classical scholarship is at
   best a byproduct of that work. Nonetheless, repro-
   duction in whole or in part is permitted for any purpose of the United States Government, and in this
   case perhaps for any purpose of the Greek government.

2. Translator's note.   That is, $5^5 = 3125$.

U. S. Controls on the Exportation of
Unclassified Technical Data
A Fabled Account

William C. Petru

From Special Libraries 60:596-600, 1969. (c) Special Libraries Association. Reprinted with permission of the author
and of Special Libraries Association.

The true, behind-the-scenes story of what really occurred on "The Day of the Great Big Paper Explosion,"
which buried the United States under three and a half feet of
paper! In this now-it-can-be-told exposé of Big Government
in Action, it is revealed how our irreplaceable national
treasures of technical know-how were prevented from leaving
our borders! And how a sneaky quasi-legal assault on the
rules and regulations controlling technical data was thwarted!
And how the very rules and regulations themselves function!
An in-depth, never-to-be-forgotten analysis of a thrilling episode in bibliographic history!

At 11:08 a. m. Pacific Standard Time, on the first
day of Spring, March 20, 1969, a curious event occurred
which will live on in history as "The Day of the Great Big
Paper Explosion." The effects of the Explosion--the term is
apt if not strictly accurate--lasted for months.

Surely, you remember the Day well: The United
States succeeded in launching the world's largest rocket precisely at the moment that the vernal equinox was passing over
Cape Kennedy, Florida. A dreadful vibration resulted from
the meeting of two mighty forces, causing the instantaneous
collapse of every known bibliographic classification and indexing scheme within the borders of the United States. Virtually every scrap of paper imparting information was forthwith
torn willy-nilly from its sheltered niche on a library shelf,
in a file drawer, in a recipe box, in a locked safe, and flung

helter-skelter to the four winds.   March being the month it
is, it was no time before all those books, letters, documents,
vendors' catalogs, pamphlets, newspaper clippings, engineering drawings, were spread--by actual sampled measurement
--an average of 3 1/2 feet deep from coast to coast and border to border.

The depth of consternation amongs librarians and
archivists (information scientists did not particularly care,
their computers not having been affected) was a marvel to
behold--breast-beating and hair-pulling being but the shallow-
est of the emotions displayed.   The reaction of the federal
government was predictable and somewhat to the point.   The
President immediately announced that X-number of dollars
and every available resource would be poured out, et cetera,
et cetera, and so forth.   Furthermore, none of the public
were to worry about the loss of this paper information because everything of real value--like tax information--was already on computers.   The government's general plan called
for the mobilization of every available snowplow to begin the
attack on the drifted paper in wedge formations . . .

Porno-Information Is Exportable?
Suddenly, in the middle of the President's address,
the Press Secretary came running in.   The Secretaries of
State, Commerce and Defense had discovered that their rules
and regulations concerning the handling of classified and unclassified information were being seriously compromised.
The regulations specified in the Industrial Security Manual
for Safeguarding Classified Information had flown out the
window along with the information they were designed to pro-
tect.   Not only was one apt to find the engineering drawings
for the building of an atomic submarine lying next to a delicious piece of pornography, but--far worse!--alien eyes
were free to dwell upon this forbidden material (the atomic
submarine, not the pornography).

Had this been the only way in which technical data
were being mishandled, the Secretaries could have closed the
borders to all travelers, permitting little information to
leave the country.   But with the Great Big Paper Explosion
the problem was that the paper was on the move, wafted as
it were on March winds.   The wafting over the United States
borders became so severe, as a matter of fact, that the
Secretaries asked the President to mobilize the snowplows
along the Canadian and Mexican borders, while minesweepers
and other vessels were commanded to drag nets up and down
the coast lines.

With the snowplows bringing a modicum of control over the inadvertent exportation of technical data, the Secretaries agreed that some sort of indoctrination program was needed for the general populace who were wading waist-deep in material for which they had no real appreciation. It was absolutely essential that some rules be followed in kicking it around.

Perhaps through frequent radio and television broadcasts of the rules and regulations affecting the exportation of technical data, the public could be aroused to the necessity of keeping these national treasures at home. The decision was made to concentrate first on unclassified information because it was found that the classified information, being obviously heavier in thought and content, had sunk to the bottoms of the piles of paper and could be worried about at a later time. In some areas where rioting college students had stirred the paper up the classified material was compromised anyway, so what difference did it make?

The more the Secretaries discussed the problem, the more they realized that it was only the regulations governing the exportation of technical data which had any meaning left under the present circumstances. A distillation of the salient regulations was needed.

The Secretary of State insisted that his rules, the International Traffic in Arms, should be used since: 1) they cover arms, ammunition, and implements of war, in which everyone is interested; 2) they contain the famous United States Munitions List; and 3) they cover both unclassified and classified data pertaining to any of the articles on the Munitions List. And all of this in one neat package only 11 pages long.

The Secretary of Commerce, a true civil-servant, immediately pooh-poohed the notion of brevity in favor of his Comprehensive Export Schedule, a fat looseleaf service containing Part 385, "Exports of Technical Data." Part 385 concerns itself: 1) only with unclassified data; 2) with all other information not included in the U. S. Munitions List; and 3) it had an intricately worked out licensing system for the exportation of technical data.

The Secretary of Defense stopped the discussion cold by saying that he didn't believe in controlling unclassified data--but if he did, all he would have to do was slap his Statement No. 2 from DoD Directive 5200.20 on it and everybody's export problem would be solved. The other Secretaries resented Defense for implying he had anything so simple, and there was a terrible row.

The President was asked to resolve the question of whose rules would save The Day of the Great Big **Paper** Explosion. He sagely called in each of the Secretaries one by one and had each answer a series of four questions: 1) the definition of technical data as provided in his regulations, 2) technical data exemptions to the regulations, 3) licensing provisions for the exportation of technical data, and 4) ease with which the regulations can be read, understood, and applied to a 3 1/2 foot pile of paper threatening to leave the borders.

The Secretary of State, eager to make the best possible impression for his department rules, carefully intoned their full title: International Traffic in Arms Regulations, Subchapter M of Chapter 1 of Title 22, by Authority of Section 414 of the Mutual Security Act of 1934. The President, unimpressed, told him to hurry up and keep to the questions.

The International Traffic in Arms Regulations (ITAR) states plainly that the term "article" shall mean any of the arms, ammunition, and implements of war and technical data relating thereto enumerated in the United States Munitions List. As used in ITAR, "technical data" means: "(a) information concerning an article on the U. S. Munitions List which enables its use, operation, maintenance, repair, overhaul, production, or manufacture, or (b) research, development, and engineering technology concerning an article on the U. S. Munitions List, or (c) any technology which advances the state-of-the-art or establishes a new art in an area of significant military applicability, or (d) classified equipment or information relating to a U. S. Munitions List article."

The whole purpose of these regulations, the Secretary of State was fond of pointing out, was to keep our good old American know-how at home. What exemption to the export controls really boiled down to was whether that information was freely available in public libraries, or by purchase at a newstand or bookstore, or had been approved for public release by government authority. If unclassified technical data does not fall within the exempted, a license issued by the Department of State is required. Applications must include five (5) copies of the technical data.

The President interrupted with a short expletive, saying that he could not have his snowplow drivers searching wildly for five copies of something in the event there was a breach in the battle at the borders. Could the rules be re-laxed to read only one copy each? ITAR didn't sound too bad, bearing in mind that it was applicable to military arti-cles only.

With this faint praise, the Secretary of State was dis-missed and the Secretary of Commerce ushered in, hugging a number of looseleaf binders which were empty because they had fallen victim to the Great Big Paper Explosion. The President saw at once that he was to be impressed with the size of the Comprehensive Export Schedule, so before it went too far, the Secretary was admonished to keep it brief.

Provisions of Part 385, "Exports of Technical Data," of the Comprehensive Export Schedule (CES) do not apply to technical data which have been officially assigned a security classification. "Technical data" within the CES means "in-formation of any kind that can be used, or adapted for use, in the design, production, manufacture, utilization, or re-construction of articles or materials. The data may take a tangible form, such as a model, prototype, blueprint, or an operating manual; or they may take an intangible form such as technical service."

Further definitions within CES state that the "export of technical data means: 1) an actual shipment or transmis-sion of technical data out of the United States; 2) any re-lease of technical data in the United States with the knowl-edge or intent that the data will be shipped or transmitted from the United States to a foreign country; or 3) the appli-cation to situations abroad of personal knowledge or techni-cal experience acquired in the United States."

When the President reminded the Secretary for the second time to keep it brief, the Secretary countered that he couldn't; after all, under discussion were the regulations controlling all unclassified technical data, except for that puny military bit left to the Department of State.

The CES provides for two types of licenses: General License GTDA and General License GTDR. General License GTDA authorizes export of technical data to all destinations --data which under ITAR were exemptions from licensing: "data released orally or visually at open conferences, lec-tures, trade shows, or other media open to the public; and publications that may be purchased without restrictions at a nominal cost or obtained without cost or are readily available at libraries open to the public." Scientific or educational data and foreign patent applications fall within this license jurisdiction also. General License GTDR is to be used when exporting data which is not exportable under provisions of General License GTDA, which include data on nuclear devices, certain electronic and aircraft commodities, and petrochemical processes.

The Secretary of Commerce, eyes glassy, continued to recite the litany of General License GTDR: "Country Group S and Z Restrictions," "Country Group W and Y Restrictions," "Technical Data Restrictions Applicable to All Destinations," "Restrictions Applicable to All Destinations Except Canada" . . .

With the word "Canada," the President leapt to his feet. If Canada as a destination was exempt from export controls of certain technical data, the President could pull back half his snowplows! The rest of the Comprehensive Export Schedule was out of the question for consideration for the general populace, of course. Too difficult to understand and so . . . comprehensive.

Zealous Librarian in Milpitas
While the President was conducting his interviews to determine what rules to follow in an indoctrination program, an incident in Milpitas, California, occurred which would soon have a direct bearing on his judgment. An innocent visitor from Canada chanced to have blown in his face the process for making porous nickel, on the restricted data list even for Canadians in the Comprehensive Export Schedule. A zealous librarian, thoroughly familiar with the rules and knowing where her duty lay, made a citizen's arrest and dragged the poor tourist--still clutching the evidence--off to jail.

In the meantime, the President called in the Secretary of Defense to find out more about the so-called simple method his Department had of controlling information. The Secretary burst in carrying nothing but a stamp pad and a rather smallish rubber stamp. These he threw down in front of the President, flatly stating that if this stamp appeared on each piece of paper lying around outside, there would be no need for the falderal of licensing or indoctrinating. The stamp was the famous Distribution Statement No. 2 from the Department of Defense Directive 5200.20, frequently called the NOFORN statement. If intended for use on unclassified material, it read:

> This document is subject to special export controls
> and each transmittal to foreign governments or for-
> eign nationals may be made only with prior approv-
> al of [controlling DoD office].

> In addition to security requirements which must be
> met, this document is subject to special export
> controls . . .

The "controlling DoD office" is the DoD activity or its
higher in-line authority under whose immediate program a
document is generated, whether the work was done in-house
or by contract.   The Secretary was quick to point out that
in this time of national emergency this definition could be
altered a bit so that his administrators could control all
technical data--DoD-sponsored or not.

The basis for Distribution Statement No. 2 (it is No.
2 in a list of five distribution statements covering various
phases of technical data) is to control information.

> that was furnished by a foreign government; com-
> mercial competition with foreign firms; the protec-
> tion of technical know-how relating to critical pro-
> ducts or manufacturing processes, tests and evalu-
> ation of military operational weapon systems and
> installations and other technology restricted by U.S.
> Mutual Security Acts.

The statement had already been placed onto all manner of
unclassified technical information--speeches, brochures, reports, sales literature--so there was no reason why it could
not be stamped onto more of the same.   And, furthermore,
Statement No. 2 has no automatic termination date.

The President sat thoughtfully . . .

Just then an aide came in to tell the President of a
radio report from Milpitas.   A federal judge had issued an
injunction against the United States government, naming the
President and the Secretaries of State, Commerce and Defense, ordering them to immediately stop enforcing all controls on the dissemination of information.   A Canadian tourist, arrested with compromising technical data in his posses-
sion, had convinced the judge that any regulations attempting
to regulate the free flow in information were patently unen-
forceable, what with all the information lying around freely
available anyway.

With the President being spared the decision of having to choose amongst the regulations, he could return to running the country. In the meantime, the librarians returned to their usual tasks of arranging and rearranging paper piles, and in no time order was restored.

You know, of course, that the Canadian tourist finally lost his case in the Supreme Court and was deported to Grande Prairie, Alberta, still not knowing what porous nickel was. The injunction against the controls on information was lifted, and along with all the other rules and regulations, the International Traffic in Arms Regulations, the Comprehensive Export Schedule, and DoD Directive 5200. 20 settled firmly back into place.

As a matter of fact, we are exactly where we were on March 20, 1969, "The Day of the Great Big Paper Explosion."

The following documents are pertinent in controlling the exportation of unclassified technical data:

1. Comprehensive Export Schedule; a compilation of official regulations and policies governing export licensing of commodities and technical data. Office of Export Control, International Commerce Bureau, U. S. Department of Commerce. Looseleaf. Available from the Superintendent of Documents.

2. Industrial Security Manual for Safeguarding Classified Information, DoD 5220. 22-M (Jul 1, 1966). Looseleaf. Change 1 (May 1, 1968). Available from the Superintendent of Documents.

3. International Traffic in Arms, subchapter M of the regulations of the Secretary of State (Departmental Reg. 108. 520, 30 F. R. 9034). As published in the Federal Register, v. 31, no. 233, pt. II, Friday, Dec. 2, 1966. Available from the Superintendent of Documents.

4. Distribution Statements (Other than Security) on Technical Documents, DoD Directive 5200. 20 (Mar 29, 1965). Change 2 (May 8, 1967). Available from local Defense Contract Administration Services Regions (DCASRs) or Department of Defense. This document references several other directives, all of which are

relevant to controlling the exportation of unclassified technical data.

For further background information on the subject, see the Journal of the National Classification Management Society (particularly 1967) and the publications of the Aerospace Industries Association.

Interplanetary Copyright

Donald F. Reines

From the Library of Congress Information Bulletin 11:13-5, August 11, 1952. Reprinted with permission of the author and the Library of Congress.

Recently the Examining Division has observed the large number of publications of all sorts dealing, either factually or fictionally, with the conquest of space, and has come to believe that the concept which H. G. Wells called "the leap in the air" is entering the consciousness of modern man. This new facet of the mind, plus the rapid growth of modern technology, has led the Examining Division to the inescapable conclusion that human beings, most probably Americans, will land on the Moon before 1960, and on Mars and Venus before 1975. In its usual forward-looking manner, the Examining Division has considered the implications of these acts insofar as they relate to the Copyright Office and the copyright law.

The very first question to be considered is the applicability of the copyright law to the Moon. Most astronomers believe the Moon is uninhabited, so it will be claimed in much the way Antarctica is now, by the various nations sending expeditions there. It will most likely be used only as a way station for trips farther out in space, but assuming some poet stationed there prints and distributes a book throughout the American colony, the question arises as to whether it can be registered, and in what class. The majority feels that it should be accepted under the conditions which apply to the territories and possessions of the United States, but the minority holds that only an ad interim registration is possible, since the Moon is most certainly outside the United States. Several have expressed merely their hopes of retiring before the first landing is made.

Mars and Venus present much more difficult questions, for on these planets we may encounter strange forms of in-

telligent life, speaking and writing in many different languages.
If they are friendly and produce objects similar to the present classes of registrable articles, will we establish copyright relations with them and register these items? If we do, the recruitment of native personnel of these planets to handle the applications in the Copyright Office becomes a necessity, at least until the languages are well known on Earth. While it is highly desirable to bring all this new material into the collections of the Library of Congress, some present members of the staff have gone on record to the effect that they will not work with anything green in color, scaly in texture, or over fifteen feet tall. As segregation has never been sanctioned here, it is felt that this problem should be brought to the attention of the Employee Relations Officer.

Moreover, it is possible some Martians and Venusians may have more than one head. In this case, would we register the work of one of these creatures as that of a single author, or would the name of each head be set down as co-author? It is important that this matter be straightened out, for more reasons than one.

Farther out in space we encounter problems of a different nature. It is apparent that the 28-year term of copyright will cause great hardship to those authors domiciled at the other end of the Galaxy, for in many cases it takes more than 28 years to reach Earth from those areas. A book published on Aldebaran and dispatched immediately to the Copyright Office would reach here in its 36th year, too late to register. The rule deduced from this is that the term of copyright must be increased in proportion to the distance we move from the Copyright Office. If this is not done there may be retaliatory measures and the breaking off of copyright relations, resulting in the works of American authors being unregistrable on Sirius, Canis Major, 23 Cygni, and other far-flung places. It will not sit well with the American publishing industry to know that its best sellers are in the public domain throughout most of the Milky Way.

We may have to leave these matters to the deliberations of the first Intergalactic Copyright Convention, but we can pass on to the reorganization of the Office necessitated by the tremendous amount of new material these planets and stars will furnish. Since the present system of examining is considered inadequate for such a work load, it has been suggested that we install a giant thinking machine, possibly occupying the entire Annex, into whose circuits we build the copyright law and all decisions made in the courts and in the Office. (It is estimated that 20,000,000,000,000,000,000 vacuum tubes should suffice.) Applications will be submitted on punched cards which will be fed into the machine and either accepted or rejected immediately. Doubtful cases which now require five or six weeks of deliberation can be cleared in one-millionth of a second, thus eliminating our backlog and our Friday afternoon reports concerning them. This alone will save 27,375,549 man-hours per year.

Since persons having a knowledge of cybernetics, nuclear physics, general semantics, non-Euclidean geometry, and electronics are not usually available in the labor market, it is expected that we will use the present staff. Mistakes will be made at first, but this is not unusual in any large scale changeover.

One suggestion for handling the mass of statistics produced by these operations is that we hire "calculating wizards," those strange persons who can perform tremendous mathematical calculations in their heads. It is felt that the fact that these wizards are usually idiots outside their ability to calculate should not be grounds for barring them from employment, since the Examining Division has never discriminated this way in the past.

We feel that, in keeping with the glorious traditions of the Copyright Office we should make every effort to solve most of these problems now, so that the pilot of the first rocket to the Moon can make his flight with a mind free of anxiety, and with the knowledge that the Service Division, the Examining Division, the Cataloging Division, and the Reference Division are all solidly behind him. And we do mean behind.

A Case History in Selective Elimination as a
Solution to the Information Crisis

William Tinker, Benjamin Evers, Paul N. Chance

From American Documentation 15:304-5, 1964. Reprinted
with permission of the American Society for Information
Science.

C. O. D. 13 February 1966[1]

Published studies on the so-called information explosion in science generally proceed from the unstated premise
that newly published research results constitute a direct in-
crement to the total store of knowledge. Since the number
of research workers and the number of published papers are

Table 1. A Comparison of the Number of Facts in Edition A
(see text) with the Number in Edition B (see text). [2]

Number of facts in Edition A	Number of facts in Edition B
7, 384, 622, 140	7, 384, 622, 141

[2] Source: Encyclopedia Britannica, A-Mc.

both demonstrably increasing (Perish's Law), this premise
leads to exponential growth rate projections for such variables as annual journal pages, costs of society publication
programs, linear feet of library shelving required, gross
weight of abstract journals, and information-transfer study
budgets.

One of us (1), in the course of a research project

[1]C. O. D. = Calculated Obsolescence Date.

on taste differentiation mechanisms in vermicula exlibris (a subject of intense interest to the library paste industry), was recently the beneficiary of one of those fortunate accidental discoveries that unexpectedly illuminate a hitherto unnoticed bypath on the main road of scientific advance. Comparative thickness measurements on two chronologically adjacent editions of the Encyclopedia Britannica revealed a difference of less than 5%, although the time-lapse was 22 years, and the predicted change (Price) should have totaled more than 10^3 pages (273.4% by weight).

Subsequent analysis showed, moreover, that this anomaly could not be accounted for by compensatory variation in any of the common physical variables of paper thickness, type size, leading, number and size of illustrations, outside dimensions of either volume or bookcase, or marginal considerations. A radically new hypothesis was thus required to account for the discrepancy.

Thus was born the concept of Historic Cancellation of Fact, and with instantaneous and understanding assistance from the National Science Foundation we proceeded to turn the undivided attention of our laboratory at Witte's End to testing it.

Taking a sample population (A-Mc) from each edition, one of us (2) assigned to each fact a coded identification number categorizing that fact in terms of its location on the McGeever spectrum of human knowledge. Upon computer comparison of the facts from each edition it was determined that the total number of facts in the two editions was nearly identical (Table 1).

Price's equations were obviously omitting some significant factor. Although the trend had been predicted to 100% accuracy, the magnitude had been grossly overestimated.

Using the lab's 14.5-33 computer and a program originally written by one of our (3) graduate students (Lajoie), one of us (4) examined the 7,384,622,141 items from the second edition (Edition B) to see how many of them were repeats of items in the first edition (Edition A). Pairing these and filing them for future study (a draft proposal has been submitted), we were left with 7,384,622 items (almost exactly .1%) which did not match. These were classified by a consulting encyclopedist as due to either:

353

1. Divergent development of continuous but noncommunicating disciplines;
2. Contradictions growing out of internal evolution of
internally communicating disciplines; or
3. Misprints.

Through the use of carefully chosen weighting factors, we were
then able to set up the first (classic) version of our Historic
Cancellation Formula:

$$\Omega = \int_{\blacktriangle}^{McC} \left[\sum_{1988}^{1990} \exp \tfrac{3}{2}\varsigma - \Bbbk \right] \qquad (1)$$

where,

ς = a constant
$\Bbbk$ = a constant

and

Ω = the Historic Cancellation Coefficient.

A mere 24 hours of computer time sufficed to demon-
strate what we had suspected all along; namely, that Ω remained absolutely fixed for all items in Class 2.   This
proved that for every item of new information uncovered by
scientific research, exactly one previously established item
is either contradicted or displaced.   This maintains $\mathcal{K}$ (the
total of human knowledge) at a constant level, and keeps the
encyclopedia from taking over the whole house.

One of us (5) has proposed a somewhat more popular-
ized version of the General Law: "For every paper we accept revealing that the earth is round, we must throw away
an old one revealing that the earth is flat."   Thus Pauli's
exclusion principle is seen to extend even to the archive.

The question may be asked: how do we in fact recognize and identify the previously established fact which is in
fact being displaced or contradicted by the new fact, and
which must be rejected in order to keep the fact-total constant?   Here again we were breaking new ground and in need
of another grant.   In due time we got it, but not before our
whole set of "noncommunicating" (Class 1) punched cards had
been attacked by several thousand escaped vermiculae exlibris, with consequent near-obliteration of the original codes

354

by enormous amounts of noise. (Let the Geometrodynamicists make their puns about wormholes; we were sick at heart.) Suffice it to say that the deck was eventually reconstituted, with only minor errors.

Our final computations revealed that the editors of the Encyclopedia had done a remarkable job of historic cancellation, but we tended to doubt that an equally thorough job was within the day-to-day capabilities of the working scientist, confronted with his normal daily ration of 627 tasks of conducting vital research and keeping his eyeglasses clean. Thus was born Project Eraser.

Under the joint sponsorship of the NSF, the AAAS, the ORNL, and the Coast Guard, we have set up complete publishing facilities here at Witte's End to gather, edit, print, and distribute free to qualified science-oriented executives and technical project leaders (advertisers please note) a daily journal known as SCRUB (Science Culling and Rejecting of Un-information Bulletin).

In our new 12-acre Un-information Dissemination Wing we have assembled a staff of experts in every field of science, whose job it is to constantly review the entire backlog of previously published scientific papers in our automated microimage files on a daily basis. Each existing paper is evaluated in the light of the new papers published the day before, and any "old" paper which has suffered obsolescence is immediately pulled from our files and republished in its entirety in SCRUB, which serves as official notice to the scientific community that the facts therein are formally declared rejected and replaced by new facts.

Each recipient of SCRUB is thus enabled to clean his own files on a daily basis and to retain in them only pertinent, relevant, certified facts, accurately representing the state of the art only 24 hours earlier.

For those whose interest in the process exceeds the merely factual and who desire to indulge in comparative or statistical analysis, there are also the SCRUB Abstracts (published weekly) and the SCRUB Annual Index, to which a SCRUB Thesaurus of the more than 25,000 indexing terms used is in preparation. All four publications will soon be available in microfilm form, and cumulation of the Abstracts and the Index is planned at five-year intervals.

In a related program, one of us (6) is studying the feasibility of Automatic SCRUB, which--through application of carefully worked out obsolescence coefficients in each major field of science--will enable journal editors of existing journals to predict a cancellation date (C. O. D.--Calculated Obsolescence Date) and print it with the abstract of the original paper for transcription to the filing record and subsequent use as an automatic disposal mechanism in automated files. We believe that on the day when Automatic SCRUB goes into operation, the Information Problem will truly be well on its way to solution.

Notes

1. Evers   3. Tinker   5. Evers or Tinker
2. Chance   4. Chance   6. Tinker? Chance?

William Tinker, Princeton University
Benjamin Evers, Yale University
Paul N. Chance, Smith College

A Minor Devil's Documentation Dictionary[1]

L. Vanby

From American Documentation 14:143-4, 1963. Reprinted with permission of the American Society for Information Science.

Abstract, n., a concrete representation in brief of the contend of some document (q. v.). Universally confused with extract, annotation, précis, excerpt, etc.

Abstract, v., the practice of producing the above. Since no one has ever defined a good abstract, the future of abstracting, professional or amateur, seems assured.

Boolean Algebra, n., a branch of logic. Unexplainably, it is felt that this might be of use to documentation, even though its results are either trivial or self-evident, or both.

Classification, n., a system of arranging similar things into a unique order, a self-evident impossibility. Another triumph of Aristotelian obfuscation.

Computer, n., an enormously overgrown on-off machine. Up to the present, it is an act of faith that a device originally designed for computing, i. e., arithmetic, can also be used in some meaningful way for lexical purposes.

Document, n., any conceivable scrap of paper with marks on it. To a documentalist (q. v.), all such scraps are of equal worth.

Document, v., see Documentation.

Documentalist, n., a harmless paper-shuffler. Not yet a professional, no longer a technician.

Documentation, n., Undefinable. It seems to consist of the logical sum of the professional activities of about 500 people.

---

[1] With a gently ironic bow to Bierce.

Education, n. , see Training.

Index, n. , a system of analyzing information in which the method used to choose categories is carefully hidden from the ultimate user; an attempt to outguess the future.

Information Retrieval, n. , the nut of it all. The exact meaning of this phrase in any particular cirumstance is reasonably obvious, even though a general definition lacks agreement. A socially useful activity, information retrieval is suspect among nonpractitioners because of overselling.

Information Theory, n. , a misleading name for an idea having a slight but useful application in this field. It is far enough past its first fashionable, or phrase-dropping, stage that one really needs to know what it is all about before discussing it.

Library, n. , a mausoleum for books. Once a historically valid idea, the march of research has completely obviated its purpose by making chimerical any idea of 'completeness' of a collection.

Literature Searching, v. , a form of detective work attempting to disguise itself as a professional activity. A useful distinction between this and information retrieval (q. v.) has been lost.

Linguistics, n. , an esoteric discipline often confused with semantics (q. v.). A friendly warning: a linguist may not know much about linguistics.

Meaning, n. , the part of a message specifically excluded in the information theory (q. v.); the only part of the message of any value.

Mechanization, v. , the attempt to do rigorously and in time-dependent fashion what has been performed artistically in the past. Difficulties of unimaginable sorts arise, naturally.

Meeting, n. , see Symposium.

Microfilm, n. , a scroll form of book in slightly reduced size. Enthusiasm for this form of storage waxes and wanes over the years.

Microcard, n. , for cowardly reasons of legal self-protection, no definition will be given of this trademark.

Redundancy, n. , a vogue-word popular among documentalists (q. r.) about 1955. It is unfortunate that a word so appropriate to this subject and its literature should have fallen into relative disuse.

Search, n. , v. , see Literature Searching.

Semantics, n. , a convenient catchall to cover ignorance of
one's own language, especially its etymology.
Already a flourishing profession of its own,
this field is likely to plague documentation
(q. v.) for years.

State of the Art, a phrase taken from the field of patents,
having nothing to do with art, and having no
very precise meaning. It seems to be wedded
firmly, as a phrase, to the word 'survey.'

Symposium, n. , a gathering ostensibly for professional purposes; often useful for job-hunting, assigna-
tions, drinking, and the like.

Thesaurus, n. , the vogue-word for 1959. Its popularity
stemmed from the success of an undoubted
genius (Roget) in another field, even though no
similar genius has appeared in this one.

Training, n. , the next step after self-instruction; the outstanding lack in the field today. Education is
never mentioned in connection with documentation.

Use-Study, n. , the practice of documentalists asking users
of information what they do with such information; the blind leading the blind.

Stinfo

Harold Wooster

From American Documentation 15:152-3, 1964.   Reprinted
with permission of the author and of the American Society
for Information Science.

As you can tell by the date, the presence of a stamp
on the envelope, and the use of 8-1/2" wide paper, this letter is being typed on my own paper, typewriter, and time.
Any opinions expressed herein will be vigorously denied from
0745 through 1615, Mondays through Fridays.

The Crawford task force (Crawford, James H. , Chairman, Task Force Report to the President's Special Assistant for Science and Technology, Scientific and Technological
Communication in the Government, Washington, April, 1962)
was apparently responsible for unleashing upon an all too
ready world the semi-acronym, Stinfo, standing for scien-
tific-technical information. Stinfo has now become a vogue
word in certain circles. As an old Scrabble player, it
seems a shame to let such a lovely stem remain unexploited.
I therefore and hereby enter a Markush claim for the following neologisms based on Stinfo, at the same time granting
permission to all and sundry to make such uses of them
(with the exception of libel suits) as they may see fit.

> Stinfoal--An undergraduate majoring in the "Informa-
> tion Sciences. "
> Stinfoam--All speeches, press releases, and papers
> containing the statement "If a piece of research
> costs less than $100,000, it is cheaper to do the
> research, ..." etc.
> Stinfodder--An elder statesman; see Stinfossil.
> Stinfoe--Ugly librarians.
> Stinfogy--One professionally concerned with docu-
> ments prior to 1962.
> Stinfolio--A thesaurus; all books with titles beginning

"Information Storage and Retrieval."

Stinfolk--The working, or indispensable level.

Stinfolly--Everyone else's information system.

Stinfone--The most useful mechanical aid to information retrieval.

Stinfood--Polyunsaturated money.

Stinfool--All but me and thee.

Stinfoolish--As in "Penny wise, stinfoolish."

Stinfop--Always first with the newest.

Stinforce--A group of individuals deprived of normal food, sleep, and social contacts, kept under bright lights in an atmosphere of rarefied thoughts and tobacco smoke (stinfug) until they have produced their quota of recommendations.

Stinform--A strait jacket.

Stinfortune--$1.98.

Stinforum--The halls of Congress, the Pentagon, the National Institutes of Health, etc.

Stinfossil--One who thinks DDC stands for Dewey Decimal Classification.

Stinfoul--Request for accurate cost accounting of unit operations.

Stinfowl--By extension from hen medic, a female documentalist.

Stinfox--Successful seeker of funds from NSF, AFOSR, ONR, ARO, DOD, CLRU, NIH, PHS, etc.

Toward the History of Documentation

Theodor B. Yerke

From <u>Special Libraries</u> 54:352-3, 1963.   Reprinted with permission of (c) Special Libraries Association.

> This important despatch was received at Bibliopolis-
> on-the-Potomac on January 7, 18,963 A. D.   It was
> transmitted by the Archaeodocument Retrieval Ex-
> pedition in Upper New York.

The discovery in Holocene sedimentary beds near the
proto-historic Lake Placid of a miraculously-preserved document entitled <u>Simplified Library School Rules</u> pushes certain
knowledge of the history of documentation almost back to the
inceptions.   The document (or "book" as its contemporaries
would have called it) is dated 1904 A. D.   That places it
clearly before the onset of the Fifth Ice Age.   The author of
the work is <u>Melvil Dewey</u>.   Now for the first time we have
conclusive indication of the famous Admiral's first name!
That he was also, as were so many in primitive times, a
self-educated man is evident from his deficient spelling.   And
of course, in those early, generalized ages, it was not unusual for a military man to dabble in documentation.

We were particularly anxious to see if this document
contained any reference to the almost-mythical Hollerith,
whom we have long regarded as the true founder of documentation.   It was always presumed that Hollerith lived near the
beginning of the 20th Christian century.   The Admiral does
not mention Hollerith in this work!   Some scholars hold that
Dewey stole the idea of information cards from Hollerith and
changed the size of them to cover his tracks.   But others
believe the Admiral invented decimal classification and 3x5
inch cards independently of Hollerith and that the two men
never even knew each other!   Communication was unbeliev-
ably bad in those days.

The most exciting thing in the ancient document occurs

on page 15, where a list of "special classes of people" appears. The list is as follows:

Heliand	Merlin
Hitopadesa	Niebelungenlied
Kabala	Renard the fox
Kalevala	Roland
Koran	Talmud
Mabinogion	Upanishads
Mahabharata	

Linguists point out that these are nearly all European or Aryan names. Further, the names in the first column are all feminine, or seem to be, and those in the second are masculine. We conclude that this is a list of wives and husbands--the true antedeluvian founders of documentation! (Except for Miss Mahabharata, the only name not linked to a man. We suspect here a prominent county librarian who remained unwed.) This list must date back almost to the Fourth Ice Age, since documentation was discovered during the recently ended interglacial epoch. Thus these hoary figures were almost mythical to documentalists of Dewey's age, which was right in the middle of the interglacial period.

The only name that can be identified with any historical event in documentation is the entry "Renard the fox." A man named Renard was leader of a library school on the western shore of the North American continent at about the time of the Admiral. We cannot explain this late-comer to the list of special persons, nor can we explain the epithet "the fox," except to note that in those ancient times persons are known to have taken a second name at maturity, usually of an animal deity or geographic feature. Another possibly recent name is Niebelungenlied. Professor Ixbitl believes that Niebelungenlied, the husband of Hitopadesa, may have been a German bibliographer.

Simplified Library School Rules contains other striking evidence of the closeness of those times to archaic thought. The instructions to documentalists include elaborate rules for the entry of noblemen and other special types of humans! Anthropomorphisms abound, in that cities, industries, and organized groups are all treated as persons! Slavery had also persisted longer than we had imagined, for there is an entry to a Sir Walter Scott's Black Dwarf. Perhaps because he belonged to a special class of persons, he was allowed to keep a slave.

Principles for primitive coding are laid down. The chief figure in this work was apparently not Hollerith but a Charles Ami Cutter. We presume "Ami" to be a transcription of the Southern dialect corruption of the word "Army." Again the military motif! The Admiral apparently felt more comfortable with his own class of people. In those days persons also took the name of their craft--Cutter no doubt descended from a line of sawyers, tailors, or harvesters. This early background of cutting things to size and purpose may have inspired him in his attempts to cut or code information to size.

Much of the instruction given in Simplified Library School Rules is almost meaningless to us now. It requires considerable effort for us really to understand that documents in these early epochs occupied considerable spatial extensions. We understand from other fragments that some of the larger libraries were thousands of square feet in extent. None of these survived the Fifth Ice Age, most having become peat deposits. The document Simplified Library School Rules itself takes up as much physical space as 1,000 years of the legislative proceedings of a major metropolitan area in a contemporary library. Professor Ixbitl has calculated that if the present totality of recorded knowledge were in macroform, as in the Admiral's day, all of our libraries would have to be removed to the moon, which same satellite they would cover to a depth of at least two miles!

As we excavate around the edges of ancient Lake Placid, it is almost certain that other valuable material about the Admiral, his life, and accomplishments will be unearthed. We are particularly anxious to find something definitive about his famous Manila folder, which is believed to be the code name of his battle plan for occupation of that former Spanish harbor.

MISCELLANEOUS VERSE

Public Documents

Harlan Hoge Ballard, Librarian and Curator,
Berkshire Athenaeum, Pittsfield, Mass.

From Library Journal 34:91-2, 1909.

Their minds unvexed by fluctuatin' stocks.
Our grandthers set great store by public doc's,
Begged from their congressman the ponderous tomes,
Perused the treasured volumes in their homes,
Read every speech by Webster or by Clay,
And read 'em in the good old-fashioned way.
Then in the evenin's, at the country store,
Uncorked the vials of the new-found lore,
And democrats and whigs exchanged their views,
And mingled argyments with village news.
But now that bosses deal out printed votes,
An' politics comes ez ready made ez coats,
When all we read is tales of greed and graft,
An' all our thinkin's done by Bryan or Taft,
The documents our fathers used to trust
Are left alone, accumulating dust,
Unless our wives or these wise girls of ours
Make 'em herbariums for pressin' flowers;
My daughter, too, you may be glad to learn,
Hez made some kind o' scrapbook out o' ehrn;
I b'lieve 'taint filled with no particular knowledge--
Mostly mementos of her days in college.
They's some keep documents to make a show
By standin' on em edgewise in a row;
Prob'ly all right--you know how 'tis yourself--
Fer nothin' looks worse than an empty shelf.
Nevertheless, so fur as I kin learn,
Most folks believe they're only fit to burn,
Though thrifty housewives think the proper caper
Is jest to sell 'em with the rags for paper.
But yet--hold on a bit! I'll tell you what--
There is one other use I most forgot;
There's congressmen, above all thought of brib'ry.

Who still present their speeches to the lib'ry.
An' libries get from many a dusty garret
Some documents from them that's glad to spare it.
So patent office and old war reports,
Old coast surveys and old decrees of courts,
Extinct committees and dead boards of health,
An ancient census of the commonwealth,
Odd volumes of old treaties with Japan,
Reports commercial and Smithsonian,
Reports of bureaus of ethnology,
And bulletins of every sort of ology.
Returns of boards of education,
Reviews of western irrigation,
Old journals of the house and senate,
The history of the Kuklux, when it
Threatened to o'errun the south,
Dry observations on the drouth,
Views of our maritime rights by Vindex;
All these and more (with never an index)
Are carted 'round to the library door,
Cause "dad don't want 'em any more!"
By reason of this ceaseless inundation
Our stacks are filled from attic to foundation.
Because they're gifts we dass'nt throw'm away;
And so the burden grows from day to day.
Such is the problem for this here convention
To solve by all its wisdom and invention;
But pounds of cure (though this 'twere rash to mention),
Ain't half as good as ounces of prevention.
When folks bring stuff we hadn't orter take,
Why don't we tell 'em so fer goodness sake?
Why load our shelves with rubbish from the tomb,
An' then complain because we're short o' room?
But since things isn't as they'd orter be,
But as they iz, I'll give you my idee:
When boats are fillin' fast, beyond a doubt,
The furst thing to be done is bail 'em out;
So 'tis with dockiments--they's wheat and chaff--
An' ef you're sinkin', overboard with half!
To change the proverb so's our case to fit,
Discrimination is the soul of wit.
Let each one judge by what his patrons need
What must be kept, from what he may be freed,
What holds true records of the town or state.
What books still live, and what are out of date.
Whether you find in volumes new or old
All dross or precious unsuspected gold,
One certain benefit you all will gain,

You'll end your task with an enlightened brain;
You'll know what's worthless in the rubbish heap,
You'll know what's worthy in the books you keep,
An' fer a help in makin' up your mind
To part with more than first you feel inclined,
Remember that the most o' what's worth while
Hez been reprinted in a better style.
Statistics sprinkled through a hundred volumes
Some handbook has condensed to twenty columns
The small type speech that in the record lurks
Stands forth in pica in the author's works,
An' bits of science scattered here and there
Are grouped in textbooks with the greatest care.
An' then there's books no sort of use to you
Others would gladly take, an' pay for too,
So, 'fore destroyin' anythin' as trash,
Try givin', tradin' or a sale for cash.
Here endeth Lesson I, "the choice of books."
Next comes "Their best arrangement," and it looks
At first as if there wasn't much to say,
Except to set 'em up the usual way,
For public documents are jest the same
Ez any other books except in name.
But I'll suggest with all becomin' deference
That documents is mostly good fer reference;
You can't expect to circulate these tomes
Ez freely ez the tales o' Mary Holmes,
No more'n you'd find a treatis' on neuralger,
Ez popular with boys as one by Alger.
Then, there's a law there's been some fuss about
That guv'ment documents must not go out.
But while, I s'pose there may be some such rule,
We haint obleeged to foller it like a mule,
For even Post, who has these things in charge,
Is willin, its restrictions to enlarge.
"Treat public documents," says Mr. Post,
"Like other reference books." This clears the coast.
We're not to circulate these books like fiction,
But if we'd lend a man a diction-
Ary over night or Sunday
If he'll return it early Monday,
We may do a similar thing, you see,
With a bulletin of geology;
Or if in a case of urgent need
We would let a man take an encycloped-
Ia, then we may lend to a studious chap
A government topographical map;
A word to the wise is verbum sap!

Still most of our documents are our own,
And were never received as a government loan;
These books we may catalogue as we choose
By Dewey or Cutter, whichever we use;
We may label and keep them apart by themselves,
Or give them their place on the classified shelves;
But whatever catalogue system it be,
Don't drop from the catalogue final u-e!
The third and last thing I am asked to explain
Is how to get at what the books contain;
Or how can we help the public to learn
To what particular page to turn?
To train up a child in the way he should go
You must travel that way yourself, you know,
So you'll hardly awaken desire for book
Upon which you have never bestowed a look.
Among these documents, neglected long,
We'll scarcely seek for poetry or song;
But almost every human thing besides
Within their dusty treasury abides.
The exploration of our western lands,
The work of master minds and master hands,
The wisest counsels for the men who toil,
The latest novelties of seed and soil,
The care of forests and the growth of trees,
The low of cattle and the hum of bees,
Our Indian tribes and all their curious ways,
Their strange religion and their children's plays,
The rich experience of our public schools,
Why children should be taught the use of tools,
Our public parks, the care of public roads,
The gypsy moth, the history of toads,
The words of statesmen and the art of war,
The story of the lighthouse on the bar,
The constitution of the United States,
The price of wheat, the present tariff rates,
Who took the prizes at the county fair,
The names of city councilmen and mayor,
The history of the nation in its prime,
Our rivers, mountains and our varied clime,
All these within these documents are found,
Besides all which in pictures they abound--
Rare pictures here of scenes forever lost,
There colored pictures fabulous in cost,
Engravings of machinery and tools,
From Corliss engines down to spinning mules;
Designs of ships and diagrams of forts,
And plans for libraries and halls and courts.

370

Jus' take one volume home and read it through
And you will know the proper thing to do.
You'll be so pleased before you reach the end
You just can't help but show it to a friend,
And when all's said there ain't no better plan
To get the proper book to the proper man.
I know there's Congress cards to help along,
And Putnam'll send 'em to you fer a song,
But as for recommendin' on 'em--pshaw!
The most that gets 'em puts 'em in a draw,
And there they'll stay till good old Gabriel comes
To rouse 'em from their dusty catacombs.
Ef someone else makes catalogues fer me,
I ain't agoin' to read the books, you see!
But if I'm more'n a label on a shelf,
I've got to find what's in 'em for myself!
I'd rather show one feller from a farm
What Riley says will do his tatters harm
Than give 10 novels to 10 city maids
Or give a boy some pirates' escapades.
I'd rather give a teacher--not a fool,
Mann's first report upon a public school
Than send her huntin' in the catalog draw,
Or hand her out the sophistries of Shaw!
The catlog's right and nes'ry in its place,
But them that tries it needs redeemin' grace!
An' jest as grammar needs a good grammarian,
So ev'ry libr'y needs a live librarian!
Get all the indexes that you can raise,
Get cards enough to fill up all your trays,
Ef folks don't read, there's jest one way to win 'em,
Fust know your books, then tell your friends what's
   in 'em.

Idle

Philip C. Blackburn

From Bedlam p. 7-8, April 7, 1930.   Reprinted by permission of the New York Public Library.

I

The Stack Chief and his friend, the Page
  Were walking through the stacks,
Comparing all the shelf-list cards
  With books--their fronts and backs.
"It is amazing," said the Page
  "The cards our shelf-list lacks."

II

If seven maidens with seven pens
  Should write for seven years
Do you suppose the Page enquired
  "This mess they then could clear?"
"I doubt it" said the Chief and shed
  A bitter salty tear.

III

"O maidens come and check with us
  The inventory--Do!
And each of you may bring four trays
  (Though we are sick with two!)
We have a stack of work today,
  And can't admire the view."

IV

"The time has come," the Stack Chief said,
  "To talk of many things:
Of lifts and misdivided books
  And slips the reader brings;
And how our monthly ratings fall,
  And why the books take wings."

V

"O maidens come and walk with us
  Along the dusty press.
Of what has happened to the books
  We each shall take a guess.
This is particularly well
  Since things are in a mess."

VI

"We can remember" quoth the maids,
  "How we were taught in school:
Whenever things are out of place,
  Then guessing is the rule.
And well they trained us in the art--
  It's such a useful tool!"

VII

Courageously, and book by book
  They checked while day was bright:
More slowly and more slowly still
  They checked 'till it was night.
Till all the books were out of place--
  Things were in order, quite.

VIII

Next day: "O will you check with us,
  Until our work is done?"
"O maidens, will you check with us?"
  But answer came there none.
And this was scarcely strange, for they'd
  Gone crazy-every one!

How A Bibliomaniac Binds His Books

Irving Browne

From his In the track of the Bookworm East Aurora, N.Y.,
Roycroft Printing Shop, 1897. p. 26-8.

I'd like my favorite books to bind
   So that their outward dress
To every bibliomaniac's mind
   Their contents should express.

Napoleon's life should glare in red,
   John Calvin's gloom in blue;
Thus they would typify bloodshed
   And sour religion's hue.

The prize-ring record of the past
   Must be in blue and black;
While any color that is fast
   Would do for Derby track.

The Popes in scarlet well may go;
   In jealous green, Othello;
In gray, Old Age of Cicero,
   And London Cries in yellow.

My Walton should his gentle art
   In Salmon best express,
And Penn and Fox the friendly heart
   In quiet drab confess.

Statistics of the lumber trade
   Should be embraced in boards,
While muslin for the inspired Maid
   A fitting garb affords.

Intestine wars I'd clothe in vellum,
   While pig-skin Bacon grasps,
And flat romances, such as "Pelham,"

Should stand in calf with clasps.

Blind-tooled should be blank verse and rhyme
    Of Homer and of Milton;
But Newgate Calendar of Crime
    I'd lavishly dab gilt on.

The edges of a sculptor's life
    May fitly marbled be,
But sprinkle not, for fear of strife,
    A Baptist history.

Crimea's warlike facts and dates
    Of fragrant Russia smell;
The subjugated Barbary States
    In crushed Morocco dwell.

But oh! that one I hold so dear
    Should be arrayed so cheap
Gives me a qualm; I sadly fear
    My Lamb must be half-sheep.

Fantasy on a Utilitarian Theme

Judith Child

From Colophon v. 2, No. 1, November 1954; and New Zealand Libraries 18:215-6, November 1955. Reprinted by permission of the author and the New Zealand Library Association.

When I build a library (which isn't very probable)
With tempting cultural vistas and edifying nooks,
And I find I'm filling up the space and running short of
      capital,
I'll solve the problem easily by leaving out the books.

The building will be spacious, with a portico and basement
Where the lower sort of readers can be stored in rental stacks,
But in the airy portico-cum-vestibule or foyer
Select non-fiction clientele will be displayed on racks.

Apart from the portico the building will be functional;
With neither walls nor ceilings to exclude the air and light.
To ensure an even heat, and subdued illumination,
We'll close it in the summer months, and open it at night.

This method of construction will be cheap and very flexible,
Allowing us to expand to an indefinite extent,
As, instead of buying property (and prices are prohibitive),
We'll lease the land for grazing at a very modest rent.

The institution will present a scene of great activity--
Its audio-visual programme is a source of special pride--
For the casual passer-by can hear the tinkling of the teacups
And have an unobstructed view of what goes on inside.

The readers will be catalogued both fully and selectively,
With staff in special cabinets reserved for juveniles,
And members of the library may borrow from the catalogue
Or spend a pleasant evening just browsing through the files.

The uninitiated may experience bewilderment
In choosing from a card-stock of ten thousand lineal feet,
But the subject-heading Millipedes will soon restore their
    confidence
With comforting suggestions of a busy city street.

A judicious use of colour, and assorted shapes and sizes
Will direct the timid users to the items they require--
Round pink cards for corporate bodies, with Refer from
    Stuff and Nonsense,
And lots of added entries for an earthquake or a fire.

There'll be space for processing, to laminate the invoices,
And special shelves provided for the card-selection tools,
And an Awful-Warning Visiblex that's labelled B-grade rental
To hold the cards not written quite according to the Rules.

We'll microfilm the issue cards and photostat the micro-
    film,
And interloan the microfilm and file the photograph
And copycat the catalogue, and catalogue the copycat,
And when demand is heavy we can microfilm the staff.

By friendly understanding with co-operating libraries,
We hope to publish supplements of various useful sorts,
To the index to the set of drawers which indexes the
    catalogue
And interfiles with finding lists of annual reports.

Innumerable adaptations readily suggest themselves
And other innovators will improve upon the scheme,
But I have written quite enough to indicate the scope of it
And sketch the variations on the no-book library theme.

The Library Mother Goose

F. K. W. Drury

From The Haystack; some reprinted in Public Libraries 30:
541, 1925; and 31:23, 1926. Reprinted with permission of
the Brown University Library.

Jingles for catalogers

Filer, Filer, all the whiler,
How does your catalog grow?
    Typed cards here
    And guide cards there
And printed ones all in a row.

Top floor hot
Bottom floor cold
Middle floor temperate
    Five days old.
None liked it hot
Some liked it cold
All were glad when the hot spell broke
    Five days old.

There was an old woman who lived in a
    shoe,
She had many books, but knew what to do:
"You sort them, arrange them, and list them
    on cards,
"And mark them all neatly, then shelve them
    by yards."

Classification is vexation,
Subject heading is as bad,

The rule for a. c.
Puzzles me,
And departments drive me mad.

———

Little Miss Elsie
Sat by the L C
    Filing her cards away;
There came an exhibit
With crowds to the limit
And frightened Miss Elsie away.

———

Sing a song of seminar,
    A room full of chaff,
Four and twenty analyticals
    For one small monograph.
When the tray was opened
    The subject cards showed off,
Wasn't that a perfect feast
    To set before a prof?

Rimes for the Order Department

Pat-a-cake, pat-a-cake, Library man,
Get me this book as fast as you can,
    Search it and order it
    And rush it for me,
And place on the shelf for Course No. 3.

———

Baa, baa, order clerk,
Have you carbon cops?
    Ay, marry, have I,
    Traysful to the tops.
One for the agent,
One for my file,
And two for the B. O.
To add to its pile.

Melodies for the Reference Department

Tom, Tom, the piper's son
Stole a book and away he run.

The deed was mean,
And Tom was seen,
And Tom went roaring to the Dean.

Old Mother Preserves went to the Reserves
To get a poor student a book;
   But when she got there
   The shelf it was bare,
Because some stude was a crook.

Jill and Jack went in the stack
To read the shelves together,
   Deep dust was found
   Where books abound
And they used pails of water.

This little book went to reserve,
This little book stayed home,
This little book had many loans,
This little book had none,
This little book cried "I'm covered with dust."
   All the way home.

Fragments from the Public Library in New York City

James Waldo Fawcett

From Bruno's Weekly Oct. 25, 1916, p. 1169.

I. --The Entrance

This is the door
By which we enter in
This great white marble mausoleum
Of dead and dying thoughts.

Come, let us pause
A moment;
Perhaps a bird will come
To drink
From the pool
At the marble lady's feet!

II. --The Magazine Room

From every corner
Of the panting earth
They come;
Men who sit
At these broad tables
Turning leaves
All day.

They are wise
More books are born
Among these paper covers
Than those who write them
Care to admit, good friend;

Few books are there
That have not once
Been merely, magazines.

III. --The Stack

There are hundreds
Of thousands of volumes
Here in this echoing vault;

And each time these volumes
Hear the attendant's even tread
They pray to their proper god
Each in his own true tongue
That they be chosen.

And when one returns
From the little pilgrimage
To the main reading room,
The others ask him:
"How is the world?"

And sometimes he replies:
"It is grey and cold.
An aged professor wanted me.
There was something of soup
In his beard."

And again he may say:
"The world is a singing place
Of sunshine and love;
I went to the hands of one
Who is fair as Heloise,
The well-beloved of Abelard."

Strange, eager hearts
Within these aging volumes . . . .

III. --The Stairway

This white descent
Frightens me;
It is so steep
And cold and white.

Some day I think
I shall not resist
The subtle temptation
To throw myself
Down the whole long flight
And scatter poppies of scarlet
Over all this adamantine coldness.

V. --The Newspaper Room

It was here
That I found her secret--
Here among these musty old records,
Here where man aids Gossip
In her war with Time.

Why do you live so long?
Yellow sheets of a day,
Why linger year on year?

Learn to forget;
Be kind.

Replies to Fragments from the Public Library
in New York City

Edmund Lester Pearson

From his column "The Librarian" in the Boston Transcript
November 9, 1916.

I. (By Captain Flanagan, Guard at the Entrance)
Yes, this is the door
By which you enter in.
But before you go out
With any dead and dying thoughts
Kindly let me look at them
To see if they have been properly charged
At the charging desk.

Some folks get absent-minded
In great white marble
What you may callems.

II. (By Mr. Ricker)
It is true.
They come from every corner
Of the aforesaid panting earth.

Some to look at magazines;
But some
Who have been dining--well--
At Shanley's.
Rush in at 9:45 P. M.
Thinking they are in the Grand Central Station.
And ask: Where is the 9.50
For Yonkers?

III. (By One of the Boys From Stack VI)
Gee! Listen to the Boob!
The attendant!

As if there was only one of us,
Why, this summer our base-ball team
Licked the Circulation Department 27 to 25.
Or would have, if their pitcher hadn't
Struck out four men in the ninth.
Next year, with Vigilante pitching, we'll
Put one over on 'em.

As for this Heloise dame
She may have been up in the Main R. R.
You can't make out the writing
On half the call-slips.

IV. (By Mr. Fedeler, Superintendent of
                    the Building)
Mr. Fawcett.
Would you mind very much
When you feel this subtle
Temptation coming over you,
To throw yourself down the whole
Long flight--
If it's all the same to you,
Would you please communicate
With me or Benson
So we can come and help you resist?
It's the devil's own job
To get those marble steps clean
And although I've got a patent preparation
That will remove spots from almost
Anything.
I'd rather not have to try it
On scarlet
Poppies.

V. (By Mr. Fox)
It is here
Comes Mr. Pearson
To see if the Transcript
Printed all of his article.

And when it does,
A smile illumines his
Handsome countenance.

Mr. Fawcett, I think I will
Give him your verses.
Printed as they are, they take up
Lots of space, and if he stings

385

The Transcript with them
He will have most enough to buy
That new tennis racquet,
For which is heart is yearning.

Verses

Hannah E. Fernald

From New Hampshire Bulletin 22:29-31, 1926. Reprinted by permission of the editor of North Country Libraries.

I
On Choosing a Novel

I cannot read the old tales, they loved so long ago,
I turn the pages over and they seem so mild
    and slow;
The style is artificial, the sentiment is worse, --
I cannot read the old tales, --I'll take a book of
    verse.

I cannot face the new tales, they make my spirit
    quail,
So much of ugliness is packed in each substantial
    tale;
The dreary people stumble on to meet their
    dreary doom,
With only cleverness to light the all-pervading
    gloom;
I cannot read the new tales, whate'er the critics
    say, --
I think I'll just relax and take a travel-book today.

II
Do They?

The puzzle-worker's here again and all his ques-
    tions too.
"What rank did Major Smith attain?
    and what did Hoover do?

Was Woodrow, Wilson's middle name?
And what was Bryan's claim to fame?

And when did Gompers die?"
From book to book I watch them speed
And wonder if they ever read,
      Even as you and I?

The puzzlers come at early morn and toil
    throughout the day,
Till dictionary leaves are torn and year-
    books all astray;
Their children gambol on the floor,
While still they con their questions
    o'er, --
"What rank did Sherman have before?
And when did Gompers die?"
I run to fetch the books they need
And wonder if they ever read,
      Even as you and I?

III
An Evening Off

How pleasant is Saturday night,
    When I've tried all the week to be good;
When I've classified all the books right,
    And filed all the cards that I should.
Then away to the bookshelves I hie,
    And choose without further ado,
A book that will make the time fly,
    With a corpse and a bloodstain or two.

Farewell to the cares of the day, --
    Tomorrow'll bring troubles, no doubt,
For the books on the shelves are astray,
    And all the new fiction is out.
There's a bindery box on the way,
    And that will mean plenty to do, --
But this is my evening to play, --
    With a corpse and a bloodstain or two.

IV.
The Red Book

I had it last year, and you got it yourself,
It stood, I recall, on a rather high shelf.
"The author?" I never remember his name.
There were several books, I believe, by
    the same.

I don't know the title. I want it again.
"What is it?" I think I've been perfectly
    plain!
"But how can you find it?" Was that what
    you said?
I told you distinctly the cover is red!

V.
A Simple Request

The gloomy ones depress her, so we
        mustn't have it sad,
    And the funny ones she thinks are
        such a bore;
She disapproves of shooting, and of language
    that is bad.
    And you <u>mustn't</u> send her one she's had
        before.

Oh, yes,--she's read 'most everything.
        all those by Ethel Dell,
    By Lincoln and by Lutz and many
        more;
Just pick her out a pleasant one,--you always
        suit her well,--
    But be <u>sure</u> it's one she hasn't had
        before.

VI.
Thoughts
On the Perversities of Alphabetical
Arrangement.

It's unprofessional, and yet
I do despise the alphabet.

The works of Mr. Edgar Guest
Upon the highest shelf must rest.
And I, to fetch them down from there,
Mount on a ladder or a chair.
I cannot put them down below,
The numbers will not have it so.
For Browning I would climb with zest,--
It makes me <u>mad</u> to climb for Guest!

And Mr. Grey, of western fame,
Is situated just the same.
In vain I proffer Henry James
And other quite distinguished names;
Conrad and Hardy, Kipling, each
Displayed within convenient reach.
The public clamors, "Give me Grey.
I want a western one today."
I leap upon the nearest chair
And perch precariously there,
Only to find, without a doubt,
The works of Mr. Grey are out!

It's unprofessional, and yet
I do detest the alphabet!

VII.
A New Book

It must be absorbing and exciting,
   It must be brilliant and fine.
It must be provocative and lively,
   And it can't have a single dull line.
For all the critics have told me so,
   And it certainly seems they ought to
     know.

(But for my part, I think it's a very
     dull book.)

It must be triumphant and enchanting,
   It must be wistful and urbane,
It must be tragic and ironic.
   And it must be revealing and sane;
For all the critics have told me so,
   And it certainly seems they ought to
     know.

(But if they hadn't, I should consider it very tiresome, and I'm rather
inclined to consider it so anyway.)

It must be dramatic and thrilling,
   It must be amazing and profound,
It must be wistful and delightful,
   And must be remarkable and sound.

For all the critics have told me so
  And it certainly seems they ought to
    know,

But there will come skeptical times
      when I
Can't help thinking the critics lie!

The Head Librarian

Sam Walter Foss

From his The Song of the Library Staff N.Y., John R. Anderson, 1906, p. 12-3.

Now my Muse prepare for business.   Plume your
    wings for loftier flight
Through the circumambient ether to a super-
    lunar height,
Then adown the empyrean from the heights
    where thou hast risen
Sing, O Muse! the Head Librarian and the joy
    that's her'n or his'n.
See him, see her, his or her head weighted with
    the lore of time,
Trying to expend a dollar when he only has a
    dime;
Tailoring appropriations--and how deftly he suc-
    ceeds,
Fitting his poor thousand dollars to his million
    dollar needs.
How the glad book agents cheer him--and he
    cannot wish them fewer
With "their greatest work yet published since
    the dawn of literature."
And he knows another agent, champing restive
    to begin
With another work still greater will immediately
    come in.
So perfection on perfection follows more and
    more sublime
And the line keeps on forever down the avenues
    of time--
So they travel on forever, stretching far beyond
    our ken,
Lifting demijohns of wisdom to the thirsty lips
    of men.

See him 'mid his myriad volumes listening to the
    gladsome din
Of the loud vociferant public that no book is
    ever "in";
And he hears the fierce taxpayer evermore lift
    up the shout
That the book he needs forever is the book for-
    ever "out."
How they rage, the numerous sinners, when he
    tries to please the saints,
When he tries to please the sinners hear the nu-
    merous saints' complaints;
And some want a Bowdlered Hemans and an ex-
    purgated Watts;
Some are shocked beyond expression at the sight
    of naked thoughts,
And he smooths their fur the right way, and he
    placates him or her,
And those who come to snarl and scratch remain
    behind to purr.
Oh, the gamesome glad Librarian gushing with
    his gurgling glee!--
Here I hand my resignation, --'tis a theme too
    big for me.

The Streamlined Library

Anne H. Hinckley

From Wilson Daily Bulletin No. 3, p. 2, June 23, 1937.
Reprinted by permission of the H. W. Wilson Company.

Let us cheer this brave new clinic
With its diagnostic view
Let us rally to our standard
That cravat of lurid hue.

It's so simple when considered--
Just a form of A B C--
And the steps that should be taken
Might be numbered 1, 2, 3.

One, locate the whole resistance;
Two, peruse it with a frown;
With the thing once analyzed,
Three, proceed to wear it down.

Camouflage with care your notice,
Use the politician's guile,
Steal the best of business methods,
And--be social all the while.

More of what the public's wanting;
Less of what it does not like;
Introduce a little conflict;
Use the neon and the mike.

Do your best to look maternal;
Wear a uniform that's snappy;
And you must give all-night service
If you'd keep your public happy.

Then we can't be blind to safety
When with borrowers we chatter;

394

Courteous must be, and cordial,
Put new gilding on old matter.

Look ahead into the future
And in 1945
You will find your old library
Has begun to look alive.

In this near and smart tomorrow
Your library will be found
Streamlined in a modern manner,
Sort of oozing from the ground.

And the walls within will rival
A most ultra cabaret;
All the patrons will be tendered
Zippy cocktails on a tray!

Great the consternation reigning
When the Neon sign shall say
"In the east and fourth floor gallery
There will be no fight today!"

Then our public will be happy
We'll be on the proper tracks;
With our staff in chorus costume
Gaily prancing from the stacks.

We'll revise our whole procedure
And now before it is too late
Get out the Houbigant and Coty,
Go forth, my friends, prognosticate.

Mansfield Center Library
1906-1929

This poem was used as an early fund-raising effort by the Mansfield Center Library, Mansfield, Connecticut. It is printed here by permission of that library's Board of Trustees.

A good date to remember--
The thirteenth of November
    And why? And how?

We're going to celebrate that day
By giving a little party. Say,
Won't you come and bring with thee
This bag with cents just twenty-three*
The age of our good Libraree?
A birthday present, don't you see,
For the Mansfield Center Libraree.
That's where the party's going to be.
Please come and drink a cup of tea.
In honor of your Libraree.
Thus helping in a pleasant way
To celebrate its natal day
From four to six P. M.   Hooray!
We'll have a jolly time.   What say?

* Come to think of it, twenty-three
  Cents isn't much for your Libraree.
  If you can do it and not holler,
  Make it fifty or a dollar.

396

Two Saints in One Act

Nina Napier

From her Library Levity Seattle, Dogwood Press, 1952. p. 29-31. Reprinted by permission of the Dogwood Press.

Fate struck as she climbed the stair one day,
With an armful of books in her usual way;

And just as she was, without preparation,
She arrived at her heavenly destination.

It happened that day Saint Peter had gone
Into town to have his halo shone,

And to keep another important date,
So he'd left Saint Paul in charge of the gate.

Paul looked out and his face was grim,
No sinner was going to get past him;

And he said: "Well, why are you standing there?
Come here and fill out this questionnaire."

So she filled in her name, her address and age,
And the state of her soul on another page,

The number of sermons to which she had listened,
And "Yes" to the question: Was she christened?

And when she had carefully answered it all,
Humbly she handed it back to Paul.

Paul took the form with a scornful look.
And entered it up in a big black book,

And he went to the files of the living and dead,
And hunted and hunted, and finally said:

397

"Well just as I thought, it's perfectly clear
You were never expected to turn up here;

And besides," he shouted, "if it comes to that,
You can't come in here without a hat!"

She picked up her books and turned to go,
When along came Saint Peter, all aglow,

Looked through the gate, and gave a shout:
"What are those books you're carrying about?"

And over his face came a wistful look,
"It's such a long time since I read a new book."

"Oh Sir," she said, "I'm sorry indeed,
I haven't a thing a saint would read,

Nothing to suit your taste in the least,
Not a single book by pope or priest."

"Hm," said Peter, "that's not what I mean,
Have you anything new by Ellery Queen?"

"Oh yes," she replied, and the saint with a grin,
Opened wide the gate, and said: "Come right in,

The Lord will welcome you into glory,
He's very fond of a mystery story."

"I see," he said, with a kind expression,
"You're a cataloguer by profession;

Librarians, I fear, to sin are prone,
So few have approached the golden throne.

But now, as a sign you've attained perfection,
I'll show you the Lord's own book collection;

How happy He'll be, how satisfied,
When He's had it properly classified!"

So the good saint led her to marble halls,
Where millions of books lined the jasper walls.

"You needn't hurry the work," said he,
"Dear child, you have all of Eternity."

Eternity waited; she sighed and said: "Well,
No wonder librarians go to Hell."

Clerihews and Other Miscellaneous Verse

Mary Pearce

From The Assistant Librarian 46:150, 152, 154; 1953; and other miscellaneous sources. Reprinted with the permission of the author and of the editor of The Assistant Librarian.

Mr. Benge,
Unimpressed by Stonehenge,
Merely lifted an eyebrow
And read something highbrow.

* * *

Henry Evelyn Bliss
Said: 'All you have to do is this:
Stick to the Order of Studies,
Buddies.'

* * *

Doctor Bray
Founded the S. P. C. K. ;
He was always passing around the hat
For things like that.

* * *

Still remembered hazily
Is James Coats of Paisiley
As the John Rylands
Of the Highlands and Islands.

* * *

Mr. Collison
Would permit no ice lollies on
Any of his premises
On pain of Nemesis.

* * *

400

Charles A. Cutter
Was heard on his deathbed to mutter:
'Librarians desiring to make use of Expansion Seven
Should apply to heaven.'

* * *

Melvil Dewey
Said: 'I guess I'm kinda screwy,
But I get sorta sentimental over the most infinitesimal
li'l decimal.'

* * *

Mr. Dudley
Got up very suddly:
Two words, one frown,
Then he sat down.

* * *

Few people at Belsize
Are blessed with gazelle's eyes;
Nor could you call Dudley
Exactly cuddly.

* * *

Edward Edwards
Never went bedwards
Without: 'God bless Panizzi
And all the Select Commizzi.'

* * *

Let us lose no time
In addressing a cordial rhyme
To Mr. Ralph Esterquest
Our distinguished midwesterguest.

* * *

Mr. Hoy
Was once a boy;
An experience the present writer
Has had denied her.

* * *

A. C. Jones
(I feel it in my bones)
Is pale as two candles
And goes in for sandals.

* * *

Grace O. Kelley
Used to tremble like jelly
Whenever she met any fans
Of Margaret Mann's.

* * *

Milton at Home
Roger Lestrange
Said: 'Isn't that your supper burning on the kitchen range?'
- A ruse that couldn't save that prim and proper critic a
Further long recital from the Areopagitica.

* * *

Mr. McClellan
Has little in common with Magellan:
He seldom cries 'Land ho!,'
Nor is his name Fernandho.

* * *

Ottmar Merganthaler
Said: 'Come into the parlour;
For I feel the time is ripe
To give the world the Linotype.'

* * *

William Morris
Lived in Epping Forris:
Which is why people's houses
Got papered with boughses.

* * *

Howard Nixon
Said: 'Have a jolly good tug at this binding, and if it still
    sticks on, --
If we are totally unable even to pull its ends orf,
--Then it was probably done by Rivière, or failing

that, Zaehnsdorf.'

* * *

Fremont Rider
Said: 'Books must get no wider;
And whoever can make them thinner
Is on to a winner.'

* * *

What a shame that Minnie Sears
Didn't spend a few years
Less on headings
And more on weddings.

* * *

Doctor Louis Shores
Is cordially yours:
Would he like to be your father?
Rather!

* * *

Mr. Shaw Wright
Dreams every night
Of finding a diary
In a medieval friary.

* * *
Or

A source of delight
To Mr. Shaw Wright
Is when an Escheat
Flutters down at his feet.

* * *

Literature hath owed
Much to the cold cathode:
A pity strips fluorescent
Make you look putrescent.

* * *

The only rhyme for intaglio

Appearing to be seraglio,
I shall attempt no explanation
Of these processes of illustration.

Miss Pearce's clerihews inspired Peter Gann to write:

Aldus of Venice
Sold classics for pennies
But he had to increase his fee
For Hypnerotomachia Poliphili.

Verses from the Bulletin Board of the
Adriance Memorial Library

Contributed by Arnold P. Sable

Supplication of a Library Clerk,
        as inspired by Odescalchi

Book! the content, circulation, state of being
Be my daily chore
Now and evermore.
Know thine own card and keep it, lest I look,
Card in hand, aghast,
And find no book!
And keep thy date slip cozy when thou wander
Or I must needs
Search file again from here to yonder.
Keep thy illustrations modest
Thus we keep our young folk honest.
Full many an art book is denuded (sic)
By borrower on a 'yield to temptation' kick!

At times I wish you stayed to gather dust
But duty calls, and circulate you must;
Wandering o'er, do thou return to me
Lest thou no more borrowed nor lended be.

Congratulation Upon My Promotion

They have promoted me
To the highest place in the library.
It was in a great hurry,
Such advancement is quite legendary.

My new place is outclass
I walk not on wood floor but on pure glass,
And have a mighty view,
If see at all--from dust that workmen blew.

405

If I look down below,
A man looks up and says: "Honey, Hellow.' "
I wear my tightest skirt,
Still, on a glassfloor it is but a flirt.

All heat of the building
Finds the top floor the best for its landing,
If I air out a bit,
Mr. B. says: "You think we heat the street?"

I can't wear a nice dress,
For by night it becomes a complete mess.
Thick dust lies everywhere
In short, my new "office" is a nightmare.

If I drop a paper
It flies through the hole that surrounds the floor
Keeps on flying deeper
Until it ends its ride in the cellar.

If at my desk working,
Each minute a patron seems bywalking.
With interested look
Asks me where he could find a certain book.

Yet, in spite of all these
Hard to believe!--I am quite at heartease.
I was promised that soon
My permanent place will be the Mens' room!

archy goes one step further

now in the evenings
when the lights are low
and there arent any strange men walking the stacks
thats the time to browse through the adriance memorial
    library
mehitabel
the things you see
for example did you know mehitabel
they have our books classified in both 827 and 828
its hard enough for a cockroach like me to open a book
let alone refer from the 827 section
to the 828 section
but toujours gai
you know me mehitabel

i dont mind some dust here or there
in the moonlight the stacks look like forest sentinels
or is that too much cliche for you mehitabel
mehitabel if only people would open their eyes
to the beauty
and wonder
about them
oh life is gai
and the dewey decimal system has its heartaches and sorrows
like the rest of life
oh i do like the local history room in the moonlight
and have you even seen the kiwanis room at dawn
who of us is adventuresome
oh mehitabel
someday ill tell you all about the dreadful things
im reading these days
about how slothful how uncaring americans now are
they dont get up to see the dawn
the beauty of life the mystery of life
one more book by vance packard and ill scream
oh by the way mehitabel
ive thought of a new game
its called hide the book cards
you get book cards from the circulation trays
and you hide them
anyplace
anywhere
i wonder if anyone will ever find the bookcard ive hidden
in the cement
in the new restrooms
mehitabel mehitabel
come trip with me through the subject reference room
well have tea by the light
by the merry merry light
of the diaphanous moon
at the carrel investment table
in between the subject reference room and the general
reference room

                                                    archy

Stopping By the Bulletin Board on a Frosty Afternoon

        Whose words those are I think I know
        But "Archy's" in his office though
        He will not see me standing here
                        407

To add my verse to those below

Our little staff must think it queer
To stop beside this board and peer
With cup in hand, or chunk of cake
"Another poem!" they'll say "Oh dear!"

They'll give their puzzled heads a shake
And little clucking noises make
"Profound" they'll murmur "Even deep!"
And thus they'll spend a coffee break

From bad to worse my stanzas creep
I fear the muse has gone to sleep
But yet, you're getting them so cheap!
But yet, you're getting them so cheap!

Miss Mehitabel Frost

Little Lyrics for Librarians

William F. Smyth

From his hand-lettered booklet Little Lyrics for Librarians
Cleveland, The Bazoo Publishing Co., 1910. Copy supplied
by the Cleveland Public Library and reprinted by permission
of that library.

A Librarian's Life

A librarian's life is the life for me,
For there's nothing at all to do, you see,
But to sit at a desk and read new books,
And admire yourself, and think of your looks.
To questioning souls one can tartly say:
"I can't be bothered with you to-day,
For I haven't finished this novel. See?"
A librarian's life is the life for me.

The Librarian's First-Born

She placed their babe upon his knee.
    He thus himself "expressioned."
"A juvenile work.   But, mercy me!
Don't loan it, dear; for can't you see--
    It hasn't been accessioned."

Oversize

It was a tall librarian
    Who wished to travel far,
So paid for a whole section
    In a Pullman sleeping car.
But the porter saw him sitting
    On his berth's soft-cushioned edge,
And yelled: "Get down! You're oversize!
    You go below the ledge!"

"Sing A Song"

Sing a song of stackrooms,
  A building full of books.
Twenty-four librarians
  Noted for their looks.
When the doors are opened
  They all begin to sing:
"You'd better draw this novel, sir.
  'Tis quite the latest thing."
The Board sits in the Boardroom
  To count Carnegie's money.
Attendants to the visitors
  Are sweet as bread and honey.
The page is in the stackroom,
  Piling books in rows,
When down falls a Blackwood's,
  And bounds off his nose.

Toohey's Original Geographic Blues

Barbara Toohey

We have a brand new building,
Our staff is young and bright
And breaking a tradition
Always fills us with delight.
But one exists
We cannot break,
For there is much
Too much at stake.
We'd be considered criminal, subversive, and unclean,
Had we not the Geographic back to 1917.

You may wonder how we got them
In a library so new,
Well, with the Geographic
You just wait, they come to you.
Each week or so
Some soul appears
Who's taken it
For twenty years.
He offers you a mildewed pile and if from these you glean,
Soon you have the Geographic back to 1917.

We're going into microfilm
To save on shelving space,
We can't find room for Harper's
Or Atlantic any place,
But on a shelf
That's six feet long,
Its place secure,
Tradition strong,
In pyroxylin-filled buckram (gold lettering on green),
We have the Geographic back to 1917.

It's a comfort just to open one,
And peruse the rich, vast store
Of hunters in pith helmets
With a captured yak or boar.
Let prices rise,
Let missiles fall,
Let riots break out
In Nepal,
The little world in which we dwell stays peaceful and
   serene
While we have the Geographic back to 1917.

The Librarian's Dream

Clara Van Sant

From Wilson Bulletin for Librarians 8:477, 1934.   Reprinted
by permission of the H. W. Wilson Company.

Believe it or not, but this story I tell,
Of a library-lady I know quite well.
She had a dream the other night,
And in this dream her soul took flight,
And ascended the golden, circular stair
That leads to Heaven, and all things fair.
At the Pearly Gates, Saint Peter sat,
Absorbed, if you please, in the U. S. Cat.
She gave her name and occupation,
With proper poise and modulation.
"Where you are from we must affix."
"Nine-seven-nine-point-four-six."
All this was written with her rank,
A regular application blank.
Two bright wings and a harp of gold,
Were given her to wear and hold.
"My labor is o'er," she softly sighed,
"On yonder cloud I'll sit and glide."
But, wait . . . a line of angels passed,
And asked her questions, thick and fast.
"Tell me, what do gypsies wear?"
"Did Cleopatra dye her hair?"
"Won't you give John the facts of life?"
"Did King Arthur have a wife?"
"Have you got plans for a motor-boat?"
"What shall I feed my Nanny-goat?"
"For a bright green lawn, which seed is best?"
"How should my daughter treat a guest?"
"How much lumber does it take
To build a lattice o'er a gate?"
"Do flying-fishes really fly?"
"What time does the bus go by?"

413

"I want figures up-to-date,
That tell how tennis players rate."
"How many islands in the ocean?"
"What causes this perpetual motion?"
For seven hours the crowd filed past,
And then--'twas nine o'clock at last.
She "chucked" the wings and harp of gold.
Her head was hot, her feet were cold.
While stumbling down the Golden Stair,
She visioned her old swivel chair.
Dreams of Heaven are mental toys.
Hence then, "vain deluding Joyes."

Ode to Illiteracy

Harold Wooster

From American Documentation 15:226, 1964.   Reprinted with permission of the author and of the American Society for Information Science.

Information is too much with us, late and soon,
Getting and reading, we lay waste our powers,
Little we keep and make it ours.
We have rotted our brains away, a sordid boon.
This Apollo, that takes us to the moon,
The tapes, that will be howling at all hours,
And are up-reeled now, like ferric towers,
For these, for everything, we're out of tune,
They move us not, Great God! I'd rather be,
Illiterate, staring at a tube outworn,
So might I, glassed by my T. V.
Have sight of Mercury, rising from the sea,
Or hear Centaur blow his noisy horn.

INDEXING

Index: There Is No Index

Stephen Leacock

Reprinted by permission of Dodd, Mead & Company, Inc.
from The Leacock Roundabout (p. 420-2) by Stephen Leacock.
Copyright 1946 by Dodd, Mead & Company, Inc.

Readers of books, I mean worth-while readers, like
those who read this volume, will understand how many difficulties centre round the making of an Index. Whether to
have an Index at all? Whether to make it a great big one,
or just a cute little Index on one page? Whether to have
only proper names, or let it take on ideas--and so on. In
short the thing reaches dimensions that may raise it to the
rank of being called the Index Problem, if nothing is done a-
bout it.

Of course one has to have an Index. Authors themselves would prefer not to have any. Having none would
save trouble and compel reviewers to read the whole book
instead of just the Index. But the reader needs it. Otherwise he finds himself looking all through the book, forwards
and then backwards, and then plunging in at random, in order to read out to a friend what it was that was so darned
good about Talleyrand. He doesn't find it, because it was in
another book.

So let us agree, there must be an Index. Now comes
the trouble. What is the real title or name of a thing or
person that has three or four? Must you put everything
three or four times over in the Index, under three or four
names? No, just once, so it is commonly understood; and
then for the other joint names, we put what is called a
cross-reference, meaning, "See this" or "See that." It
sounds good in theory, but in practice it leads to such results as--Talleyrand, see Perigord . . . and when you hunt
this up, you find--Perigord, Bishop of, see Talleyrand.
The same effect can be done flat out, with just two words,

419

as Lincoln, see Abraham . . . Abraham, see Lincoln.
But even that is not so bad because at least it's a closed
circle. It comes to a full stop. But compare the effect,
familiar to all research students, when the unclosed circle
runs like this, each item being hunted up alphabetically, one
after the other--Abraham, see Lincoln . . . Lincoln, see
Civil War . . . Civil War, see United States . . . United
States, see America . . . America, see American History
. . . American History, see also Christopher Columbus,
New England, Pocahontas, George Washington . . . the thing
will finally come to rest somehow or other with the dial
pointing at see Abraham Lincoln.

But there is worse even than that. A certain kind of
conscientious author enters only proper names, but he indexes them every time they come into his book, no matter
how they come in, and how unimportant is the context. Here
is the result in the Index under the Letter N:

Napoleon--17, 26, 41, 73, 109, 110, 156, 213, 270, 380,
460. You begin to look them up. Here are the references:
Page 17--"wore his hair like Napoleon."
Page 26--"in the days of Napoleon."
Page 41--"as fat as Napoleon."
Page 73--"Not so fat as Napoleon."
Page 109--"was a regular Napoleon at Ping-pong."
Page 110--"was not a Napoleon at Ping-pong."
Page 156--"Napoleon's hat."
Pages 213, 270, 380, 460, not investigated.

Equally well meant but perhaps even harder to bear is
the peculiar kind of index that appears in a biography. The
name of the person under treatment naturally runs through
almost every page, and the conscientious index-maker tries
to keep pace with him. This means that many events of his
life get shifted out of their natural order. Here is the general effect:

John Smith: born. p. 1: father born. p. 2: grandfather
born. p. 3: mother born. p. 4: mother's family leave Ireland.
p. 5: still leaving it. p. 6: school. p. 7: more school. p. 8: dies
of pneumonia and enters Harvard. p. 9: eldest son born. p. 10:
marries, p. 11: back at school. p. 12: dead. p. 13: takes his degree. p. 14: . . .

Suppose, then, you decide to get away from all these
difficulties and make a Perfect Index in which each item
shall carry with it an explanation, a sort of little epitome

of what is to be found in the book. The reader consulting the volume can open the Index, look at a reference, and decide whether or not he needs to turn the subject up in the full discussion in the book. A really good Index will in most cases itself give the information wanted. There you have, so to speak, the Perfect Index.

Why I know about this is because I am engaged at present in making such an Index in connection with a book on gardening, which I am writing just now. To illustrate what is meant, I may be permitted to quote the opening of the book, and its conversion into Index Material:

As Abraham Lincoln used to say, when you want to do gardening, you've got to take your coat off, a sentiment shared by his fellow enthusiast, the exiled Napoleon, who, after conquering all Europe, retaining only the sovereignty of the spade in his garden plot at St. Helena, longed only for more fertilizer.

As arranged for the Index, the gist, or essential part of this sentence, the nucleus, so to speak, appears thus:

Abraham Lincoln; habit of saying things, p. 1; wants to do gardening, p. 1; takes his coat off, p. 1; his enthusiasm, p. 1; compared with Napoleon, p. 1.

Coat; taken off by Abraham Lincoln, p. 1.

Gardening; Lincoln's views on, p. 1; need of taking coat off, for, p. 1; Napoleon's enthusiasm over, p. 1; see also under spade, sovereignty, St. Helena.

Napoleon; his exile, p. 1; conquers Europe, p. 1; enthusiastic over gardening, p. 1; compared with Lincoln; retains sovereignty of spade, p. 1; plots at St. Helena, p. 1; longs for fertilizer, p. 1; see also Europe, St. Helena, fertilizer, seed catalogue, etc., etc. . . .

That's as far as I've got with the sentence. I still have to write up sovereignty, spade, sentiment, share, St. Helena, and everything after S. There's no doubt it's the right method, but it takes time somehow to get the essential nucleus of the gist, and express it. I see why it is easier to do the other thing. But then sin is always easier than righteousness. See also under Hell, road to, Pavement, and Intentions, good.

A Selective Subject Index

                            424